13.50

WITHDRAWN

THE WORLD OF DREAMS

BY

HAVELOCK ELLIS

'Sleep has its own world'

BOSTON AND NEW YORK
HOUGHTON MIFFLIN COMPANY
1922

Republished by Gale Research Company, Detroit, 1976

Library of Congress Cataloging in Publication Data

Ellis, Havelock, 1859-1939.
　The world of dreams.

　　Reprint of the 1922 ed. published by Houghton Mifflin, Boston.
　Includes bibliographical references and index.
　1. Dreams.　I. Title.
BF1078.E5　　　1976　　　154.6'3　　　　75-43879
ISBN 0-8103-3780-0

PREFACE

THERE are at least four different ways of writing a book on dreams. There is, for instance, the *literary* method. In this way one goes to books or to the memories of other people for one's material, and so collects a great number of more or less wonderful stories. I have rejected this method, for it is entirely untrustworthy. Dreams are elusive at the best; only a very careful observer can set down a dream faithfully, even directly after it has occurred, and no one can safely entrust a dream to memory.

There is, again, what I may call the *clinical* method of studying dreams by the personal observation and collection of facts, with summation and analysis of the results. On a large scale, with the aid of the *questionnaire*, this method has been especially carried on in the United States, notably at Clark University under the inspiration of Dr. Stanley Hall. A strict and scientific adherence to the clinical method of studying dreams has resulted in Professor Sante de Sanctis's book *I Sogni* (first edition 1899), which is, on the whole, the best book on dreams published in recent years.

Then there is the *experimental* method, which, not content with mere objective study of the phenomena, endeavours to interfere with them and to find out the results of interference. This method may be combined with other methods of studying dreams. In its pure form it has in recent years been especially practised by the late Mourly Vold. Its results are not without interest, but they do not cover a large part of the field, and they are not altogether reliable. Dreaming activity is so fluid and suggestible—and this is notably so when experimenter and subject are the same person—that interference with the phenomena deforms them, and we cannot be sure that by experiment we have really learned much about the life of dreams.

There is, finally, the *introspective* method. This may be said to be the earliest of the more scientific methods of studying dreams. Maine de Biran was here a pioneer, and Maury, in his famous book, *Le Sommeil et les Rêves* (1861), which inaugurated the modern study of dreams, adopted a mainly introspective method, though he was not always quite successful in avoiding the fallacies of that method. It is in France that this method has been most frequently and most successfully cultivated.

Professor Sigmund Freud's *Die Traumdeutung* (first edition, 1900), may be said to belong to the introspective class, though to a special division which Freud himself terms psycho-analytic. This is undoubtedly the most original, the most daring, the most challenging of recent books on dreams, and is now the text-book of a whole school of investigators. It is not a book to be neglected, for it is written by one of the profoundest of living investigators into the obscure depths of the human soul.

Even if one rejects Freud's methods as unsatisfactory and his facts as unproved, the work of one so bold and so sincere cannot fail to be helpful and stimulating in the highest degree. If it is not the truth it will at least help us to reach the truth.

The little book now presented to the reader belongs mainly to the introspective group of dream studies, though not to the psycho-analytic variety. It is based on data which have accumulated beneath my hands during more than twenty years, and some of the ideas developed in it were put forward in a paper 'On Dreaming of the Dead,' *Psychological Review*, Sept. 1895; in 'A Note on Hypnagogic Paramnesia,' *Mind*, No. 22, 1896; and in 'The Stuff that Dreams are made of,' *Popular Science Monthly*, April 1899. The book is not the outcome of experiment or of any deliberate concentration of thought on dreaming. I have simply noted down dream experiences,—most often in myself, less often in immediate friends,—directly they have occurred, usually on awakening in the morning. The few unimportant exceptions to the rule are duly noted. By maintaining this rule I have been able to satisfy myself that everything I have set down is reasonably accurate. Such a method certainly tends towards the exclusion of peculiar and exceptional dreams. This I do not greatly regret. I am chiefly interested in the problems of normal dreaming; they are sufficiently puzzling and mysterious and they properly present themselves for explanation first. I do not wish it to be understood that I question the existence of telepathic and other abnormal dream experiences. That is not the case. But it so happens that under the conditions I have laid down I have not met with any dreams that clearly and decisively belong to this abnormal class. Such few possible examples as have come under my immediate observation (in no case as personal experiences) are slight, and, moreover, sometimes of too intimate a character for full exposition.

Thus my contribution to the psychology of dreaming is simple and unpretentious; it deals only with the fundamental elements of the subject. I do not make this statement entirely in a spirit of humility. It seems to me that in the past the literature of dreaming has often been overweighted by bad observation and reckless theory. By learning to observe and to understand the ordinary nightly experience of dream life we shall best be laying the foundation of future superstructures. For, rightly understood, dreams may furnish us with clues to the whole of life.

HAVELOCK ELLIS.

CONTENTS

CHAPTER I

INTRODUCTION

PAGE

The House of Dreams—Fallacies in the Study of Dreams—Is it possible to Study Dreams?—How Fallacies may be Avoided —Do we always Dream during Sleep?—The Two Main Sources of Dreams with their Sub-divisions, . . . 1

CHAPTER II

THE ELEMENTS OF DREAM LIFE

The Spontaneous Procession of Dream Imagery—Its Kaleidoscopic Character—Attention in Dreams—Relation of Drug Visions and Hypnagogic Imagery to Dreaming—Colour in Dreams—The Fusion of Dream Imagery—Compared to Dissolving Views—Sources of the Imagery—Various types of Fusion—The Sub-Conscious Element in Dreaming— Verbal Transformations as Links in Dream Imagery—The Reduplication of Visual Imagery in Motor and other Terms, 20

CHAPTER III

THE LOGIC OF DREAMS

All Dreaming is a Process of Reasoning—The Fundamental Character of Reasoning—Reasoning as a Synthesis of Images—Dream Reasoning Instinctive and Automatic— It is also Consciously carried on—This a result of the Fundamental Split in Intelligence—Dissociation—Dreaming as a Disturbance of Apperception, ... 56

CHAPTER IV

THE SENSES IN DREAMS

All Dreams probably contain both Presentative and Representative Elements—The Influence of Tactile Sensations on Dreams—Dreams excited by Auditory Stimuli—Dreams aroused by Odours and Tastes—The Influence of Visual Stimuli—Difficulty of distinguishing between Actual and Imagined Sensory Excitations—The Influence of Internal Visceral Stimuli on Dreaming—Erotic Dreams—Vesical Dreams—Cardiac Dreams and their Symbolism—Prodromic Dreams—Prophetic Dreams, ... 71

CHAPTER V

EMOTION IN DREAMS

Emotion and Imagination—How Stimuli are transformed into Emotion—Somnambulism—The Failure of Movement in Dreams—Nightmare—Influence of the approach of Awakening on imagined Dream movements—The Magnification of Imagery—Peripheral and Cerebral Conditions combine to produce this Imaginative Heightening—Emotion in Sleep also Heightened—Dreams formed to explain Heightened Emotions of unknown origin—The fundamental Place of Emotion in Dreams—Visceral and especially Gastric disturbance as a source of Emotion—Symbolism in Dreams—The Dreamer's Moral Attitude—Why Murder so often takes place in Dreams—Moral Feeling not Abolished in Dreams though sometimes Impaired, ... 94

CHAPTER VI

AVIATION IN DREAMS

Dreams of Flying and Falling—Their Peculiar Vividness—Dreams of Flying an Alleged Survival of Primeval Experiences—Best explained as based on Respiratory Sensations combined with Cutaneous Anæsthesia—The Explanation of Dreams of Falling—The Sensation of Levitation sometimes experienced by Ecstatic Saints—Also experienced at the Moment of Death, ... 129

CONTENTS

CHAPTER VII

SYMBOLISM IN DREAMS

PAGE

The Dramatisation of Subjective Feelings Based on Dissociation—Analogies in Waking Life—The Synæsthesias and Number-forms—Symbolism in Language—In Music—The Organic Basis of Dream Symbolism—The Omnipotence of Symbolism—Oneiromancy—The Scientific Interpretation of Dreams—Why Symbolism prevails in Dreaming—Freud's Theory of Dreaming—Dreams as Fulfilled Wishes—Why this Theory cannot be applied to all Dreaming—The Complete Form of Symbolism in Dreams—Splitting up of Personality—Self-objectivation in Imaginary Personalities—The Dramatic Element in Dreams—Hallucinations—Multiple Personality—Insanity—Self-objectivation a Primitive Tendency—Its Survival in Civilisation, ... 148

CHAPTER VIII

DREAMS OF THE DEAD

Mental Dissociation during sleep—Illustrated by the Dream of Returning to School Life—The Typical Dream of a Dead Friend—Examples—Early Records of this Type of Dream—Analysis of such Dreams—Atypical Forms—The Consolation sometimes afforded by Dreams of the Dead—Ancient Legends of this Dream Type—The Influence of Dreams on the Belief of Primitive Man in the Survival of the Dead, . 194

CHAPTER IX

MEMORY IN DREAMS

The Apparent Rapidity of Thought in Dreams—This Phenomenon largely due to the Dream being a Description of a Picture—The Experience of Drowning Persons—The Sense of Time in Dreams—The Crumpling of Consciousness in Dreams—The Recovery of Lost Memories through the Relaxation of Attention—The Emergence in Dreams of Memories not known to Waking Life—The Recollection of Forgotten Languages in Sleep—The Perversions of Memory in Dreams—Paramnesic False Recollections—Hypnagogic Paramnesia

—Dreams mistaken for Actual Events—The Phenomenon of Pseudo-Reminiscence—Its Relationship to Epilepsy—Its Prevalence especially among Imaginative and Nervously Exhausted Persons—The Theories put forward to Explain it—A Fatigue Product—Conditioned by Defective Attention and Apperception—Pseudo-Reminiscence a reversed Hallucination, ... 212

CHAPTER X

CONCLUSION

The Fundamental Nature of Dreaming—Insanity and Dreaming—The Child's Psychic State and the Dream State—Primitive Thought and Dreams—Dreaming and Myth-Making—Genius and Dreams—Dreaming as a Road into the Infinite, 261

INDEX, ... 283

THE WORLD OF DREAMS

CHAPTER I

INTRODUCTION

The House of Dreams—Fallacies in the Study of Dreams—Is it Possible to Study Dreams?—How Fallacies may be Avoided—Do we always Dream during Sleep?—The Two Main Sources of Dreams with their Subdivisions.

WHEN we fall asleep we enter a dim and ancient house of shadow, unillumined by any direct ray from the outer world of waking life. We are borne about through its chambers, without conscious volition of our own; we fall down its mouldy and rotten staircases, we are haunted by strange sounds and odours from its mysterious recesses; we move among phantoms we cannot consciously control. As we emerge into the world of daily life again, for an instant the sunlight seems to flash into the obscure house before the door closes behind us; we catch one vivid glimpse of the chambers we have been wandering in, and a few more or less fragmentary memories come back to us of the life we have led there. But they soon fade away in the light of common day, and if a few hours later we seek to recall the strange experiences we have passed through, it usually happens that the visions of the night have already dissolved in memory into a few shreds of mist we can no longer reconstruct.

A

THE WORLD OF DREAMS

For most of us our whole knowledge ends here. Our dreams are real enough while they last, but the interests of waking life absorb us so entirely that we rarely have leisure, and still less inclination, to subject our sleeping adventures, trivial and absurd as they must usually seem, to the careful tests which waking intelligence is accustomed to subject more obviously important matters to. The world of dreams and the mysterious light which prevails there [1] are abandoned entirely to our sleeping activities.

This leading characteristic of dream life—the fact that it takes place in another and more shadowy world and in a different kind of consciousness [2]—has led

---

[1] The subdued quality of the light in normal dreaming—the usual absence of sunshine and generally even of colour—has long been noted. 'We never dream of being in the sunshine,' says Henry Dircks (*Lancet*, 11th June 1870, p. 863), though too absolutely; 'light and shade form no requisite elements. . . . The liveliest and most impressive dream is, in reality, a true night scene, very dubiously lighted up, and in which the nearest objects are those which we principally observe and which most interest us.'

[2] As some writers give a rather special meaning to the word 'consciousness,' I may say that I simply mean by it (as defined by Baldwin and Stout in the *Dictionary of Philosophy and Psychology*) 'the distinctive character of whatever may be called mental life,' or, as Professor Stratton puts it, in defence of this broad definition (*Psychological Bulletin*, April 1906), 'consciousness designates the common and generic feature of our psychic acts.' Dreaming then becomes, as defined by Baldwin and Stout, 'conscious process during sleep.' It should be added that there is much uncertainty about any definition of consciousness. Bode ('Some Recent Definitions of Consciousness,' *Psychological Review*, July 1908) thinks it 'a matter for legitimate doubt' whether any definition of consciousness can be adequate, and Mercier (art. 'Consciousness' in Tuke's *Dictionary of Psychological Medicine*) boldly proclaims—quite justly, I think—that 'consciousness is not susceptible of definition,' for we can never go behind it or outside it. That we have to admit various kinds, or at all events various degrees, of consciousness will become clear in our discussion of dreaming.

to the criticism of the study of dreams from the scientific side. We cannot really study our dreams, these objectors say, because we—that is to say, our waking consciousness—cannot come sufficiently closely in contact with them. Dreams, it is argued, are inevitably transformed in our hands ; what we are studying is not our dreams, but only our waking, and probably altogether false, impressions of our dreams. There is a certain element of truth in this objection. It is very difficult, indeed impossible, to recall exactly, and in their proper order, even the details of a real adventure which has only just happened to us. It is, obviously, incomparably more difficult to recall an experience which took place, under such shadowy conditions, in a world so remote from the world of waking life. There is, further, the very definite difficulty that we only catch our dreams for a moment by the light, as it were, of the open door as we are emerging from sleep. In other words, our waking consciousness is for a moment observing and interpreting a process in another kind of consciousness, or even if we assert that it is the same consciousness it is still a consciousness that has been working under quite different conditions from waking consciousness, and accepting data which in the waking state it would not accept. For the student of dreams it must ever be a serious question how far the facts become inevitably distorted in this process. Sleeping or waking, it is probable, our consciousness never embraces the whole of the possible psychic field within us. There are, when we are dreaming as well as when we are awake—as will become clearer in the sequel—subconscious, or imperfectly conscious, states just below our consciousness, and exerting an influence upon it.[1] Our latent psychic possessions, among which dreams move, would seem to be by no means always at the same depth ; the specific gravity of consciousness, as it were, varies, and these latent elements rise or fall, becoming nearer to the conscious surface or falling further away from it. But the greatest change must take place when the waking surface is reached and the outer world breaks on sleeping consciousness. In that change there is doubtless a process of necessary and automatic transformation and interpretation. We may picture it, perhaps, as somewhat the same process as when a person skilled in both languages takes up a foreign book and reads it out in his own tongue. With practice the reader may become unconscious that he is transforming everything, that the words he utters are different from the words he sees, and that he even transposes their order, some-

[1] By ' subconscious ' is meant, as defined by Baldwin and Stout, ' not clearly recognised in a present state of consciousness, yet entering into the development of subsequent states of consciousness.' Some psychologists strongly dislike the word ' subconscious.' They are even disposed to argue that there is no subconscious mind, and that before and after the stage of ' awareness,' psychic facts only exist as ' dispositions of brain cells.' The psychologist, however, as such, has no concern with brain cells which belong to the histologist. When we occupy ourselves with dreams we realise at every step that it is possible for psychic states to exist and to affect our ' awareness,' while at the same time they are not immediately within the sphere of that ' awareness.' Psychic states of this kind seem most properly termed ' subconscious,' that is to say slightly, partially, or imperfectly conscious. Any objection to so precise and convenient a term for a real phenomenon seems, indeed, to belong to the sphere of personal idiosyncrasy into which we have perhaps no right to intrude.

times putting in the middle of a sentence the verb he sees at the end.

Yet even if we admit that the passage from sleeping to waking consciousness involves a change as complete as this—and it is probable, as we shall see, that some such change sometimes takes place—for a faithful interpreter the sense still remains the same. It is impossible to believe that the witness of waking consciousness to the nature of the visions it has caught at the threshold between sleeping and waking life is false, and the most convincing evidence of this is the utter unlikeness of these visions to the data of ordinary waking life.

But even this conclusion has been subjected to severe criticism which we have to face before we proceed further. Foucault, an acute investigator of dream psychology—carrying to its extreme point a position more partially and tentatively stated by Delbœuf and Tannery—has denied that our dreams, as they finally present themselves to waking consciousness, at all correspond to the psychic process in sleep upon which they are founded, and he especially insists that the logical connections are superadded.[1] He considers that dreaming is an 'observation of memory' made under such conditions that 'it would be very imprudent to regard the remembrance of the dream as reproducing faithfully the mental state of sleep.' During sleep, he believes, our dream ideas proceed, concurrently, it may be, but separately and independently; at the moment when awakening begins, the mind, as an act

---

[1] Foucault, *Le Rêve*, 1906.

of immediate memory, grasps the plurality of separate pictures and applies itself spontaneously to the task of organising them according to the rules of logic and the laws of the real world, making a drama of them as like as possible to the dramas of waking life.[1] He agrees with Goblot that ' the dream we remember is a waking thought,' and with Tannery that ' we do not remember our dreams, but only the reconstructions of them we effected at the moment of waking.' It is after awakening, Foucault concludes, that the dream develops, and its final shape depends on the period at which it is noted down ; ' the evolution of the dream after awakening is a logical evolution, dominated and directed by the instinctive need to give a reasonable appearance to the *ensemble* of images and sensations present to the mind, and to assimilate the representation of the dream to the system of representations which constitutes our knowledge of the real world.' [2]

In arguing his thesis, Foucault makes much of the modifications which can be proved to take place if any one is asked to repeat a dream at intervals of months. Under the influence of time and repetition a dream becomes more coherent and more conformed to reality. In illustration Foucault presents two versions of an insignificant dream in which a lady imagines that she is out with her husband for a drive, and in the course of it experiences a natural need which she seeks an opportunity to satisfy ; the details of the first version were highly improbable ; some months later they had

---

[1] Foucault, *op. cit.*, ch. iv.   [2] Foucault, *op. cit.*, p. 49.

INTRODUCTION

become much more like what might have occurred in real life. Such a process, Foucault thinks, is taking place from the first in the making of dreams as we know them awake.

There are, undoubtedly, facts which may seem to support Foucault's argument that the logic of the dream, as we know it, is not in the original dream, but is introduced afterwards. Thus I once dreamed in the morning that I asked my wife if she had been into a certain room, and that she replied, 'Can't get in.' I immediately awoke and realised that my wife had actually spoken these words, not to me, but to an approaching servant, in anticipation of a message about entering a neighbouring room of which the door was locked. It is thus evident that although it seemed to me in my dream that the question came first and the answer followed in the ordinary course, in reality the answer came first. The question was a theory, supplied automatically by sleeping intelligence and prefixed to the answer, in which order they both appeared to sleeping consciousness, that is to say, in the only way in which sleeping consciousness can ever be known, as translated into waking consciousness.[1]

It must be borne in mind that such a dream as I have recorded—in which an actual sensory experience is introduced, untransformed, as a foreign body into sleeping consciousness—is not a typical dream. Dreams are, however, without doubt of various kinds, and we

[1] This occasionally retrospective character of dreams has long been known, and was referred to by the writer of an article on 'Dreams and Dreaming' in the *Lancet* for 24th November 1877.

may well admit that there is a class of dreams formed in this way. That supposition will, indeed, be helpful in explaining several dreams I shall have to record. The process is much the same as when a nervous person receives a telegram, and at once assumes that some dreaded accident has occurred, and that the telegram is the announcement of it. The craving for reasons is instinctive, and the dreamer's sense of logic even dominates his sense of time.

But Foucault's argument is that waking consciousness effects this logical construction of the dream. Here his position is weak and incapable of proof. It is, indeed, contrary to all the tests we are able to apply to it. If it is the object of the logic of our dreams to make them conformable to our waking experience, that end, we must admit, is in most cases very far from being attained. In their original form, as Foucault views the matter, our dreams are simple dissociated images. In that shape they would present nothing whatever to shock the consciousness of waking life. The logic, hypothetically introduced solely to make them conformable to real life, is frequently a preposterous logic such as the consciousness of waking life could not accept or even conceive. This fact alone serves to throw serious doubt upon the theory that it is waking consciousness which impresses its logic upon our dreams.

Nor, again, is there any analogy, and still less identity, between the process whereby we grasp a dream when we awake, and the process whereby the memory of a dream is transformed during months of waking life.

INTRODUCTION

The latter is part of a general process affecting all our memories in greater or less degree. I visit, for instance, a foreign cathedral, and take careful note of the character and arrangement of buttresses and piers; a few months later, if I have failed to set the facts down, my memory of them will become uncertain, confused, and incorrect. But I need not, therefore, lose faith in the tolerable exactitude of my original impressions. In the same way, we cannot argue that the shifting memory of a dream during a long period of time throws the slightest doubt on the accuracy of our original impression of it. We never catch a dream in course of formation. As it presents itself to consciousness on awakening there may be doubtful points and there may be missing links, but the dream is, once for all, completed, and if there are doubtful points or missing links we recognise them as such. We make no attempt to supply a logic that is not there, and we never see any such process going on involuntarily. I should, indeed, myself be inclined to say that there is always a kind of gap between sleeping consciousness and waking consciousness; the change from the one to the other kind of consciousness seems to be effected by a slight shock, and the perception of the already completed dream is the first effort of waking consciousness. The existence of such a shock is indicated by the fact that, even at the first moment of waking consciousness, we never realise that a moment ago we were asleep. As soon as we realise that we are awake it seems to us that we have already been awake for an uncertain but distinct period of time ; some people, indeed, especially old people, on awaking, feel this so strongly that they deny they have been asleep. It once happened to me to be in the neighbourhood of a dynamite factory at the moment when a very disastrous explosion occurred ; at the time my back was to the factory, and I am quite unable to say how long an interval occurred between the shock of the explosion and my own action in turning round to observe the straight shaft of smoke and solid material high in the air ; there was a gap in consciousness, an interval of unknown and seemingly considerable length, caused by the deafening shock of the explosion, although it is probable that my action in turning round was almost or quite instantaneous. It seems to me that the transition from sleeping consciousness to waking consciousness occurs in a similar manner on a smaller scale.

Although the view of Foucault that the dream is logically organised after sleep has ended seems, when we examine the evidence in its favour, to be unacceptable, we may still admit that, in some cases at all events, the dream only assumes final shape at the moment when sleeping consciousness is breaking up, that the dream, as we know it, is a final synthetic attempt of sleeping consciousness as it dissolves on the approach of waking consciousness. Sleeping consciousness, we may even imagine as saying to itself in effect : ' Here comes our master, Waking Consciousness, who attaches such mighty importance to reason and logic and so forth. Quick ! gather things up, put them in order—any order will do—before he enters to take possession.' That is to say, in other words, that as sleeping consciousness comes nearer to the threshold of waking consciousness it is possible that the need for the same kind of causation or sequence which is manifested in waking consciousness may begin to make itself felt even to sleeping consciousness. Even this assumption seems, however, as regards most dreams, to be extravagant. In any case, and at whatever stage the dream is finally constituted, we are not entitled, it seems to me, to believe that any stage of its constitution falls outside the frontiers of sleep. It is satisfactory to be able to feel justified in reaching this conclusion. For if dreams were chiefly or mainly the product of waking consciousness they would certainly lose a considerable part of their significance and interest.

Even, however, when we have reached this conclusion the path of the student is still far from easy. The undoubted fact that in any case the difficulties of observing and recording dreams are very great cannot fail to make us extremely careful. Although the dreams of some persons, who may be regarded as themselves of vivid and dramatic temperament, seem to be habitually vivid and dramatic to an extent which, in my own case, is extremely rare, one is usually justified in feeling a certain amount of suspicion in regard to dream-narratives which are at every point clear, coherent, connected, and intelligible. Dreams, as I know them on awaking from sleep, occasionally present episodes to which these epithets may be applied, but on the whole they are full of obscurities, of uncertainties, of inexplicable lacunae. The memory of dream events is lost so rapidly that one is constantly obliged to leave the exact nature of a detail in doubt. One seems to be recalling a landscape seen by a lightning flash. It is for this reason that I have made it a rule only to admit dreams which are noted very shortly, and if possible immediately, after the moment of awakening. It is further of importance in recording one's dreams, to note the emotional attitude experienced during the dream as well as any physical sensations felt on awakening. The attitude of dream consciousness towards dream visions usually varies from that of waking consciousness, although the normal extent of the difference is a disputable point. When I read dream narratives of landscapes which, as described, appear at every point as beautiful and impressive to waking consciousness as they appeared to dreaming consciousness, I usually suspect that, granting the good faith and accuracy of the narrator, we are really concerned, not with dreams in the proper sense, but with visions experienced under more abnormal conditions, and especially with drug visions. In the present inquiry I am only concerned to ascertain the most elementary and fundamental laws of the dream world, as they occur in fairly ordinary and normal persons, and therefore it becomes necessary to be very strict as to the conditions under which they were recorded. It is the most ordinary dreams that are most likely to reveal the ordinary laws of

INTRODUCTION 13

dream life, but for this end it is necessary that they should be recorded with the greatest accuracy attainable.

I am myself neither a constant nor, usually, a very vivid dreamer, and in these respects I am probably a fairly ordinary and normal person ; the personal material which I have accumulated, though it spreads over twenty years, is not notably copious. Nor have I ever directed my attention in any systematic and concentrated manner to my dream life. To do so would be, I believe, to distort the phenomena. I have merely recorded any significant phenomena as they occurred.

To remark that one is not a constant dreamer is not to assert that dreaming is rare, but merely that one's recollection of it is rare. Though we may only catch a glimpse of our latest vision of the night as we leave the house of sleep, it may well be that there were many earlier adventures of the night which are beyond the reach of waking consciousness. Sometimes, it is curious to note, we become vaguely conscious, during the day, for the first time, of a dream we have had during the night. Many psychologists, as well as metaphysicians—fearful to admit that the activity of the soul could ever cease—believe that we dream during the whole period of sleep ; this has of recent years been the opinion of Vaschide, Foucault, Näcke, and Sir Arthur Mitchell, as it formerly was of Sir Benjamin Brodie, Sir Henry Holland, and Schaaffhausen. In earlier days Hippocrates, Descartes, Leibnitz, and Cabanis seem to have been of the same opinion. On the other hand, Locke, Macnish, and Carpenter held that deep sleep is dreamless ; this is also the opinion of Wundt, Beaunis, Strümpell, Weygandt, Hammond, and Jastrow. Moreover, there are some people, like Lessing, who, so far as they know, never dream at all. My own personal experience scarcely inclines me to accept without qualification the belief that we are always dreaming during sleep. I find that my remembered dreams tend to be correlated with some slight mental or physical disturbance, and therefore it seems to me probable that, if dreams are continuous during sleep, they must, during completely undisturbed sleep, be of an extremely faint and shadowy character. To return to a metaphor I have before used, we may say that sleeping consciousness in its descent from the surface of the waking life may fall to a point at which its specific gravity being practically the same as that of its environment, a state approaching complete repose is attained.[1] It cannot of course be said that the failure to remember dreams is any argument against their occurrence. It is well known that when the psychic activity of sleep assumes a definitely motor shape, as in talking in sleep and in somnambulism, it

[1] The old French case (quoted by Macnish) of a woman, with a portion of her skull removed, whose brain bulged out during dreams but was motionless in dreamless sleep, as well as the more recent similar case known to Hammond (*Treatise on Insanity*, p. 233), supports the belief that the psychic activity which is not manifested in remarkable dreams is probably at the most of a very shadowy character. Even during waking life psychic activity often falls to a very low ebb; Beaunis, who has investigated this question ('Comment Fonctionne mon Cerveau,' *Revue Philosophique*, January 1909), describes a condition which he names 'psychic twilight' and regards as frequently occurring.

is very rare for any recollection to remain on awakening, though we cannot doubt that psychic activity has been present. In the same way the dream that we remember when awakened from sound sleep by another person is by no means always due to that awakening. This is shown by the fact that if we were turning round or making other movements just before being thus awakened, the dream we remember—in one such case a dream of making one's way with difficulty between a sofa and a chair—may have no relation to the circumstance of the awakening, but clearly be suggested by the movements made during sleep, though these movements themselves remain unknown to waking consciousness. The movements of dogs during sound sleep—the rhythmical lifting of the paws, the wagging of the tail—point in the same direction.[1]

The fact that failure of memory by no means proves the absence of dreaming may be illustrated, not only by the forgetfulness of what takes place during hypnotic sleep, but by what we sometimes witness during partial anaesthesia maintained by drugs. This was well shown in a case I was once concerned with, where it was necessary to administer chloroform (preceded by the alcohol-chloroform-ether mixture) for a prolonged period during a difficult first confinement. The drug

[1] Lucretius long ago referred to the significance of this fact (lib. iv. vv. 988-994), and he stated that the hallucination persisted for a time even after the dog had awakened. I have never myself been able to see any trace of such hypnagogic hallucination or delusion in dogs who awake from dreams, though I have frequently looked for it; it always seems to me that the dog who seemingly awakes from a dream of hunting grasps the fireside facts of life around him immediately and easily.

was not given to the point of causing complete abolition of mental activity, and the patient talked, and occasionally sang, throughout, referring to various events in her life, from childhood onwards. The sensation and the expression of pain were not altogether abolished, for slight cries and remarks about the discomfort and constraint imposed upon her were sometimes mingled in the same sentence with quite irrelevant remarks concerning, for instance, trivial details of housekeeping. Confusions of incompatible ideas also took place, as during ordinary dreaming. 'Where is the three-cornered nurse,' she thus asked, 'who does not mind what she does?' There was also the abnormal suggestibility of dream consciousness. The questions of bystanders were answered but always with a tendency to agree with everything that was said, this tendency even displaying itself with a certain ingenuity as when in reply to the playful random query: 'Were you drunk or sleeping last night?' she answered, with some hesitation: 'A little of both, I think.' To the casual observer, it might seem that there was a state of full consciousness on the basis of which a partial delirium had established itself. Yet on recovery from the drug there was no recollection of anything whatever that had taken place during its administration, and no sense of the lapse of time.

Fantastic and marvellous as our dreams may sometimes be, they are in practically all cases made up of very simple elements. It is desirable that we should at the outset have a provisional notion as to the sources of these simple elements. Most writers on dreams hold that there are two great sources from which these elements are drawn : the vast reservoir of memories and the actual physical sensations experienced at the moment of dreaming, and interpreted by sleeping consciousness. Various names have been given to these two groups, the recognition of which is at least as old as Aristotle.[1] Thus Sully calls them central and peripheral, Tissié, psychic and sensorial, Foucault, imaginative and perceptive. Fairly convenient names are those adopted by Miss Calkins, who calls the first group representative, the second group presentative, meaning by representative ' connected through the fact of association with the waking life of the past,' and by presentative ' connected through sense excitation with the immediate present.'[2]

The representative group falls into two subdivisions, according as the memories are of old or of recent date ; these subdivisions are often quite distinct, recent dream memories belonging—probably with most people —to the previous day, while old dream memories are usually drawn from the experience of many years past, and frequently from early life. In the same way presentative impressions fall into two subdivisions,

[1] This classification of the sources of dreams has, however, been generally accepted for little more than a century. At an earlier period it was not usually believed to cover the whole ground. Thus Des Laurens (A. Laurentius) in the sixteenth century, in his treatise on the Disease of Melancholy (insanity), says that there are three kinds of dreams : (1) of Nature (*i.e.* due to external causes) ; (2) of the mind (*i.e.* based on memories); and, above both these classes, (3) dreams from God and the devil.

[2] M. W. Calkins, ' Statistics of Dreams,' *American Journal of Psychology*, April 1893.

according as they refer to external stimuli present to the senses, or to internal disturbances within the organism. It is scarcely necessary to observe that any or all of these four sub-groups, into which the whole of our dream life may be analysed, may become woven together in the same dream.

I have called the classification 'provisional' because, though it is convenient to adopt it for the sake of orderly arrangement, when we come to consider the matter it will be found that the material of dreams is in reality all of the same order, and purely psychic, though it may be differentiated in accordance with the character of the stimulus which evokes the psychic material of which it is made. Strictly speaking, the source of the dream as a dream can only be central, and a truly presentative dream is impossible. If our senses receive an impression, external or internal, and we recognise and accept that impression for what we should recognise and accept it when awake, then we cannot be said to be dreaming. The internal and external stimuli which act upon sleeping consciousness are not a part of that consciousness, nor in any real sense its source or its cause. The ray of sunlight that falls on the dreamer, the falling off of his bedclothes, the indigestible supper he ate last night—these things can no more 'account' for his dream than the postman's knock can account for the contents of the letter he delivers. Whatever the stimuli from the physical world that may knock at the door of dreaming consciousness, that consciousness is apart from them, and stimuli can only reach it by undergoing transformation. They must put off the character which they wear as phenomena of the waking world ; they must put on the character of phenomena of another world, the world of dreams.

CHAPTER II

THE ELEMENTS OF DREAM LIFE

The Spontaneous Procession of Dream Imagery—Its Kaleidoscopic Character—Attention in Dreams—Relation of Drug Visions and Hypnagogic Imagery to Dreaming—Colour in Dreams—The Fusion of Dream Imagery—Compared to Dissolving Views—Sources of the Imagery—Various types of Fusion—The Subconscious Element in Dreaming—Verbal Transformations as Links in Dream Imagery—The Reduplication of Visual Imagery in Motor and other Terms.

PERHAPS the most elementary fact about dream vision is the perpetual and unceasing change which it is undergoing at every moment. Sight is for most of us the chief sensory activity of sleeping as it is of waking life ; the commonest kind of dream is mainly a picture, but it is always a living and moving picture, however inanimate the objects which appear in vision before us would be in real life. No man ever gazed at a dream picture which was at rest to his sleeping eye as are the pictures we gaze at with our waking eyes. So far as my own experience is concerned, I have rarely in sleep seen a sentence, a word, a letter written on a sheet of dream-paper which was not changing beneath the eye of sleep. I dream, for instance, that I wish to stamp a letter, and look in my pocket-book for a penny stamp ; I am able to find stamps of other values, I am able to find penny stamps that are torn or defaced or of an

THE ELEMENTS OF DREAM LIFE 21

antiquated type disused thirty years ago ; all sorts of stamps, as well as little pictures resembling stamps, develop and multiply beneath my gaze ; the stamp I seek remains unfound, probably because it had appeared at the beginning of the series and suggested all the rest. That is indicated by another dream (experienced, it may be noted, during the early stage of a cold in the head) : I have to catch a train ; I see my hat hanging on a peg among other hats, and I move towards it ; but as I do so it has vanished ; and I wander among rows of hats, of all shapes and sizes, but not one of them mine. Sleeping consciousness is a stream in which we never bathe twice, for it is renewed every second. It is this as much as any characteristic of the visual dream—for the mainly auditory or motor dream often presents less difficulty in this respect—which makes it so difficult to recall and reproduce. We are, as it were, gazing at a constantly revolving kaleidoscope in which every slightest turn produces a new pattern, somewhat resembling that which immediately preceded it—so that, if the kaleidoscope were conscious we should say that each picture had been suggested by the preceding pattern—but yet definitely novel.[1]

Delbœuf has denied that this process ever involves any real metamorphosis of images ; he regarded it as

[1] The simile of the kaleidoscope for the most elementary process of dreaming has often suggested itself. Thus in an article on dreaming in the *Lancet* (24th November 1877) we read : ' The combinations are new, but the materials are old, some recent, many remote and forgotten. . . . The turn of the kaleidoscope is instantaneous and any new idea thrown into the field, perhaps in the act of turning, becomes an integral part of the picture.'

an illusion due to rapid succession of distinct images which are afterwards combined in memory. That view is not, however, tenable ; apart from the fact that it makes the illegitimate assumption that our recollection of a dream is entirely unreliable, it must be remembered that (as Giessler has pointed out) the shock of emotional horror or surprise that frequently accompanies such dreams suffices to prove the reality of the metamorphosis. Thus I once, as a youth, had a vivid dream of an albatross that became transformed into a woman, the beautiful eyes of the albatross taking on a womanly expression, but the bird's beak only being imperfectly changed into a nose as the bird-woman murmured, ' Do you love me ? ' In this case the vivid surprise of the dream was precisely associated with the simultaneous existence of the two sets of characters.

It is not, however, necessary that there should be any metamorphosis of dream images, nor even that the procession of dream imagery should be continuous. And whether or not there is metamorphosis of images, whether the imagery is continuous or discontinuous, it seems to me that we must admit the possibility of its spontaneous character. That is, indeed, a debated, and, it may be admitted, a debateable point. Thus Foucault[1] accounts for the multiplication of almost similar images sometimes witnessed in dreams as due to *desire* ; we see a number of things because we desire to possess a number of these things, and he explains a

---

[1] Foucault, *Le Rêve*, p. 182.

THE ELEMENTS OF DREAM LIFE 23

dream of Delbœuf's, of a procession of lizards, as due to the fact that Delbœuf was a collector of lizards, in the same way as he would explain the dreams of thirsty people who imagine they are drinking repeated glasses of water or wine. I am quite unable to accept this explanation. The shifting and multiplication of dream imagery, as in the procession of lizards, is a fundamental and elementary character of spontaneous mental imagery, and is constant in some drug visions, notably those occasioned by mescal.[1] The repetition of imaginary drinks in the dreams of a thirsty man belongs to another more special class in explanation of which desire may be more properly invoked; it is merely the expression of the fact that after the imaginary drink the dreamer remains thirsty, and the suggested image is therefore repeated.

That in some cases there is what we may call a deliberate subconscious selection in the imagery presented to consciousness in dreams, there can be no doubt. But mental imagery is deeper and more elemental than any of the higher psychic functions even when exerted subconsciously. Just as the immense procession of continuous and totally unfamiliar imagery which is evoked by the action of mescal on the visual centres has no more connection with the subject's volition or desires than the procession of the starry skies, so likewise, we seem bound to admit, it may be in the case of a succession of separate images in

[1] This is in accordance with the view of Wundt, who attributes this multiplication of imagery to the retinal element.

dreams. It is nearly always possible to find a link of connection between any two images chosen at random, and the link is often a real subconscious link, but not necessarily so. Discontinuous images may arise, it seems probable, from a psychic basis deeper than choice, their appearance being determined by their own dynamic condition at the moment. We must, as Baron Mourre [1] not quite happily puts it, take into account ' the physiological state of ideas.' If we hold to the belief that dreaming is based on a fundamental and elementary tendency to the formation of continuous or discontinuous images, which may or may not be controlled by psychic emotions or impulses, we shall be delivered from many hazardous speculations.

When we thus start with the recognition of a more or less spontaneous procession of images as the elemental stuff of dreams, one of the first problems we encounter is the relation of attention to that imagery. What is the degree and the nature of the attention we exert in dreams ?

'Sleep from the psychological point of view,' says Foucault, 'is a state of profound distraction or total inattention.' And Mourre shows by dreams of his own that any exercise of will in dreaming leads to awakening, and that the deeper the sleep the more absent is volition from dreams. Hence the involuntary wavering and perpetually mere meaningless change of dream imagery. Such concentration as is possible during sleep usually

---

[1] Baron Charles Mourre, ' La Volonté dans le Rêve,' *Revue Philosophique*, May 1903.

THE ELEMENTS OF DREAM LIFE 25

reveals a shifting, oscillating, uncertain movement of the vision before us. We are, as it were, reading a sign-post in the dusk, or making guesses at the names of the stations as our express train flashes by the painted letters. It is this factor in dreams which causes them so often to baffle our analysis. There is thus a failure of sleeping attention to fix definitely the final result— a failure which itself may evidently serve to carry on the dream process by suggesting new images and combinations. It can scarcely be said, however, that the question of attention in dreams is thus settled. It would be inconceivable that the terrible occurrences that may overtake us in dreams and the emotional turmoil aroused should be accompanied by 'total inattention and distraction.' Nor can it be said that that supposition agrees with the vivid memory which our dreams sometimes leave. We can probably account for the phenomena much more satisfactorily by adopting Ribot's useful distinction between voluntary attention and spontaneous attention.[1] Voluntary or artificial attention is a product of education and training. It is directed by extrinsic force, is the result of deliberation, and is accompanied by some feeling of effort. It always acts on the muscles and by the muscles; without muscular tension there can be no voluntary attention. Spontaneous or natural attention, on the other hand, is that more fundamental kind of attention which exists anteriorly to any education or training, and is the only kind of attention which animals and

[1] Ribot, *Psychologie de l'Attention*, 1889, chs. i. and ii.

young children are capable of. It may be weak or strong, but always and everywhere it is based on emotional states; every creature moved by pleasure and pain is capable of spontaneous attention under the influence of those stimuli. These two kinds of attention are at the opposite poles from each other, and are incompatible with each other. There can be no doubt that, as Ribot himself pointed out, it is voluntary attention that is defective (though it may not always be entirely absent) in dreams;[1] the muscular weakness and inco-ordination of sleep involve this lack of attention which is indeed an essential condition of the restoration and repose of sleep. But all the characters of spontaneous attention are present. The attention we exercise in dreams is mainly of this fundamental, automatic, involuntary character, conditioned by the emotions we experience, and for the most part escaping all the efforts of our voluntary attention. Further, it has been ably argued by Leroy that a similar state of involuntary automatic attention, with concomitant diminution or disturbance of voluntary attention, is a necessary condition for the appearance of the visual and auditory hallucinations abnormally experienced in the waking state.[2]

[1] Maine de Biran, perhaps the earliest accurate introspective observer of dreaming, noted the absence of all voluntary active attention. Beaunis regards attention as possible in dreams, but fails to distinguish between different kinds of attention.

[2] B. Leroy, ' Nature des Hallucinations,' *Revue Philosophique*, June 1907. As regards the importance of the absence of voluntary attention in the production of visual images, it may be remarked that even the after-image of a bright object in waking life is much more vivid when it occurs in a

THE ELEMENTS OF DREAM LIFE 27

There is, then, at the basis of dreaming a seemingly spontaneous procession of dream imagery which is always undergoing transformation into something different, yet not wholly different, from that which went before. It seems a mechanical flow of images, regulated by associations of resemblance, which sleeping consciousness recognises without either controlling or introducing foreign elements. This is probably the most elementary form of dreaming, that which is nearest to waking consciousness, and that in which the peripheral and retinal element of dreaming plays the largest part.

The fundamental character of this spontaneous self-evolving procession of imagery is indicated by the significant fact that it tends to take place whenever the more retinal and peripheral part of the visual apparatus is affected by the exhaustion of undue stimulation, or even when the organism generally is disturbed or run down, as in neurasthenic conditions.[1] The most obtrusive and familiar example of visual imagery is furnished by the procession of perpetually shifting and changing after-images which continue to evolve for a considerable time after we have looked at the sun or

state of inattention and distraction. I noticed this phenomenon some years ago, especially when studying mescal, and in recent years it has been recorded by J. H. Hyslop (*Psychological Review*, May 1903).

[1] We must be cautious in assuming that such imagery is purely retinal. Scripture ('Cerebral light,' *Studies from the Yale Psychological Laboratory*, vol. v., 1899) argues that even the so-called 'retinal light' or '*eigenlicht*' is cerebral, not retinal at all, since it is single and not double, and differs from after-images, which are displaced by pressure on eyeball. This view is perhaps too extreme in the opposite direction.

other brilliant object.[1] Less striking, but more intimately akin to the imagery of dreams, are the hypnagogic visions occurring as we fall asleep, especially after a day during which vision has been unusually stimulated and fatigued, though they do not seem necessarily dependent on such fatigue. Most vivid and instructive of all is the procession of visual imagery evoked by certain drugs. Of these the most remarkable and potent, as well as the best for study, is probably mescal, which happens also to be the only one with which I am myself well acquainted.[2] This substance provokes a constant succession of self-evolving visual imagery which constantly approaches and constantly eludes the semblance of real things; in the earlier stages these images closely resemble those produced by the kaleidoscope, and they change in a somewhat similar manner. Such spontaneous evolution of imagery is evidently a fundamental aptitude of the visual apparatus which many very slightly abnormal conditions may bring into prominence.

The power of opium is somewhat similar, and, as De Quincey long since pointed out, such power is simply a revival of a faculty usually possessed by children, although, judging from my own experiences with mescal, drugs exert it in a far more vivid and potent degree than that in which it usually occurs in the child.

[1] For a full and interesting study of these, see S. J. Franz, 'After-images' (Monograph Supplements to *Psychological Review*, vol. iii., No. 2, June 1899). He agrees with those who regard after-images as entirely retinal in origin.

[2] See Havelock Ellis, 'A New Artificial Paradise,' *Contemporary Review*, January 1898; *ib.* ' Mescal ; A Study of a Divine Plant,' *Popular Science Monthly*, May 1902.

THE ELEMENTS OF DREAM LIFE

The psychologists of childhood have not often investigated this phenomenon,[1] but so far as my own inquiries go, all or nearly all persons have possessed, when children, the power of seeing visions in the dark on the curtain of the closed eyelids, perhaps the representation of fairy tales they had read, perhaps merely commonplace processions of individuals or events, a tendency sometimes appearing for the same figure to recur again and again. I think it is fairly certain that the so-called ' lies ' of children, told in good faith, are in part due to the occasional eruption of this faculty into daylight life. People who deny that they ever possessed this power have, almost certainly, only forgotten. I should myself be inclined to deny that I had ever had any such visionary faculty if it were not

[1] G. E. Partridge, however (' Reverie,' *Pedagogical Seminary*, April 1898), has investigated hypnagogic phenomena in 826 children. They were asked to describe what they saw at night with closed eyes before falling asleep. Among these children 58·5 per cent. of those aged from thirteen to sixteen saw things at night in this way ; of those aged six the proportion was higher, 64·2 per cent. There seemed to be a maximum at about the age of ten, and probably another maximum at a much earlier age. Stars were most frequently mentioned, being spoken of by 151 children, colours by 145, people and faces 77, animals 31, scenes of the day 21, flowers and fruit 18, pictures 15, God and angels 13. Partridge calls these phenomena hypnagogic ; while, however, the hypnagogic visions of adults may well be a relic of children's visions, the latter have much greater range and vitality, for they are not confined to the moment before sleep, and the child sometimes has a certain amount of control over them. E. Guyon has studied hypnagogic and allied visions in children in his Paris thesis, *Sur les Hallucinations Hypnagogiques*, 1903. He believes that children always find them terrifying. That, however, is far from being the case and is merely due to a pre-occupation with morbid cases, which naturally attract most attention. (This is also illustrated by the examples given by Stanley Hall, ' A Study of Fears,' *American Journal of Psychology*, 1897, pp. 186 *et seq.*) The visions of the healthy child are not terrifying, and he accepts them in a completely matter-of-course way. He is no more puzzled or troubled by his waking dreams than by his sleeping dreams.

that I can recall one occasion of its presence, at about the age of seven, when sleeping with a cousin of the same age ; we amused ourselves by burying our heads in the pillows and watching a connected series of pictures which we were both alike able to see, each announcing any change in the picture as soon as it took place. This fact of community of vision served to impress on my mind the existence of a faculty of which otherwise I can recall no trace.[1]

Of these various groups of allied phenomena, that which more especially concerns us in the investigation of dreams is the group of phenomena most strictly called hypnagogic, belonging, that is to say, to the ante-

[1] The earliest detailed, though not typical, description of this phenomenon I have met with is by Dr. Simon Forman, the astrologer, in his entertaining *Autobiography*, written in 1600. He says that, as a child of six, 'So soon as he was always laid down to sleep he should see in visions always many mighty mountains and hills come rolling against him, as though they would overrun him and fall on him and bruise him, yet he got up always to the top of them and with much ado went over them. Then should he see many great waters like to drown him, boiling and raging against him as though they would swallow him up, yet he thought he did overpass them. And these dreams and visions he had every night continually for three or four years' space.' He believed they were sent him by God to signify the troubles of his later years. De Quincey accurately described the phenomenon in 1821, in his *Confessions of an English Opium-Eater* : ' I know not whether my reader is aware, that many children, perhaps most, have a power of painting, as it were, upon the darkness, all sorts of phantoms : in some, that power is simply a mechanic affection of the eye ; others have a voluntary or a semi-voluntary power to dismiss or to summon them, or, as a child once said to me when I questioned him on this matter, " I can tell them to go and they go; but sometimes they come, when I don't tell them to come." ' E. H. Clarke (*Visions*, 1878, pp. 212-216) discussed the ability of children to see visions, and pointed out the element of will in this ability. It seems unusual for auditory impressions to intrude, though J. A. Symonds (biography by Horatio Brown, vol. i. p. 7), in describing his own night-terrors as a child, speaks of phantasmal voices which blended with the caterwauling of cats on the roof.

THE ELEMENTS OF DREAM LIFE 31

chamber of sleep, when the senses are in repose and waking consciousness is slipping away, or else when, as we leave the world of dreams, waking consciousness is flowing back again. This state has been known from very ancient times. Aristotle referred to it, and in the dawn of modern scientific thought Hobbes described allied phenomena.[1] The strictly psychological study of hypnagogic visions seems to have begun with Baillarger.[2] Then, some years later, Maury, who had a rich personal experience of such phenomena, devoted a chapter to the hypnagogic state, and gave it its recognised name.[3]

Hypnagogic imagery, there can be little doubt, is not a purely ocular phenomenon, even when it is stimulated by ocular fatigue. It is a mixed phenomenon, partly retinal and partly central. That is to say that the eye supplies entoptic glimmerings, and the brain, acting on the suggestions thus received, superposes mental pictures to those glimmerings.[4] They are thus

[1] 'From being long and vehemently attent upon geometrical figures,' Hobbes says after referring to the after-images of the sun (*Leviathan*, part i., ch. 2), 'a man shall in the dark (though awake) have the images of lines and angles before his eyes: which kind of fancy hath no particular name; as being a thing that doth not commonly fall into men's discourse.'

[2] Baillarger, 'De l'Influence de l'Etat Intermédiaire à la veille et au sommeil sur la Production et la Marche des Hallucinations,' *Annales Médico-Psychologiques*, vol. v., 1845.

[3] Maury, *Le Sommeil et les Rêves*, 1861, pp. 50-77. Good descriptions of hypnagogic imagery are given by Greenwood, *Imagination and Dreams*, pp. 16-18, and Ladd, 'The Psychology of Visual Dreams,' *Mind*, 1892. See also Sante di Sanctis, *I Sogni*, pp. 337 *et seq*.

[4] This is the explanation offered by, for example, Delage (*Comptes-rendus de l'Académie des Sciences*, vol. cxxxvi., No. 12, pp. 731 *et seq.*). It is accepted by Guyon and others. Delage insists on the retinal element since he finds that hypnagogic images follow the movements of the eye.

analogous to the pictures we may see in the fire or in the clouds. It must be added that the other senses also furnish corresponding rudiments which are filled in by the central activity ; this is notably the case with faint buzzings and sounds in the ear, and in addition, muscular twitches and internal visceral sensations, all these becoming more prominent as the attentive activity of waking life subsides.[1]

What is the relation of hypnagogic imagery to dreams ? Johannes Müller, the great physiologist, long ago identified them, as previously had Gruithuisen and Burdach, while Maury—who himself possessed, however, a somewhat abnormal and irritable nervous system—regarded hypnotic imagery as furnishing the whole of the formative element of dreams, as being ' the embryogeny of dreams ' ; he frequently found that images which appeared to him in this way before going to sleep reappeared in dreams. This is supported by Mourly Vold, who made experiments on himself, and by fixing images as he fell asleep dreamed of the same images. Goblot, however, while regarding hypnagogic imagery as analogous with dream imagery, denies that it is identical. Since the hypnagogic state is the porch to sleep and dreams—the praedormitium, as Weir Mitchell terms it—we can scarcely fail to admit with Maury that hypnagogic imagery presents us with the germinal stuff of dreams. If it is not identical with the fully formed dream, it is still the early stage of dreaming.

[1] Similarly, under chloroform, Elmer Jones found that vision is at first stimulated.

THE ELEMENTS OF DREAM LIFE

This is certainly the view suggested by my own experience, even though I have never definitely recognised a dream as related to a previous hypnagogic image. It has, however, occasionally happened to me that as I have begun to lose waking consciousness a procession of images has drifted before my vision, and suddenly one of the figures I see has spoken. This hallucinatory voice occurring before I was fully asleep has startled me into full waking consciousness, and I have realised that, while yet in the hypnagogic stage, I was assisting at the birth of a dream.

There is one point, it may be noted in passing, at which dreams do not usually correspond with some of the phenomena with which we may most naturally compare them. I refer to their presentation of colour. In the dreams of most people colour is rare. We seem usually, from this point of view, to remember a dream as we would remember a photograph, or, if any colour at all is present, a tinted drawing. Judging from my own experience, I should say that it is difficult to decide whether the absence of colour is due to its actual absence from the dream imagery, or merely to its failure to make any impression on memory. Some careful observers have, however, stated that the colour of their dream imagery is definitely grey. Thus Beaunis states that his dream imagery is usually *en grisaille*, like an image recalled in the waking state, though occasionally the colour is vivid, and Dr. Savage says that in his dreams colour is rarely or never present. 'I see landscapes of black and white, and flowers assume their true form, but not their colours.'[1] This greyness of dream imagery corresponds to the disappearance of colour under chloroform anaesthesia. 'So long as the eyes could be held open voluntarily,' says Elmer Jones, 'vision seemed quite normal, save that the colours of the spectrum faded out into a grey band.' Even in the early stage of some insanities also, as Stoddart has found, some degree of colour-blindness is present.[2] Grace Andrews states, indeed, that in nearly half of her own visual dreams colour sensations were included. This seems to me exceptional. In my own experience, the emergence of a single colour, which usually strikes me as beautiful, is not rare. I see, for instance, a friend drinking wine copiously from a large goblet, and I judge by the colour of the wine that it is hock, or I am impressed by the shimmering grey tone of the poplin dresses worn by a group of ladies, which seems to indicate that the tone of the whole picture was not grey. I am inclined to think that when colour in a dream becomes more pronounced than this, the dream is not normal, but is associated with some degree of cerebral disturbance, and especially the presence of headache. This would agree with the fact that persons subject to migraine are liable to visual colour phenomena. As an example of a vivid colour dream associ-

[1] G. H. Savage, 'Dreams: Normal and Morbid,' *St. Thomas's Hospital Gazette*, February 1908.

[2] *British Medical Journal*, 11th May 1907. The actual hallucinations of the insane are usually coloured normally. Head, however, finds (*Brain*, 1901, p. 353) that the waking visual hallucinations sometimes associated with visceral disease are always white, black, or grey, and never coloured or even tinted.

ated with headache, I may bring forward the following : I dreamed that an artist of note, with whom I am acquainted, was painting my portrait. (The pose of the portrait was standing, but I was lying down ; this, however, caused me no surprise.) I saw the colours of the picture with great vividness, and I noted the extreme rapidity with which the artist painted ; thus the red and black pattern of the necktie he had given me was suddenly changed to a totally different blue pattern, and the whole picture then appeared as a harmony of blues, the rapidity with which the artist effected these changes impressing me as very remarkable. In another dream in which I saw a painter occupied on a picture, a landscape representing sunrise, memory recalled the effect of light as vivid, but no definite sense of colour remained. This seems to me the normal condition of things in the ordinary dreams of most persons, colour, when it occurs, or when it is remembered, being for the most part confined to a single object or a single tint, and often being associated with a feeling of aesthetic pleasure.

In ordinary dreaming there is usually something more than a spontaneous procession of related imagery. There is a more definitely central and psychic element. There is association, not only by obvious resemblance, but by contiguity, usually the casual contiguity of images received during the previous day, which forces together images related to each other indeed, but by no means obviously. Dreaming consciousness embodies and actively co-ordinates definite, and not merely random, images. The passive and spontaneous flow of imagery is thus modified in its course.

The image of the magic lantern well illustrates this character of dream experiences. The movement of the cinematograph, indeed, scarcely corresponds to that fusion of heterogeneous images which marks dream visions. Our dreams are like dissolving views in which the dissolving process is carried on swiftly or slowly, but always uninterruptedly, so that at any moment two (often, indeed, more) incongruous pictures are presented to consciousness, which strives to make one whole of them, and sometimes succeeds, and is sometimes baffled. Or we may say that the problem presented to dreaming consciousness resembles that experiment in which psychologists pronounce three wholly unconnected words and require the subject to combine them at once in a connected sentence. It is unnecessary to add that such analogies fail to indicate the subtle complexity of the apparatus which is at work in the manufacture of dreams.

By this mechanism of dreaming, isolated impressions, or else impressions which have a resemblance or a connection which is not obvious to the waking intelligence, flow together in dreams to be welded into a whole. There is produced, in the strictest sense, a *confusion*. For instance, a lady, who in the course of the day has admired a fine baby and bought a big fish for dinner, dreams with horror and surprise of finding a fully developed live baby sewed up in a large cod-fish. Again, a lady who had been cooking in the course of the day and in the evening had read a scientific description of the way birds obtain and utilise their food, such as fruit and snails, dreams at night that she has discovered when out walking a kind of animal-fruit, a damson containing a snail within it, which she views with delight as admirably adapted for culinary purposes. Another lady, after carving a duck at dinner, dreams that she is trying to cut off a duck's leg, but seems to realise in her dream at the same time that it is really her husband's neck she is hacking at.[1] In a dream of my own, children's heads took the form and shape of flowers of various shapes and hues, though mainly of the composite order (like chrysanthemums), and their eyes looked out from between the petals.

It must be added that in a very considerable proportion of cases the combinations produced in dreams are far more plausible than in any of the instances just narrated ; the whole dream may thus easily follow as commonplace and matter-of-fact a course as in real life. Thus, after going to live in a new neighbourhood, I dreamed that I entered a shop belonging to a certain firm, and saw there an employé who, in real life, to my knowledge, had previously left another shop belong-

[1] The transformation of birds into human beings seems peculiarly common in dreams. I have referred to this point elsewhere (*Studies in the Psychology of Sex*, vol. i. 3rd ed., p. 193). It is an interesting and doubtless significant fact that the same transformation is accepted in the myths of primitive peoples. Thus, according to H. H. Bancroft (*Native Races of the Pacific*, vol. i. p. 93), a pantomime dance of the Aleuts represents the transformation of a captive bird into a lovely woman who falls exhausted into the arms of the hunter.

ing to the same firm; an entirely probable combination was thus effected, and the dream conversation that followed was equally natural and probable. We do not go out of our way in dreams to invent absurdities; we simply accept the data presented to us, dealing with them as rationally as the intellectual instruments at our disposal may permit.

The dream constituted by the falling together of trivial reminiscences is not always, however, as commonplace and plausible as in the dream just narrated. In other cases the falling together of equally trivial reminiscences may constitute a fantastic and imaginative picture altogether outside waking experience or waking thought. Thus I dream that it is my duty to watch beside a great king while he sleeps. He lies on a huge bed, fully clothed and booted, and with a great crimson mantle thrown over him. I am permitted to lie on the edge of the bed outside the mantle, but must on no account close my eyes, for I must be ready to respond at once to his call. The elements of such a picture are obviously so simple and commonplace that it is not surprising that I could not find that even one of them had been specially present to waking consciousness. Yet the picture that at that particular moment they fell together to compose—like the broken fragments of coloured glass in a kaleidoscope—is altogether alien alike to my experience and to my imagination.

The source of the common confusion of dream imagery is to be found in very varying motives. In a large proportion of cases, what we witness is merely the flowing together of impressions which have no real resemblance, but which happen to have been received at nearly the same time, and to admit of being fused ; thus, in one case, occupation during the day partly in the fowl-yard and partly in the garden, led a lady to the dream project of breeding chickens by planting fowls' heads. Very frequently, however, there is a real resemblance in the two objects combined, although it is not a resemblance which would ever present itself to waking consciousness. The fowl-yard will supply another instance of this confusion also. I went to sleep thinking of a friend who was that night to stay at a certain hotel I had never seen. I dreamed that I saw the hotel in question ; its façade was not unlike that of a common type of hotel, but the roof was flat and at no very great height from the ground, so that I was able to overlook the building and see into all the windows, an arrangement that struck me as bad. My ability to overlook the building was not, however, accompanied by any perception of its diminutiveness. On awakening I remembered that my wife had received a chicken incubator the day before, and we had examined it in the evening. The image of the hotel had fused with the image of the incubator.

In another dream of the same type I imagined that I was with a dentist who was about to extract a tooth from a patient. Before applying the forceps he remarked to me (at the same time setting fire to a perfumed cloth at the end of something like a broomstick, in order to dissipate the unpleasant odour) that it was the largest tooth he had ever seen. When extracted I found that it was indeed enormous, in the shape of a caldron, with walls an inch thick. Taking from my pocket a tape measure (such as I carried in waking life), I found the diameter to be not less than twenty-five inches ; the interior was like roughly-hewn rock, and there were sea-weeds and lichen-like growths within. The size of the tooth seemed to me large, but not extraordinarily so. It is well known that pain in the teeth, or the dentist's manipulations, cause those organs to seem of extravagant extent ; in dreams this tendency rules unchecked ; thus a friend once dreamed that mice were playing about in a cavity in her tooth. But for the dream just quoted, there was no known dental origin ; it arose solely or chiefly from a walk during the previous afternoon among the rocks of the Cornish coast at low tide, and the fantastic analogy, which had not occurred to waking consciousness, suggested itself during sleep.

In another dream, illustrating the same kind of confusion of images having a real resemblance unnoticed in waking life, I seemed to see on a table a small hand-gong of a common type, struck by a hammer, but on striking it repeatedly, it produced flashes of light instead of the sounds normally produced by a gong. I concluded that the instrument must be out of order and called some one to attend to it, whereupon we proceeded to deal with it as though it were a diminutive battery of the kind used to work electric bells. The

THE ELEMENTS OF DREAM LIFE 41

gong was one familiar to me at the time in daily life ; on the previous day I had casually observed that it was misplaced. In my dream I discovered a resemblance which actually exists between a gong of the type in question and the lever-handle for turning on the electric light, soothing a certain doubt by saying to myself in my dream that the instrument served both for the production of sound and of light. This link of connection led to the association of an electric battery with the hand-gong, as well as to the attribution to the gong of light-giving properties.[1]

Such a dream serves as a transition to another very common kind of confusion of imagery in which two altogether unlike images are amalgamated through each happening to have in the mind a link of connection with some third idea. I dreamed that my wife's dog— a dog who, in real life, was constantly getting into trouble—had killed a child in the neighbouring town. On going thither I entered a butcher's shop, and saw the child lying on a table, mutilated and bleeding. After a time, however, I learned that it was not a child, but a pig that had been killed, and what I had previously taken for a child was now visibly a dead pig. I felt ashamed of my mistake, and the sympathy I had experienced now seemed excessive, especially when the butcher remarked that it was all right as he had been

---

[1] It is noteworthy that this marked tendency in dreams to discover analogies, although doubtless a tendency of primitive thought, is also a progressive tendency. ' The conquests of science,' says Sageret (' L'Analogie Scientifique,' *Revue Philosophique*, January 1909), ' are the conquests of analogy.'

fattening the pig and meant to kill it soon anyhow. Then the pig was cut open, though it made daring attempts to come to life again, during which I awoke. It is clear how, in this case, the idea of the butcher's shop served as a bridge from the image of the child to the image of the pig. Again, after a day in which I had received a letter from a lady, unknown to me, living in France, and later on had written out a summary of a criminal case in which a detective had to go over to France, I dreamed that some one told me that the lady I had heard from was a detective in the service of the French Government, and this explanation, though it seemed somewhat surprising, fully satisfied me. Here, it will be seen, the idea of France served as a bridge, and was utilised by sleeping consciousness to supply an answer to a question which had been asked by waking consciousness.

The confusion of imagery may be more remote, embodying abstract ideas and without reference to recent impressions. Thus I dreamed that my wife was expounding to me a theory by which the substitution of slates for tiles in roofing had been accompanied by, and intimately associated with, the growing diminution of crime in England. I opposed this theory, pointing out the picturesqueness of tiles, their cheapness, and greater comfort both in winter and summer, but at the same time it occurred to me as a peculiar coincidence that tiles should have a sanguinary tinge suggestive of criminal bloodthirstiness. I need scarcely say that this bizarre theory had never suggested itself to my waking thoughts. There was, however, a real connecting link in the confusion—the redness, and it is a noteworthy point, of great significance in the interpretation of dreams, that that link, although clearly active from the first, remained subconscious until the end of the dream, when it presented itself as an entirely novel coincidence.

I dreamed once that I was with a doctor in his surgery, and saw in his hand a note from a patient saying that doctors were fools and did him no good, but he had lately taken some *selvdrolla*, recommended by a friend, and it had done him more good than anything, so please send him some more. I saw the note clearly, not, indeed, being conscious of reading it word by word, but only of its meaning as I looked at it ; the one word I actually seemed to see, letter by letter, was the name of the drug, and that changed and fluctuated beneath my vision as I gazed at it, the final impression being *selvdrolla*. The doctor took from a shelf a bottle containing a bright yellow oleaginous fluid, and poured a little out, remarking that it had lately come into favour, especially in uric acid disorders, but was extremely expensive. I expressed my surprise, having never before heard of it. Then, again to my surprise, he poured rather copiously from the bottle on to a plate of food, saying, in explanation, that it was pleasant to take and not dangerous. This was a vivid morning dream, and on awakening I had no difficulty in detecting the source of its various minor details, especially a note received on the previous evening and containing a dubious figure, the precise nature of which I had used my pocket lens to determine. But what was *selvdrolla*, the most vivid element of the dream? I sought vainly among my recent memories, and had almost renounced the search when I recalled a large bottle of salad oil seen on the supper table the previous evening; not, indeed, resembling the dream bottle, but containing a precisely similar fluid. *Selvdrolla* was evidently a corruption of 'salad oil.' This dream illustrates the uncertainty of dream consciousness, but it also illustrates at the same time the element of certainty in dream *subconsciousness*. Throughout my dream I remained, consciously, in entire ignorance as to the real nature of *selvdrolla*, yet a latent element in consciousness was all the time presenting it to me in ever clearer imagery. We see that the subconscious element of dream life treats the conscious part much as a good-natured teacher treats a child whose lesson is only half learned, giving repeated clues and hints which the stupid child understands only at the last moment, or not at all. It is, indeed, a universal method, the method of Nature with man, throughout the whole of human evolution.

It will be seen that at this point we are brought into contact with another characteristic of dream life: there is often more in dreams than dreaming consciousness is able to realise. On the one hand, the elements of dream life are drawn from a wider field than is normally accessible to waking consciousness; on the other hand, the focus of dream consciousness is

THE ELEMENTS OF DREAM LIFE 45

narrower than that of waking consciousness, and cannot apperceive all that is going on. There is at once more extension and more contraction than in the psychic life of the waking world. A very large part of the psychic life of sleep is outside our power, and some of it is even beyond our sight.

It will be observed that the perpetual movement and the constant fusion of images which constitute the most fundamental character of dream life really combine two characteristics which, abstractly regarded, are distinct. The tendency of the dream image to be ever changing, ever putting forth some new feature which more or less radically alters its nature, is not a phenomenon of precisely the same nature as the tendency for two definite images, well known to waking consciousness, to become fused together, consciously or unconsciously, in dreams. Practically, however, there is no line of demarcation. What happens is that the image is ever spontaneously changing, and that each change is at once recognised by dreaming consciousness as a known object. Thus I dreamed that I was in a drawing-room and saw a beautiful and attractive woman with an unusually low evening dress entirely revealing the breasts; then, between the breasts, three additional nipples appeared, and I realised in my dream that here was a case of supernumerary breasts of sufficient scientific interest to be carefully examined later on; and then, as I gazed, I saw a number of little fleshy nipple-like protuberances on the body, and thereupon I realised that I was really looking at a case of the rare skin disease termed *molluscum fibrosum*. Thus the perpetually wavering and developing image is at the same time a succession of quite different images. On the other hand, when we seem to have a fusion of two definite images, what we really see in most cases is one image melting into the other and gradually losing its earlier character. In either case the process is the same interplay of automatic peripheral imagery and central ideas, whether the new image is brought into focus by, as it were, a current in consciousness, or is merely suggested by a spontaneous change in the previous image. How far the image suggests the idea or the idea the image, it is extremely difficult in most cases to say. The phenomenon we witness is a perpetually dissolving view; the vital process behind that phenomenon we must usually be content to be ignorant of.

It sometimes happens that the dream image is slowly transformed without the dreamer realising the transformation. Thus an image of a doll may take on the character of a human being. In a dream of this kind—possibly suggested by Villiers de l'Isle Adam's *L'Eve Future*, though that book had not been recently in my mind—I imagined that a lady of my acquaintance (whose identity I could not recall on awakening) had taken a fancy to possess an artificial woman, constructed with vast ingenuity and at enormous expense. The skin and hair seemed real as I noted with a certain horror on observing the breasts and armpits, but in places—I noticed especially one arm—

THE ELEMENTS OF DREAM LIFE 47

the creature was as defective as an ill-made doll. It was, however, able to walk with a little support, and, most remarkable of all, it gave intelligent answers to questions ; this alone it was that caused me a certain surprise. What at the beginning of the dream had only been an artificial image was evidently becoming a real human being, and one can readily believe that such stories as that of Pygmalion's statue may have been suggested by dream experiences.

The dream is mainly a dissolving view, because for most of us it is above all a visual phenomenon. Those people who, in their dreams, at all events, if not also in waking life, are largely of auditory type, experience dreams in which words play exactly the same shifting, developing, and dissolving part played by images in the persons of more markedly visual type. In their dreams they resemble those insane people who, in some feeble and confusional states, manifest echolalia and confabulation, their ideas drifting along the associational paths of least resistance suggested by every random word they hear. Maury records successions of dream imagery strung together in a similar manner by a procession of verbal transformations ; thus in one oft-quoted dream the scenes were connected by the words, *kilomètre, kilos, Gilolo, Lobelia, Lopez, loto*.[1] In such a case the procession of verbal auditory imagery constitutes the basis of the dream. This is probably rare. In most people the basis of the dream is furnished by visual imagery, and auditory images only occasion-

[1] Maury, *Le Sommeil et les Rêves*, p. 115.

ally form an associative link, being more usually subordinated to the visual elements.

The speech peculiarities of dreams have been very thoroughly investigated by Kraepelin,[1] who has brought together two hundred and eighty-one examples, partly observed in himself, though they are not common, and Kraepelin considers that the hearing centres fall more deeply asleep than the visual centres, the eyes being already sufficiently protected by the lids.[2] Kraepelin classifies the speech disturbances of dreams into two great groups : (1) *paraphasia*, or disturbance of word-finding, where the idea is associated with a wrong word, which is sometimes a new formation[3]; and (2) *disorders of oration*, in which the peculiarity lies, not in the words, but in their order. The speech disturbances of dreams, Kraepelin remarks, spring from deep disturbance of thought, such as occur in sensorial aphasia, and, as in such aphasia, the dreamer thinks his nonsense is quite clear and reasonable. Much the same may occur in alcoholic delirium and in *dementia præcox*.

The invention of new words probably occurs frequently in dreams, without leaving a clear trace in

[1] Kraepelin, ' Ueber Sprachstörungen im Traume,' *Psychologische Arbeiten*, Bd. v., 1906, pp. 1-104 ; cf. Lombard, ' Glossolalie,' *Archives de Psychologie*, July 1907.

[2] This is confirmed by the fact that under chloroform anaesthesia hearing is the first sense to be lost and vision the last (Elmer Jones, ' The Waning of Consciousness under Chloroform,' *Psychological Review*, January 1909).

[3] It may be recalled as not without significance that the formation of new words is fairly common among young children ; see, *e.g.*, an interesting correspondence in *Nature*, 26th March and 9th April 1891.

THE ELEMENTS OF DREAM LIFE 49

memory, and still more frequently, perhaps, as in the 'selvdrolla' dream, already recorded, there are seeming new verbal formations which are really mere corruptions of imperfectly realised words. An example of a definite and precise new word seems to be furnished by the following dream, which was at all points vivid and precise. I saw quite close to me a huge tawny bird, with an orange bill. The creature got up and moved away, seeming as large as an ostrich. I asked a lady, standing by, who had some ornithological knowledge, what the bird was, and she replied that she thought it was a *jaleisa*. Then I asked the same question of a poor woman who was passing, curious to know what she would answer; she said, 'Oh, it's a kind of starling.' There was no doubt in my dream as to the spelling of 'jaleisa,' but I am quite unable to account for the word.[1] It so happened, however, that before I went to bed I had been reading one of Calderon's plays, and I imagine that this pseudo-Spanish word had formed itself in my brain among the echoes of Calderon's enchanting music. The question arises as to why that ignorant old woman should have called the jaleisa a starling. It seems just possible that the more familiar name was suggested by the last syllable of the strange bird's name, the association being verbal. It is equally possible, and perhaps more likely, that the association followed by the more usual visual channel, and that the jaleisa's orange beak suggested the large orange beaks of newly hatched

---

[1] It can scarcely be derived from the unfamiliar word *chalizah*, the Hebrew name for the levirate

starlings, which had once, many years previously, vividly attracted my attention.

A probable illustration of the influence of verbal association in diverting the current of a dream is seen in the harrowing narrative that follows : A lady dreamed that she went to an entertainment which turned out to be a kind of revival meeting, presided over by a lady, and full of uproar. It was suddenly realised that Hell was underneath the hall, and a man, supposed to be a slave, was torn to pieces and cast into Hell. A lady present was so much affected by the scene that she threw herself into a pool of water, and was drowned, her body being afterwards pulled out by a working man with a pitchfork. The dreamer was so overcome by these tragic events that she felt that there was nothing left but to commit suicide. Resolving to drown herself, she went to a lighthouse (which, however, somewhat resembled a bathing machine) on a height, in order to throw herself down into the sea. It was of an exquisite green tint, extremely lovely and attractive, but she had not the courage to leap in. She thought it might give her courage if she had a good meal first, so she returned to the hall and joined the lady who had presided over the meeting. They sat down to a dish of roast mutton, but, as they were eating, suddenly looked at each other with mutual understanding ; they realised that they were eating the woman who had been drowned, and, it will be remarked, had been pulled out of the water by a fork. It was possible to account for every element of which this dream was made up, but

THE ELEMENTS OF DREAM LIFE

Its tragic character was unsupported by anything in waking life, and entirely native to the dream. The possibility of any guiding link between 'Hell' and 'hall' had not presented itself to the dreamer, nor had it occurred to me when I set down the dream as here reproduced. It must be noted, however, that the revival meeting would itself tend to suggest the idea of Hell. It seems probable that verbal associations usually play only a subordinate part.

Sometimes the verbal links of association in dreams, far from introducing tragedy, lead, by the conjunction of two words of the same sound, to puns. Thus a dreamer imagined that he and some friends were looking at a house with its bedroom or bedrooms open to the air, the front wall being gone, and they were laughing at the comical effect when a mysterious voice came saying, 'A three-walled bedroom is a side-burst stor(e)y.' As the dreamer awoke, he found himself laughing at this juxtaposition of the idea of the storey of a house-side split open, and the idea of a side-splitting story. The conditions of psychic activity during sleep—when ideas drift together from widely separated regions along channels of association which are usually held closed by the higher intellectual processes—seem, indeed, to be specially favourable to the production of puns and allied forms of witticism.[1] They may, there-

[1] Thus I have rarely ever attempted parody when awake, but once when at Montserrat, with thoughts far from humorous fields, I dreamed of making a parody (I am not quite clear of what) apparently suggested by the goose-pond in the cloisters of Barcelona Cathedral.

fore, be properly regarded as closely associated with subconscious activity.¹

A verbal link is seen in the following 'recipe' invented on another occasion by the same dreamer :—

> 'Call in the tipcat, cut off its tail;
> Fold up some eggs in a saucepan;
> Sit on the rest, like an elderly male,
> And gulp down the whole as a horse can.'

It is evident that the tipcat suggested a cat's tail, while the suggestion of a cooking recipe in 'cut off its tail' led on to eggs and saucepan; the eggs suggested 'sitting,' while 'gulp,' as the dreamer noted, appeared as 'gallop,' and suggested the horse. The ease with which the whole fell into a completely rhymed doggerel stanza is due to the fact that the dreamer is a poet.²

A more common phenomenon in my experience than association by verbal clues is a transference from visual terms into the terms of some other sense, and a repetition in that form. Thus a lady dreams that a large and very beautiful picture resembling tapestry forms itself before her, and in it she sees herself, only much more beautiful in shape, standing by a tree, and on the other side of the tree an old friend is standing, while there are a crowd of people around. Then she sees her friend touch her on the arm. At the same time the dreamer feels the touch. The visual image is reduplicated in a motor form. Such a phenomenon is doubt-

---

[1] This point of view has been specially developed by Freud, *Der Witz und seine Beziehung zum Unbewussten*.

[2] It may be noted that somewhat similar doggerel verse is sometimes made by the insane; see, *e.g.*, *Journal of Mental Science*, April 1907, p. 284.

THE ELEMENTS OF DREAM LIFE

less a natural result of the special conditions of dream life. In waking life the senses are working co-ordinately, and if we see ourselves touched we shall probably feel ourselves touched. But in dreams the body is a vision, and not our real body, and when we see it touched, we realise we ought to feel it touched, and a tactile sensation is thus suggested and experienced.

There are, however, other reduplications to which this explanation will not apply. Thus I imagined I was sitting at a window, at the top of a house, writing. As I looked up from my table I saw, with all the emotions naturally accompanying such a sight, a woman in her nightdress appear at a lofty window some distance off, and throw herself down. I went on writing, however, and found that in the course of my literary employment—I am not clear as to its precise nature—the very next thing I had to do was to describe exactly such a scene as I had just witnessed. I was extremely puzzled at such an extraordinary coincidence; it seemed to me wholly inexplicable. Again I dreamed that I was coming up the Thames (apparently in a steamboat), reading a novel, written by a friend, which was the history of some one who arrives in England coming up the Thames to London, by what I felt to be an extraordinary coincidence, in exactly the same way as I was at the moment. Then I found myself seemingly at the end of a London pier, with the river rippling at my feet, and in front the superb panorama of London; exactly the scene which, in less detail, was described in the book. Such dreams, reduplicating the imagery in a new sensory medium, are fairly common, with me at all events. The association is less that of analogy than of sensory media, as of the visual image becoming a verbal motor image. In other cases a scene is first seen as in reality, and then in a picture. Thus I dreamed that I was witnessing the performance of an orchestra, and observed that all the players had instruments of ancient pattern which, I understood, had been in constant use for several hundred years ; I could recall the shapes of many on awaking, and none of them were quite modern ; I could not, however, recall the character of the music, which seemed to make no impression on me, since I was absorbed in observing the shapes of the instruments. I specially observed an old framed engraving hanging on the wall, in my dream, representing precisely one of the instruments played on, and I understood that it was called a *bourdon*.[1] It is interesting to observe the profound astonishment with which sleeping consciousness apperceives such simple reduplication.

In dreams planes of existence that in waking life are fundamentally distinct are brought together, so that events belonging to different planes move on the same plane, and even become combined. Acting and life, the picture and the reality, are no longer absolutely distinct. Art and life flow in the same channel. The reason, doubtless, is that for the dreamer the world of waking life, the world of things as they are to the

---

[1] There was no known origin for this dream, and the word *bourdon* had no conscious associations for my mind ; I was not even definitely aware that it is used in a musical sense.

waking senses, is closed and cannot even be completely recalled. So that all modes of representation are strictly on the same level, and it is, therefore, perfectly natural and logical that they should stand side by side and merge into one another.

CHAPTER III

THE LOGIC OF DREAMS

All Dreaming is a Process of Reasoning—The Fundamental Character of Reasoning—Reasoning as a Synthesis of Images—Dream Reasoning Instinctive and Automatic—It is also Consciously carried on—This a result of the Fundamental Split in Intelligence—Dissociation—Dreaming as a Disturbance of Apperception.

IN dreams we are always reasoning. That is a general characteristic of dreams which is worth noting, because its significance is not usually recognised. It is sometimes imagined that reason is in abeyance during sleep.[1] So far from this being the case, we may almost be said to reason much more during sleep than when we are awake. That our reasoning is bad, often even preposterous, that it constantly ignores the most elementary facts of waking life, scarcely affects the question. All dreaming is a process of reasoning. That artful confusion of ideas and images which, at the outset, I referred to as the most constant feature of dream mechanism is nothing but a process of reasoning, a perpetual effort to argue out harmoniously the absurdly limited and incongruous data present to sleeping consciousness. Binet, grounding his conclusions on hypnotic experiments, finds that reasoning is the funda-

[1] Freud brings together (*Traumdeutung*, pp. 38 *et seq.*) some of the different opinions regarding reasoning in dreams.

THE LOGIC OF DREAMS

mental part of all thinking, the very texture of thought.[1] It is founded on perception itself, which already contains all the elements of the ancient syllogism. For in all perception, as Binet plausibly argues, there is a succession of three images, of which the first fuses with the second, which, in its turn, suggests the third. Now this establishment of new associations, this construction of images, which, as we may easily convince ourselves, is precisely what takes place in dreaming, is reasoning itself.

Reasoning may thus be regarded as a synthesis of images suggested by resemblance and contiguity, indeed a sort of logical vision, more intense even than actual vision, since it is capable of producing hallucinations. To reasoning all forms of mental activity may finally be reduced; mind, as Wundt has said, is a thing that reasons. Or, as H. R. Marshall puts it, 'reason is a mode of instinct.'[2] When we apply these general statements to dreaming, we may see that the whole phenomenon of dreaming is really the same process of image formation, based on resemblance and contiguity. Every dream is the outcome of this strenuous, wide-ranging instinct to reason. The supposed 'imaginative faculty,' regarded as so highly active during sleep, is the inevitable play of this automatic logic.

[1] 'Reasoning,' says Binet (*La Psychologie du Raisonnement*, 1886, p. 10), speaking without reference to dreaming, but in words that are exactly applicable to it, ' is an organisation of images determined by the properties of the images alone ; it suffices for the images to be put in presence and they become organised ; reason follows with the certainty of a reflex.'

[2] H. R. Marshall, *Instinct and Reason* ; *ib.* ' Reason a Mode of Instinct,' *Psychological Review*, March 1899.

The syllogistic arrangement of dream imagery is carried on in an absolutely automatic manner ; it is spontaneous, involuntary, without effort. Sleeping consciousness, though all the time it is weaving the data that reach it into some pattern of reason with immense ingenuity, is quite unaware that it is itself responsible for the arguments thus presented. In the evening, before going to bed, I glance casually through a newspaper ; I see the usual kind of news, revolutionists in Russia, Irish affairs, crimes, etc. ; I see also a caricature of the Liberal Party as a headless horseman on a barren plain. During sleep these unconnected impressions revive, float into dream consciousness, and spontaneously fall into as reasonable a whole as could be expected. I dream that by some chemical or mechanical device a man has succeeded in conveying the impression that he is headless, and is preparing to gallop across some district in Russia, with the idea of making so mysterious an impression upon the credulous population that he will be accepted as a great religious prophet. I distinctly see him careering across sands like those of the seashore, but I avoid going near him. Then I see figures approaching him in the far distance, and his progress ceases. I learn subsequently that he has been arrested and found to be an Irish criminal. A coherent story is thus formed out of a few random impressions.

All such typical dreams are syllogistic. There is, that is to say, as Binet expresses it, the establishment of an association between two states of consciousness

THE LOGIC OF DREAMS

by means of an intermediate state which resembles the first, is associated with the second, and by fusing with the first associates it with the second. In this dream, for instance, we have the three terms of (1) headless horseman, (2) revolutionary crime, and (3) Russia and Ireland. The intermediate term, by the fact that it resembles the first, and is contiguous in the mind with the third, seems to fuse the first and the third terms, so that the headless horseman becomes an Irish criminal in Russia. In dreaming life, as in waking life, our minds are always moving by the construction of similar syllogisms, marked by more or less freedom and audacity.

It is unnecessary to multiply examples of the instinctive and persistent efforts on the part of the sleeping mind to construct a coherent whole out of the incongruous elements that come before it; nearly every dream furnishes some proof of this profoundly rooted impulse.[1] It is instructive, however, to consider the nature and the limitations of dreaming reason.

This rationalisation and logical construction of imagery, it is necessary to realise, occurs at the very threshold of sleeping consciousness. The dreamer makes no effort to arrange isolated imagery; the arrangement has already occurred when the imagery comes to the focus of sleeping consciousness; so that this reasoning and arranging process is so fundamental and instinctive that it occurs in a region which may be

---

[1] Some of the most methodically absurd examples of dreaming logic cannot be effectively brought forward, as they are so personal that they require much explanation to make them intelligible.

said to be subconscious to dreaming consciousness. If it were not so our dreams would never be real to us, for even dreaming consciousness could not accept as real a hallucination which it had itself arranged. In this sense it is true that, to some extent, our dreams are often based on an ultimate personal and emotional foundation.[1]

But this ingeniously guided and rationalised confusion of imagery by no means covers the whole of the reasoning process in dreams. This is a double process. It is first manifested subconsciously in the formation of dream imagery, and then it is manifested consciously in the dreamer's reaction to the imagery presented to him. Every dream is made up of action and reaction between a pseudo-universe and a freely responding individual. On the one side there is the irresistibly imposed imagery—really, though we know it not, conditioned and instinctively moulded by our own organism—which stands for what in our waking hours we may term God and Nature ; on the other side is the Soul struggling with all its might, and very inefficient means, against the awful powers that oppose it. The problem of the waking world is presented over again

---

[1] Delacroix ('Sur la Structure Logique du Rêve,' *Revue de Metaphysique*, November 1904), in opposition to Leroy and Tobolowska, goes so far as to say that 'the sense of the dream, the interpretation of the image, is given in the image, before the image, if one may say so ; we are not concerned with a mere procession of images without internal connection, but are introduced into a pre-established organisation ; wholes are decomposed and not separate elements united.' We have to remember that in dream life as in waking life the action is twofold ; in either world when our psychic activity is of low intensity we combine external images into a fairly objective picture ; when psychic activity is intense external images are subdued and controlled by that activity.

THE LOGIC OF DREAMS

in this battle between the dreaming protagonist and his dreamed fate. Both of these elements are instinctively reasoned out, consciously or subconsciously; both are imperfect fragments from the rich reservoir of human personality.

The things that happen to us in dreams, the pseudo-external world that is presented to sleeping consciousness—the imagery, that is, that floats before the mental eye of sleep—are a perpetual source of astonishment and argument to the dreamer. A large part of dreaming activity is concerned with the attempt to explain and reason out the phenomena we thus encounter, to construct a theory of them, or to determine the attitude which we ought to take up with regard to them. Most dreams will furnish evidence of this reasoning process.

Thus a lady dreamed that an acquaintance wished to send a small sum of money to a person in Ireland. She rashly offered to take it over to Ireland. On arriving home she began to repent of her promise, as the weather was extremely wild and cold. She proceeded, however, to make preparations for dressing warmly, and went to consult an Irish friend, who said she would have to be floated over to Ireland tightly jammed in a crab basket. On returning home she fully discussed the matter with her husband, who thought it would be folly to undertake such a journey, and she finally relinquished it, with great relief. In this dream—the elements of which could all be accounted for—the association between sending money and the post-office, which would at once occur to waking consciousness, was closed; consciousness was a prey to such suggestions as reached it, but on the basis of those suggestions it reasoned and concluded quite sagaciously.

Again (after looking at photographs of paintings and statuary, and also reading about the theatre), I dreamed that I was at the theatre, and that the performers were acting and dancing in a more or less, in some cases completely, nude state, but with admirable propriety and grace, and very charming effect. At first I was extremely surprised at so remarkable an innovation ; but then I reflected that the beginnings of such a movement must have long been in progress on the stage unknown to me ; and I proceeded to rehearse the reasons which made such a movement desirable. On another occasion, I dreamed that I was in the large *plaza* of a Spanish city (Pamplona possibly furnishing the elements of the picture), and that the governor emerged from his residence facing the square and began talking in English to the subordinate officials who were waiting to receive him. The real reason why he talked English was, of course, the simple one that he spoke the language native to the dreamer. But in my dream I was extremely puzzled why he should speak English. I looked carefully into his face to assure myself that he was not really English, and I finally concluded that he was speaking English in order not to be understood by the bystanders. Once more, I dreamed that I was looking at an architectural drawing of a steeple, of quite original design, somewhat in the shape of a cross, but very elongated. I attempted in

THE LOGIC OF DREAMS

my dream to account for this elongation, and concluded that it was intended to neutralise the foreshortening caused when the steeple would be looked at from below.

There is, we here see afresh, a fundamental split in dreaming intelligence. On the one side there is the subconscious, yet often highly intelligent, combination of imagery along rational although often bizarre lines. On the other side is concentrated the conscious intelligence of the dreamer, struggling to comprehend and explain the problems offered by the pseudo-external imagery thus presented to it. One might almost say that in dreams subconscious intelligence is playing a game with conscious intelligence. In a dream previously narrated (p. 43) subconscious intelligence offered to my dreaming consciousness the mysterious substance *selvdrolla*, and bid me guess what it was; I could not guess. And subconscious intelligence presented the drawing of the elongated steeple, and I was able to offer an explanation which seems fairly satisfactory. So that, in the world of dreams, it may be said, we see over again the process which, James Hinton was accustomed to say, we see in the universe of our waking life; God or Nature playing with man, compelling him to join in a game of hide-and-seek, and setting him problems which he must solve as best he can. It may well be, one may add, that the dream process furnishes the key to the metaphysical and even, indeed, the physical problems of our waking thoughts, and that the puzzles of the universe are questions that we ourselves unconsciously invent for ourselves to solve.

We can never go behind the fantastic universe of our dreams. The validity of that universe is for dreaming consciousness unassailable. We may try to understand it and explain it, but we can never deny it, any more than we can deny the universe of our waking life, however we may attempt to analyse it. Dreaming consciousness never realises that the universe that confronts it springs from the same source as itself springs. I dreamed that a man was looking at his own house from a distance, and on the balcony he saw his daughter and a man by her side. 'Who is that man flirting with my daughter?' he asked. He produced a field-glass, and, on looking through it, he exclaimed: 'Good Heavens, it's myself!' Dreaming consciousness accepted this situation with perfect equanimity and solemnity. In the dream world there is, indeed, nothing else to do. We may puzzle over the facts presented to us; we may try to explain them; but it would be futile to deny them, even when they involve the possibility of a man being in two places at the same time.[1]

Only to a few people there comes occasionally in dreams a dim realisation of the unreality of the ex-

---

[1] A somewhat similar mistaken self-detachment may even occur momentarily in the waking condition. Thus Jastrow (*The Subconscious*, p. 137) refers to the 'lapse of consciousness' of a lady student who, while absorbed in her work, heard outside the door the shuffling of rubber heels such as she herself wore, and said 'There goes ——,' naming herself. That delusion was no doubt due to the eruption of a dream-like state of distraction. As regards the visual phantasm of the self (which has sometimes been seen by men of very distinguished intellectual power) it may be noted that it is favoured by the conditions of dream life. Our dream imagery is all pictural, sometimes even to dream consciousness, and to see oneself in the picture is, therefore, not so very much more remarkable than it is in waking life to come upon oneself among a bundle of photographs.

THE LOGIC OF DREAMS

perience : ' After all, it does not matter,' they are able to say to themselves with more or less conviction, ' this is only a dream.' Thus one lady, dreaming that she is trying to kill three large snakes by stamping on them, wonders, while still dreaming, what it signifies to dream of snakes,[1] and another lady, when she dreams that she is in any unpleasant position—about to be shot, for instance—often says to herself: ' Never mind, I shall wake before it happens.'

I have never detected in my own dreams any recognition that they are dreams. I may say, indeed, that I do not consider that such a thing is really possible, though it has been borne witness to by many philosophers and others from Aristotle and Synesius and Gassendi onwards. The phenomenon occurs ; the person who says to himself that he is dreaming believes that he is still dreaming, but one may be permitted to doubt that he is. It seems far more probable that he has for a moment, without realising it, emerged at the waking surface of consciousness.[2] The only approach to a recognition of dreaming as dreaming that I have

[1] As regards the significance of snakes in dreams, it may be remarked that the followers of Freud regard them as being, in the dreams of women, as they are in the speech and myths of primitive peoples, erotic symbols (*e.g.* Karl Abraham, *Traum und Mythus*, 1909, p. 19). It must be remembered, however, that this erotic symbolism is but a small part of the emotional interest aroused by snakes which are an extremely common source of fear, especially in the young. See *e.g.* Stanley Hall, ' A Study of Fears,' *American Journal of Psychology*, 1897, pp. 205 *et seq*.

[2] It may even occur that a person partly wakes up, perceives what is going on around him, converses about it, falls asleep again, and imagines in the morning that the whole episode was a dream. Hammond, who also denies that we can dream we are dreaming, gives a case in illustration (*Treatise on Insanity*, p. 190).

experienced, is connected with the reduplication that may sometimes occur, and the sense of a fatalistic predetermination. Thus I dreamed (with nothing that could suggest the dream) that I was one of a group of people who, as I realised, were carrying out a drama in which by force of circumstance I was destined to be the villain, having, by bad treatment, been driven to revenge. I knew at the outset how events would turn out, and yet, though it seemed real life, I felt vaguely that it was all a play that was merely being rehearsed. I had attained in the world of dreams to the Shakespearian feeling that it was all a stage, and I merely a player. So we may become the Prosperos of the life of dreams.[1]

This quality of dreaming consciousness is a manifestation, and the chief one, of what is called *dissociation*.[2] In dissociation we have a phenomenon which runs through the whole of the dreaming life, and is scarcely less fundamental than the process of fusion by which the imagery is built up. The fact that the

---

[1] The vision of the dream world we thus attain corresponds exactly to the philosophy of life set forth by Jules de Gaultier, perhaps the most subtle and original of living thinkers; according to Gaultier the psychic improvisation which has created the spectacle of the world has, as it were, sworn 'never to recognise itself beneath the masks it has assumed, in order to retain the joy of an unending play of the unforeseen.'

[2] Dissociation may be defined as a condition in which, in the words of Tannery (*Revue Philosophique*, October 1898), ' the various organisms of the brain which in the waking state accomplish distinct functions with satisfactory agreement are, on the contrary, in a state of semi-independence.' There is, in Greenwood's words (*Imagination in Dreams*, p. 41), a ' loosening of mental bonds,' corresponding to the relaxation of muscular tension which also occurs before going to sleep.

THE LOGIC OF DREAMS

reasoning of dreams is usually bad, is due partly to the absence of memory elements that would be present to waking consciousness, and partly to the absence of sensory elements to check the false reasoning which, without them, appears to us conclusive. That is to say, that there is a process of dissociation by which ordinary channels of association are temporarily blocked, perhaps by exhaustion of their conductive elements, and the conditions are prepared for the formation of the hallucination. It is, as Parish has argued, in sleep and in those sleep-resembling states called hypnagogic that a condition of dissociation leading to hallucination is most apt to occur.[1]

Thus it is that though the psychic frontier of the sleeping state is more extended than that of the normal waking state, the focus of sleeping consciousness is more contracted than that of waking consciousness. In other words, while facts are liable to drift from a very wide psychic distance under our dreaming attention, we cannot direct the searchlight of that attention at will over so wide a field as when we are awake. We deal with fewer psychic elements, though those elements are drawn from a wider field.

The psychology of 'attention' is, indeed, a very

[1] Edmund Parish, *Hallucinations and Illusions: A Study of the Fallacies of Perception* (Contemporary Science Series), 1897. It is significant to observe that in hysteria, which may be regarded as presenting a condition somewhat analogous to sleep, dissociation also occurs. 'Hysteria,' says Janet (*The Major Symptoms of Hysteria*, 1907, p. 332), one of the greatest authorities, 'is a form of mental depression characterised by the retraction of the field of personal consciousness and a tendency to the dissociation and emancipation of the system of ideas and functions that constitute personality.'

disputed matter.[1] There is no agreement as to whether it is central or peripheral, motor or sensory. As we have seen in the previous chapter, it seems reasonable to conclude, according to a convenient distinction established by Ribot, that spontaneous attention is persistent during sleep, but voluntary attention is at a minimum. In some such way, it seems, whatever theory of attention we adopt, we have to recognise that in dreams the attention is limited.

Such a position is fortified by the conclusion of those who look at the problem, not so much in terms of attention as in terms of apperception. Apperception, according to Wundt, differs from perception in that while the latter is the appearance of a content in consciousness, the former is its reception into the state of attention. Or, as Stout defines it, apperception is ' the process by which a mental system appropriates a new element, or otherwise receives a fresh determination.' [2] Apperception is, therefore, the final stage of attention, and ultimately, as Wundt remarks, it is one with will. Apperception and will, as most psychologists consider, like attention, are enfeebled and diminished, if not abolished, in sleep.

In dreams, it thus comes about, we accept the facts

[1] The theories of attention are lucidly and concisely set forth by Nayrac, ' Le Processus et le Mécanisme de l'Attention,' *Revue Scientifique*, 7th April 1906.

[2] G. F. Stout, *Analytic Psychology*, vol. ii. p. 112. In the *Dictionary of Philosophy and Psychology*, again, Stout and Baldwin define apperception as ' the process of attention in so far as it involves interaction between the presentation of the object attended to, on the one hand, and the total preceding conscious content, together with pre-formed mental dispositions, on the other hand.'

THE LOGIC OF DREAMS

presented to us—that is the fundamental assumption of dream life—and we argue about those 'facts' with the help of all the mental resources which are at our disposal, only those resources are frequently inadequate. Sometimes they are startlingly inadequate, to such an extent, indeed, that we are unaware of possibilities which would be the very first to suggest themselves to waking consciousness. Thus the lady who wished to send a small sum of money to Ireland is not aware of the existence of postal orders, and when she decides to convey the money herself, she is not aware of the existence of boat-trains, or even of boats; she might have been living in palaeolithic times. She discusses the question in a clear and logical manner with the resources at her disposal, and reaches a rational conclusion, but considerations which would be the first to occur to waking consciousness are at the moment absent from sleeping consciousness; whole mental tracts have been dissociated, switched off from communication with consciousness; they are 'asleep,' even to sleeping consciousness.[1]

The result is that we are not only dominated by the suggestion of our visions, but we are unable adequately to appreciate and criticise the situations which are presented to us. We instinctively continue to reason, and to reason clearly and logically with the material at

---

[1] A very similar state of things occurs in some forms of insanity, especially in the less profound states of mental confusion, when, as Bolton remarks ('Amentia and Dementia,' *Journal of Mental Science*, July 1906, p. 445), we find 'certain associated remnants of former experience combined into a sequence according to the normal laws of mental association.'

our disposal, but our reasoning is hopelessly absurd. We perceive in dreams, but we do not apperceive; we cannot, that is to say, test and sift the new experience, and co-ordinate it adequately with the whole body of our acquired mental possessions. The phenomena of dreaming furnish a delightful illustration of the fact that reasoning, in its rough form, is only the crudest and most elementary form of intellectual operation, and that the finer forms of thinking involve much more than logic. 'All the thinking in the world,' as Goethe puts it, 'will not lead us to thought.'

CHAPTER IV

THE SENSES IN DREAMS

All Dreams probably contain both Presentative and Representative Elements—The Influence of Tactile Sensations on Dreams—Dreams excited by Auditory Stimuli—Dreams aroused by Odours and Tastes—The Influence of Visual Stimuli—Difficulty of distinguishing between Actual and Imagined Sensory Excitations—The Influence of Internal Visceral Stimuli on Dreaming—Erotic Dreams—Vesical Dreams—Cardiac Dreams and their Symbolism—Prodromic Dreams—Prophetic Dreams.

At the outset I adopted provisionally the usual classification of dreams into two classes: the peripheral or presentative group, excited by a stimulus from without, and the central or representative group, having its elements in memories. If, however, we look carefully at the matter, in the light of the experiences which we have encountered, it will be found that this classification, however superficially convenient it may be, fails to correspond to any radical duality of dream phenomena. When we closely question our dream experiences, it ceases to be clear that they really fall into two groups at all.

On the one hand, it would appear that most, perhaps, indeed, all dreams that are sufficiently vivid to be clearly remembered on awakening, have received an initial stimulus from some external, or at all events, peripheral source.[1] There is something unusual or uncomfortable in the sleeper's position, or he has been subjected to some slight unusual strain which has modified his nervous condition, or there has been some deviation from his usual diet, or a physiological stress of some kind is making itself felt within him—careful self-questioning constantly reveals the actual or probable existence of some external or certainly peripheral stimulus of this kind. So that we seem entitled to say that in all dreams there is probably a presentative element.

On the other hand, an even more cursory investigation of our dream life suffices to show that in every dream there is also a representative element. No dream can be said to be strictly and literally presentative. If, when I am seemingly asleep, a person speaks to me, and I become conscious that he is present and speaking,

---

Although I reached this conclusion independently, as a result of the analysis of dream experiences, I find that it was set forth at a much earlier period by Wundt. 'Men are accustomed to regard most of the phantasms of dreams as hallucinations,' he writes (*Grundzüge der Physiologischer Psychologie*, vol. iii.), ' but most dream representations are apparently illusions, initiated by the slight sensory impressions which are never extinguished in sleep.' Weygandt, in his brief but excellent book, *Entstehung der Traüme*, fully adopts this view, although I scarcely think he is always successful in his attempts to demonstrate it by his own dreams; such demonstration is necessarily often difficult or impossible because, apart from the dream itself, we seldom know what sensory impressions are persisting in our sleep. C. M. Giessler (*Die Physiologische Beziehungen der Traumvorgänge*, 1896, p. 2), who also proceeds from Wundt, likewise regards dreams as in general the more or less orderly and successive revival of psychic vestiges of waking life, conditioned by inner or outer excitations. Tissié (in *Les Rêves*, 1898), again, declares that ' dreams of purely psychic origin do not exist,' and Beaunis (*American Journal of Psychology*, July-October 1903) also believes that all dreams need an internal or external stimulus from the organism.

I am not entitled to say that I 'dream' it. A consciousness which perceives facts in the same way as they may be perceived by waking consciousness is not a dreaming consciousness. So that there are, in the literal sense, no presentative dreams. What happens is that the stimulus, instead of being presented directly to consciousness, and recognised for what it is to waking consciousness, serves to arouse old memories and ideas which dream consciousness accepts as a reasonable explanation of the external or peripheral stimulus. The stimulus may be said to be, in a sense, the cause of the dream, but the dream itself remains central, and as truly a combined picture of mental images as though there were no known peripheral stimulus at all.

Thus, while it is true that the division of dreams into two classes corresponds to a recognisable distinction, it is yet a superficial and unimportant distinction. It is likely that all dreams have a peripheral or presentative element, and certain that they all have a central or representative element. This will become clearer if we now proceed to discuss those dreams which have, demonstrably, their exciting cause in some external or internal organic stimulus.

The world which we enter through the portal of sleep presents such obvious and serious limitations that we are apt to under-estimate its real richness and variety. In some respects, indeed, we can accomplish in sleep what is beyond our reach awake. Thus it sometimes happens that we reason better in sleep than when awake, that we may find in dreams the solutions of difficulties which escape us awake, and that we may remember things which, when awake, we had forgotten. But even within the ordinary range of experience, it is interesting to note that our dreams contain the same elements as our waking life. The sensory activities which stir us during the day are equally active, though in strange transformations, in the world of dreams.

It is probable that all the senses may furnish the medium through which stimuli may reach sleeping consciousness; though touch and hearing are doubtless the main channels to dream life. The eyes are closed, so that while the chief parts of our dream life are in terms of vision, direct visual stimuli can only be a very dim and uncertain influence. But no sense is absolutely excluded from activity in dreams.[1]

Heat or cold sensations and pressure sensations, as well as their anaesthetic absence, undoubtedly play an important part in explaining various kinds of dreams. They do not necessarily result in rememberable dreams, even although it is possible that they still affect the current of sleeping consciousness. It is possible to press and massage the body of a sleeper all over, gently but firmly, without interrupting sleep. When the pressure

---

[1] Thus W. S. Monroe ('Mental Elements of Dreams,' *Journal of Philosophy*, 23rd November 1905) found that in nearly three hundred dreams of fifty-five women students of the Westfield Normal College (Massachusetts), visual imagery appeared in sixty-seven per cent. dreams, auditory in twenty-six per cent., tactile in eight per cent., motor in five per cent., olfactory in a little over one per cent., and gustatory in rather under one per cent. In the results of observation recorded by Sarah Weed and Florence Hallam (*American Journal of Psychology*, April 1896) the sensory imagery appears in the same order of frequency and approximately in the same proportions.

THE SENSES IN DREAMS 75

reaches a considerable degree of vigour, the sleeper may move a muscle, perhaps the lips, even an arm, may go so far as to half wake and move the whole body. All these movements suggest that they have accompaniments on the psychic side, yet, on finally awakening, the sleeper may be unable to recall any memory of the occurrence, or any vestige of a dream.

In a certain proportion of cases, however, a dream results. Thus a lady dreams that, with a number of other people, she is on board a ship which is rocking heavily, and on awakening she finds that her large dog is on the bed, vigorously scratching himself. The ship has clearly been the theory invented by sleeping consciousness to account for the unfamiliar sensations of movement.

When living in the south of Spain, I awoke early one morning, and heard a mosquito buzzing. I fell asleep again and dreamed that a huge insect—as large as a lobster, but flat like a cockroach, and scarlet in colour—had alighted on my hand. The creature had two long horns, and from each of these proceeded numerous very long and delicate filaments which were inserted into my hand to a considerable depth. I had to cut the creature in half, and draw away the forepart, which was attached to my hand, with great care lest I should leave portions of the filaments in the flesh. This animal seemed all the more unpleasant because it was noiseless, and its attacks, I thought, imperceptible. I appeared to be attacked by a succession of them. On awakening, there was irritation of the left wrist, as though the mosquito had bitten me, although I had long ceased to be bitten by mosquitoes. This dream, it will be seen, corresponds in an unusually close way to the idea of a presentative dream ; imagination followed reality in presenting an insect as the cause of the sensation experienced (possibly because I had actually heard the mosquito when awake), but still, as in all dreams, the process was mainly central, and imagination was freely exercised in creating a creature adequate to explain the doubtless vague and massive cutaneous sensations transmitted to sleeping consciousness.[1]

Perhaps one of the commonest skin sensations to excite dream formation is that of cold due to disturbance of the bed coverings. The following example may serve as an illustration of this class. I dreamed that I was in an hotel, mounting many flights of stairs, until I entered a room where the chambermaid was making the bed ; the white bedclothes were scattered over everything, and looked to me like snow ; then I became conscious that I was very cold, and it appeared to me that I really was surrounded by snow, for the chambermaid remarked that I was very courageous to come up so high in the hotel, very few people venturing to do so on account of the great cold at this height. I awoke to find that it was a cold night, and that I was entangled in the sheets, and partly uncovered. Nothing else

[1] In another case, a sensation of irritation in the palm led to a dream of being scratched by a cat. Guthrie mentions (*Clinical Journal*, 7th June 1899) that as a child he used to dream of being tortured by savages by being slowly tickled under the arms when unable to move; he sweated much at night, and considers that the tickling thus caused was the source of the dreams.

had occurred to suggest this dream which sleeping consciousness had elaborated out of the two associated ideas of altitude and snow in order to explain the actual sensations experienced. It is noteworthy that, as in the dream just before narrated, there was here also a link with reality, this time furnished by the disarranged bedclothes.[1]

The auditory experiences of dreams, to a greater extent perhaps than those involving the sense of touch, may be based on spontaneous disturbances within the sensory mechanism. This is notably also the case with visual experiences, and in many respects the conditions in the ear are analogous. Apart from increased resonance of the ear, or hyperaesthesia of the auditory nerve, producing special sensitiveness to sounds, an increased flow of blood through the ear, as well as muscular contractions and mucous plugs in the external ear, furnish the faint rudimentary noises which, in sleep, may constitute the nucleus around which hallucinations crystallise. Disease of the ear may obviously act in the same way, but, even apart from actual disease, various nervous disturbances favour the production of auditory hallucinations during sleep, and, in marked cases, even awake.

We may dream of listening to music in the absence of all external sounds having any musical character. In such cases, no doubt, the actual conditions

---

[1] The corresponding sensation of heat can also, of course, be experienced in sleep, alike whether the stimulus comes from the brain or the skin. Thus I dreamed that, not knowing whether some water was hot or cold, I put my finger into it and felt it to be distinctly hot.

within the auditory mechanism are suggesting music to the brain, but the resulting music seems usually to be less definite, less rememberable, than when it forms around the nucleus of an external series of sounds. In many of these cases it is probable that we do not hear music in our dream ; we are simply under conditions in which we imagine that we hear music. Thus, on going to bed soon after supper, but not perceptibly suffering from indigestion, I dreamed that I was present at a public meeting combined with an orchestral concert. A speech was to be made by a man who looked like an old sailor or soldier, and meanwhile the orchestra was playing. The speaker—unaccustomed, I gathered, to the etiquette of such a meeting—suddenly interrupted the orchestra by a remark, and the surprised conductor stopped the performance for a moment and then continued, subsequent remarks by the speaker failing to affect the music, which continued to the end, becoming more lively and vigorous in character. But what the music was, I knew not at the time, nor could I recall any fragment of it on awakening. It is even possible that such a dream is mainly visual, and that no hallucinatory music is heard, its occurrence being merely deduced from the nature of the vision.

If the dreams evoked by sounds within the ear are usually difficult to trace in normal persons under ordinary circumstances, this is not the case with dreams suggested by sounds which strike the ear from without. These constitute one of the most interesting groups of dreams as well as one of the easiest to explain, and

THE SENSES IN DREAMS

they are very frequent.[1] Their mechanism may, indeed, be observed under some circumstances even in the waking state. In some persons, music, a voice, a bird's song, even a word, a comment, arouse phantoms of colour and form, light and shade, coloured clouds, streams, waves, etc. The phenomena are especially rich when produced by an orchestra. Such 'music-phantoms,' as they are termed, are a special and freer development of the narrow and rigid phenomena of 'colour-hearing.' They have been studied by Dr. Ruths.[2] We have to remember that music possesses a fundamental motor basis. As Dauriac remarks, music may be defined as 'movement clothed with sound.'[3] It tends to produce movement, or, failing movement, to produce motor imagery.[4]

Dreams excited by definite external auditory stimuli may be of various character. A not uncommon source —especially for those who live on a wind-swept coast—is the occurrence of storms. A lady dreams, for instance, that her little dog has fallen off a high cliff and that she

[1] The ease with which musical sounds can be applied during sleep and the beneficial results on emotional tone have suggested their therapeutic use. Leonard Corning ('The Use of Musical Vibrations before and during Sleep,' *Medical Record*, 21st January 1899) is regarded as the pioneer in this field.

[2] Ch. Ruths, *Experimental-Untersuchungen über Musikphantome*, 1898.

[3] Dauriac, 'Des Images Suggérées par l'Audition Musicale,' *Revue Philosophique*, November 1902.

[4] De Rochas has described and reproduced the gestures and dances of his hypnotised subject, Lina, under the influence of music. Ribot (*L'Imagination Créatrice*, pp. 177 *et seq.*, 291 *et seq.*) has discussed the imagery suggested by music and points out that it is most pronounced in non-musical subjects. Fatigue and over-excitement are predisposing conditions in the production of this imagery, as is shown by MacDougall (*Psychological Review*, September 1898) in his own experience.

hears his shrieks; it was an extremely windy night, and her window was open. The dream has some resemblance to one which Burdach recorded that he shared with a companion in an hotel during a storm; they both dreamed they were wandering at night among high precipices.

On one occasion I awoke in the middle of a windy night imagining I had been listening to an opera of Gluck's (which in reality I had never heard), and experiencing all the sense of delicious waves of melody which one actually experiences in listening to such operas as *Alceste*. A fragment of a melody I had heard in the dream still persisted in my memory on awaking, so that I could mentally repeat it, when it seemed as agreeable as in the dream, though unfamiliar.

The following dream had also a similar origin. I imagined that I was assisting at a spectacle of somewhat dubious erotic character, in company with other persons who, out of modesty, covered their faces with their hands with the decorous gesture which recalled (as dream consciousness evidently realised) that of people during prayer in church. Thereupon a beautiful voice was heard in the background loudly chanting a versicle of the Te Deum. This awoke me, and I seemed to realise when half awake that the voice I had heard in the dream was a real voice. There had, however, been no real voice, only the loud howling of the wind and the beating of the rain on the window panes.

Once, on a very windy night, and when, perhaps, suffering a trifling disturbance of health—for there was slight pleurodynic pain the next morning—I dreamed

THE SENSES IN DREAMS

I was quietly at home with friends, when suddenly the sky became illuminated. We found that this was due to steady and continuous lightning, a state of things which remained throughout the dream, the sky presenting the appearance of a cracked and crushed sheet of melting ice.[1] By and by, fragments of buildings and similar debris were whirled past in the air, and I caught sight of a woman driven above me by her skirts. We now realised the imminent approach of a terrific cyclone which, at any moment, might carry the house and ourselves away. I remembered no more.

Yet another dream may be mentioned as likewise directly due to a violent storm and the rattling of a window near my bed. The latter sound evidently recalled to sleeping consciousness the sound of the rattling window of a railway train, and I dreamed that I was travelling to Berlin with a medical friend. There were the accompaniments, not unfamiliar in dreams, of rushing along interminable platforms, and up and down endless stairs, finding myself in a carriage of the wrong class, with, in consequence, more wandering along corridors, and finally finding that my friend had been left behind. The character of the dream may have been influenced by slight indigestion. In this dream, unlike those already recorded as due to external stimuli, the elements of the dream were not the pure invention of dreaming imagination, but compacted entirely of ideas that had been recently familiar.

[1] One is tempted to think that this lightning may have been a symbolistic transformation of lancinating neuralgic pains, magnified, as sensations are apt to be, in sleep.

The following dream was due to an auditory stimulus of different character. I dreamed that I was listening to a performance of Haydn's *Creation*, the orchestral part of the performance seeming to consist chiefly of the very realistic representation of the song of birds, though I could not identify the note of any particular bird. Then followed solos by male singers, whom I saw, especially one who attracted my attention by singing at the close in a scarcely audible voice. On awakening, the source of the dream was not immediately obvious, but I soon realised that it was the song of a canary in another room. I had never heard Haydn's *Creation*, except in fragments, nor thought of it at any recent period; its reputation as regards the realistic representation of natural sounds had evidently caused it to be put forward by sleeping consciousness as a plausible explanation of the sounds heard, and the visual centres had accepted the theory.

However far-fetched and improbable our dreams may seem to the waking mind, they are, from the point of view of the sleeping mind, serious and careful attempts to construct an adequate theory of the phenomena. The imagery is sought from far afield only to fit the facts more accurately. Thus a lady dreamed that her dog was being crushed out flat in a large old-fashioned box-mangle. She awoke to find that water from a burst pipe was falling from the ceiling on to the floor on the landing outside her door, close to where the dog had his bed. She had never seen a mangle of this kind since she was a child, or had any occasion to think of it, but the rhythm and sound of it somewhat resembled that of the falling water.

One more example of an auditory dream may be given. I dreamed that I was back in a schoolroom of my boyhood, with two or three of the present masters. The room had been entirely changed, and it contained much new school apparatus and, notably, on a table, several miniature engines, of different character, actually working. I said to the masters that I wished all these apparatus had been there twenty years ago (a considerable under-estimate of the actual interval since I left that schoolroom), so that I might have enjoyed the benefit of them. 'All life is made up of machinery,' I found myself uttering aloud as I awoke, 'and unless you understand machinery you can't understand life.' It was not till some moments later that I became conscious of a faint whirring sound which puzzled me till I realised that it was the sound of distant machinery entering through the open window. This had, undoubtedly, suggested the engines of the dream, though I had not been conscious in my dream of hearing any sounds, and the small size of the dream engines corresponded to the faintness of the actual sounds.

Dreams aroused by odours do not usually seem to occur except on the experimental application of them to the sleeper's nostrils, and experiments in this direction are not usually successful.[1] Occasionally, however,

---

[1] In some experiments by Prof. W. S. Monroe on twenty women students at Westfield Normal School a crushed clove was placed on the tongue for ten successive nights on going to bed. Of 254 dreams reported as following there were seventeen taste dreams and eight smell dreams, and three of

smell dreams occur without any traceable sensory source, and Grace Andrews, for instance, records a dream of the sea, accompanied by the seashore odour, ' a pure and rich sensation of smell.' In my own case olfactory dreams have been rare and insignificant.

Taste, as we usually understand it, really involves, as is well known, an element of smell, and taste dreams of this kind seem to occur from time to time under the influence of any slight disturbance of the mucous membrane of the mouth or slight indigestion. It is possible that the latter element was present in the following dream : I imagined that, following the example of a friend, I gave some cigarettes to a tramp we had casually met, and that, in return, we felt compelled to drink some raw gin he carried. I did so with some misgiving as to the possible results of drinking from a tramp's flask, but although in real life I had not tasted gin for many years, the hot burning taste of the spirit was very distinct. On awakening, my lips seemed hot and dry, and it was doubtless this labial sensation which led dream consciousness to seek a plausible explanation in cigarettes and spirits. Although the spirit seemed to

---

these dreams actually involved cloves. The clove also influenced dreams of other classes ; thus, as a result of the burning sensation in the mouth, one dreamer imagined that the house was on fire (W. S. Monroe, ' A Study of Taste Dreams,' *American Journal of Psychology*, January 1899). It has indeed been found, by Meunier, specially easy to apply olfactory stimuli during sleep and so improve the emotional tone (R. Meunier, ' A Propos d'onirothérapie,' *Archives de Neurologie*, March 1910). Meunier found that in his own case tuberose always called out agreeable dreams full of detail, though in another subject the dreams were always unpleasant. In hysterical subjects essence of geranium provoked various agreeable dreams followed by a pleasant emotional tone during the following day.

have the specific flavour of gin, it is always difficult, if not impossible, in dream sensations, to distinguish between what one feels and what one merely concludes that one feels. In such a case, that is to say, it remains doubtful whether the labial sensation evokes the specific hallucination of gin, or whether it merely suggests to sleeping consciousness that the gin has been tasted, much as it is possible to suggest to the hypnotised person that the substance he is tasting is a quite different substance, that salt is sugar, or that water is wine.

As with dreams of smell, it is not always possible to detect any external stimulation as the cause for a taste or pseudo-taste dream.[1] This may be illustrated by a dream which belongs strictly to the tactile class; I dreamed that I called upon a medical acquaintance whose assistant I found in a dark surgery. I absently took up a broken medicine bottle and put it to my mouth, when my friend came in. I spoke to him on some medical topic, but he entered his carriage, and was driven off before he had time to answer me. I then found that my mouth was full of fragments of broken colourless glass, which I carefully removed. This dream was constructed, in the manner which has been often illustrated in the previous pages, of small separate incidents which had occurred during the immediately preceding days. One of the incidents

---

[1] Titchener ('Taste Dreams,' *American Journal of Psychology*, January 1895) records taste dreams by auto-suggestion, and Ribot (*Psychology of the Emotions*, p. 142) thinks there can be no doubt dreams of both taste and smell can occur without objective source.

was the fact that I had myself smashed a little coloured (not colourless) glass and carefully picked up the fragments. But the vividest part of the dream was the sensation of broken glass in the mouth, and on awaking no sensation could be detected in the mouth. So that though the most plausible explanation of such a dream would be the theory that the recent experience with broken glass had suggested to sleeping consciousness the explanation of an unpleasant sensation actually experienced in the mouth, there was nothing whatever to support that theory.

The falling of light on the closed eyes, or the half opening of the eyes, has been found to serve as a visual stimulus to dreams, but I have myself no decisive evidence on this point.[1] In the case of a lady who dreamed that a lover was in her room, and that suddenly the door opened, and she saw her mother standing before her with a bright light, which awoke her, she could find nothing in the room, no light, to account for the dream. It is, of course, unnecessary for a dream of a bright light to be actually produced by an external visual stimulus accompanying the dream, for the spontaneous retino-cerebral activity itself produces sensations of light. Thus, on the night after a pleasant walk in a country lane through which the setting sun

---

[1] Hammond (*Treatise on Insanity*, p. 229) knew a gentleman who dreamed he was in heaven and surrounded by dazzling brilliance, awaking to find that the smouldering fire had flared up. Weygandt dreamed that he was gazing at 'living pictures' illuminated by magnesium light, and awoke to find that the morning sun had just appeared from behind clouds and was flooding the room with light. See also Parish, *Hallucinations and Illusions*, p. 52.

THE SENSES IN DREAMS

shone, I dreamed that I was walking along a lane in which I saw a bright light and my own vast shadow in front of me. It would seem that, on the whole, the curtain of the eyelids effectually shuts out light from the eye during sleep, and that the sense which is more active during the day than any other is the most carefully guarded of all during the night. The peculiarly delicate and unstable nature of the chemical basis of vision makes up for this protection from external stimulation, and by its spontaneous activity ensures that even in dreams vision is the predominant sense.

What we find as regards the part played in dreams by excitations arising from the external specific senses holds good also for excitations arising from internal organic sensations. The main difference is that the stimuli which reach sleeping consciousness from the organs within the body—the stomach, heart, lungs, sexual apparatus, bladder, etc.—are usually more vague and massive, more difficult to recognise and identify, than are the more specific sensory stimuli which reach us from without. These visceral excitations may be transformed within the brain into imagery so unlike themselves that we may refuse to recognise them, and must frequently experience some amount of hesitation. Evidence of this fact will come before us in due course later on. I only wish to refer here to the more obvious part played in dreams by sensations arising within the body.

We should expect that the visceral processes to be

translated most clearly and directly into dreaming consciousness would be, not those which are regular and continuous, but those which assert themselves, more or less imperiously, at intervals. This is actually the case. The heart, for instance, probably plays a part in dreams only when disturbed in its action, and even then nearly always a very transformed part. On the other hand, when the impulses of the generative system arise in sleep to manifest themselves in erotic dreams, the resulting imagery is usually very clear, and with very definite and recognisable sexual associations. Erotic dreams are, indeed, in both men and women, among the most vivid of all dreams, and the most emotionally potent.[1]

The bladder, again, is an internal organ which makes its functional needs felt only at intervals, and thus, when those needs occur during sleep, they become conscious in imagery which easily recalls the source of the stimulus. It may, indeed, be said that vesical dreams are full of instruction in the light they throw on the psychology of dreaming. This has long been well known to writers on dreams. Thus Scherner, many years ago, insisted on the interest and importance of vesical dreams. In women, especially, he regarded them as very frequent and developed, most dream stories of women, he considered, containing symbolic representations of this organic irritation. Water, in some form or another, is naturally the commonest

[1] I have discussed erotic dreams in the study of 'Auto-erotism' in the first volume of my *Studies in the Psychology of Sex* (third edition, revised and enlarged, 1910).

symbol. In Scherner's opinion, also, all dreams of fish playing in the water are vesical dreams.[1]

In its simplest form the vesical dream is what Freud would term a wish-dream of infantile type, frequently in the magnified form common in dreams, and sometimes transferred from the dreamer himself to become objectified in another person, or even an inanimate object.[2] There is, however, a very important difference according to whether these dreams take place in an adult or in a young child. In the adult it almost invariably happens that the dream act remains merely a dream act, and no corresponding motor impulse is transmitted to the bladder. But when such dreams occur to very young children, in whose brains the motor inhibitory mechanism is not yet fully established, it not infrequently happens that the motor impulse is transmitted and the expulsive action of the bladder is set up in sympathy with the imagery of the dream; thus is established the condition known as nocturnal enuresis. As the young brain develops, and inhibition becomes more perfect, these vesical dreams cease to exert any actual effect on the bladder, even when, as sometimes happens, they continue to occur at intervals

---

[1] K. A. Scherner, *Das Leben des Traums*, 1861, pp. 187 *et seq.* Volkelt some years later (*Die Traum-Phantasie*, 1875, p. 74) pointed out the occurrence of somewhat similar vesical symbolisms (including in the case of women a filled knitting-bag) in dream life, though he regarded visions of water as the most usual indication in such dreams. Vesical dreams may, of course, contain other elements; see *e.g.* an example given by C. J. Jung, ' L'Analyse des Rêves,' *L'Année Psychologique*, 15th year, 1909, p. 165.

[2] A typical dream of this kind, of sufficient importance to be embodied in history, occurred several thousand years ago to Astyages, King of the Medes, and has been recorded by Herodotus (Book I. ch. 107).

in adult life.¹ Occasionally, both in those who have and those who have not suffered from nocturnal enuresis in childhood (especially women), vesical dreams of this character may occur without even any real distension of the bladder. In some of these cases the dream can be shown to be due to a reminiscence or suggestion from the waking life of the previous day. Dreams stimulated by organic sensations from within are thus found to resemble those proceeding from sensory sensations from without in that they are both exactly simulated by dreams which are mainly of central origin.

When we turn to those internal organs of the body which normally carry on their functions in a constant and equable manner, seldom or never obtruding themselves into the sphere of consciousness, any disturbance of function seems much less likely to be translated into dream consciousness in a simple and direct form. It is sufficient to take the example of the heart. When the heart is acting normally any consciousness of its action is as rare asleep as awake. Even when cardiac action is disturbed, either by disease or by temporary excitement, dream consciousness seldom realises the physical cause of the disturbance. Occasionally, indeed, the cardiac disturbance may reach sleeping consciousness without any very remote transforma-

---

¹ In the study of Auto-erotism mentioned in a previous note I have brought forward dreams illustrating some of the points in the text, and have also discussed the analogies and contrasts between vesical and erotic dreams. The fact that nocturnal enuresis is associated with vesical dreams, though referred to by Buchan in his *Venus sine Concubitu* more than a century ago, is still little known, but it is obviously a fact of clinical importance.

THE SENSES IN DREAMS

tion; thus a lady dreams that she is fainting while really breathing in a slightly laboured and spasmodic way; but at another period the same lady, at a time when she was suffering from some degree of heart weakness, dreamed one night, when the trouble was specially marked, that she was driving sweating horses up a steep hill, urging them on with the whip in order to avoid an express train which she imagined was behind her. This dream of sweating and panting horses climbing a hill has been noted by various observers to occur in connection with heart trouble.[1] The real difficulty of the panting and struggling heart instinctively finds its apparent explanation in a familiar spectacle of daily life.

In another case a dreamer awoke from a disturbed sleep associated with indigestion, having the impression that burglars were tramping upstairs, but immediately realised that the tramp of the burglars' feet was really the beating of her own heart. Somewhat similarly, when suffering from headache, I have dreamed of hammering nails into a floor, a theory obviously invented to account for the thump of throbbing arteries.

An interesting group of phenomena connected with the sensory influences discussed in this chapter is furnished by the premonitions of physical disorders and diseases sometimes experienced in dreams. A physical disturbance may reach sleeping consciousness many hours, or even days, before it is perceived by

[1] So, for instance, the asthmatic patient of Max Simon (*Le Monde des Rêves*, p. 40) who, during an attack, dreamed of sweating horses attempting to draw a heavy waggon uphill.

waking consciousness, and become translated into a more or less fantastic dream. This has been recognised from of old, and Aristotle, for instance, observed that dreams magnify sensory excitations, and pointed out that they were thus useful to the physician in diagnosing symptoms not yet perceptible in the waking state. Thus Hammond knew a gentleman who, before an attack of hemiplegic paralysis, repeatedly dreamed that he had been cut in two down the middle line, and could only move on one side, while a young lady who dreamed she had swallowed molten lead, though quite well on awaking, was attacked by severe tonsilitis toward midday. Erythematous conditions of the skin, as has been pointed out to me by Dr. Kiernan, who has met with numerous cases in point, play an especial part in generating these dreams. Jewell, again, mentions a girl who dreamed, three days before being laid up with typhoid fever, that some one threw oil over her and set light to it. Macario, who was, perhaps, the first to record and study scientifically the dreams of this class, termed them prodromic.[1]

'Prophetic' dreams, in which the dreamer foresees, not a physical condition which is already latent, but an external occurrence, belong to an entirely different

---

[1] Forbes Winslow also recorded cases (*Obscure Diseases*, pp. 611 *et seq.*), and many examples were brought together by Hammond (*Treatise on Insanity*, pp. 234 *et seq.*). Vaschide and Piéron discuss the matter and bring forward thirteen cases (*La Psychologie du Rêve*, pp. 34 *et seq.*). Féré recorded two cases in which dreams were the precursory symptoms of attacks of migraine (*Revue de Médecine*, 10th February 1903). Various cases, chiefly from the literature of the subject, are brought together by Paul Meunier and Masselon (*Les Rêves et leur Interprétation*, 1910).

THE SENSES IN DREAMS

class, and need not be discussed in detail here, since they are usually fallacious. A fairly common experience of this kind is the dream of an unknown person who is afterwards met in real life. These dreams fall into two groups : in the first the 'prophecy' is based on a failure of memory, the dreamer having really seen the person before ; in the second, the subsequent 'recognition' of the person is due to the emotional preparation of the dream, and the concentrated expectation. Sante de Sanctis, who points this out, gives an experience of the kind which happened to the distinguished novelist, Capuana, who had a vivid dream of a dark lady, with expressive eyes, and three days after met the lady of his dream in the street.[1] Women, in a state of emotional expectation, have often mistaken dead (or even living) persons for missing husbands or children, and any one who has observed how, when a noted criminal flies from justice, he is soon 'recognised,' from his portrait, in the most various parts of the world, will have no difficulty in believing that it is easily possible to 'recognise' people from dream portraits, which are much vaguer than photographs. That there are other prophetic dreams, less easy to account for, I am ready to admit, though they have not come under my own immediate observation.

[1] Sante de Sanctis, *I Sogni*, p. 380.

CHAPTER V

EMOTION IN DREAMS

Emotion and Imagination—How Stimuli are transformed into Emotion—Somnambulism—The Failure of Movement in Dreams—Nightmare—Influence of the approach of Awakening on imagined Dream Movements—The Magnification of Imagery—Peripheral and Cerebral Conditions combine to produce this Imaginative Heightening—Emotion in Sleep also Heightened—Dreams formed to explain Heightened Emotions of unknown origin—The fundamental Place of Emotion in Dreams—Visceral and especially Gastric disturbance as a source of Emotion—Symbolism in Dreams—The Dreamer's Moral Attitude—Why Murder so often takes place in Dreams—Moral Feeling not Abolished in Dreams though sometimes Impaired.

WHETHER the influences which stimulate our dreams arise from without or from within the organism, they are always filtered and diffused through the obscured channels of perception. They reach the brain at last in a vague and massive shape which may or may not betray to waking analysis the source from which they arise, but will certainly have become so changed in these organic channels that their affective tone will be predominant. They are, that is to say, largely transformed into *emotion*. And, when so transformed, they become the origin of what we regard as the imaginative element in dreams.[1]

[1] The dependence of sleeping imagination on emotion of organic origin was long ago clearly seen and set forth by the acute introspective psychologist, Maine de Biran (*Œuvres Inédites*, 'Fondements de la Psychologie,' p. 102).

EMOTION IN DREAMS

Sleep is especially favourable to the production of emotion because while it allows a considerable amount of activity to sensory activities, and a very wide freedom to the imagery founded on sensory activities, it largely and in many directions inhibits motor activity. The actions suggested by sensory excitation cannot, therefore, be carried out. As soon as the impulse enters motor channels it is impeded, broken up, and scattered in a vain struggle. This process is transmitted to the brain as a wave of emotion.

Sometimes, indeed, as we know, motor co-ordinations, usually inhibited in sleep, are not so inhibited. The dreamer is able to execute, perfectly or imperfectly, some action which, really or in imagination, he desires to execute. He is then said to be in a state of somnambulism. The somnambulist, in the wide sense of the word, is not necessarily a person who walks in his sleep, but any person in whom a group of co-ordinated muscles is sufficiently awake to respond more or less adequately to the motor impulse from the sleeping brain. To talk in sleep is a form of somnambulism. When the motor channels are thus unimpeded, there is usually no memory of a dream on awaking. The impulses that reach consciousness can be, as it were, quickly and easily drained off to the surface of the nervous system, and they tend to leave no deep impress on consciousness.

'I worked late last night,' writes a lady, a novelist, 'went to bed, and dropped into a dead kind of sleep. When I woke this morning about seven a funny thing had happened. Two candles were burning in my room. When I went to bed I had only one burning, and I know I put that out. Now, there were two burning side by side as if I had been writing, and they had evidently been burning only an hour or so, I must have got up and lighted them in my sleep.'[1] The actions carried out in the somnambulistic condition are not usually co-ordinated with the action of higher emotions : thus, a young woman was impelled by a distended bladder, while still asleep, to get out of bed and proceeded to carry out the suggested action, but without further precautions, on to the floor ; she was only awakened by an exclamation from her sister, who had been aroused by the sound. We seem to see that under a strong stimulus—unfinished work in one case, vesical tension in the other—the motor centres have awakened to activity in the early morning while the higher centres are still soundly asleep. If the second sleeper had not been awakened, in neither case would any memory of the incidents have remained.[2] There has been no struggle, and no resultant emotions have, therefore, been aroused to impress consciousness. It is evident that the lack of adaptation between sensory and motor activity is an

---

[1] Jastrow (*The Subconscious,* p. 206) relates a similar case observed in a girl student.
[2] Herbert Wright, who finds that in children night-terrors are apt to be associated with somnambulism, points out that when the somnambulism replaces the night-terrors it leaves no memory behind (*British Medical Journal,* 19th August 1899, p. 465). An interesting study of movement in normal and morbid sleep has been contributed by Segre (' Contributo alla Conoscenza dei Movimenti del Sonno,' *Archivio di Psichiatria,* 1907, fasc. 1.).

important factor in dreams, and contributes to impart to them their emotional character.

In somnambulism we have a state which is in some respects the reverse of that usual in dreams. The higher centres are, indeed, split off from the lower centres, but it is the former that are asleep and the latter are awake, whereas in ordinary dreaming the higher centres are acting in accordance with their means, while the lower centres are quiescent. Somnambulism is an approximation to a condition found in some diseases of the brain when, as a result of lesion of the higher nervous levels, we have a mental state — the ideatory apraxia of Liepmann — in which the muscular system carries out plans, but the plans are defective because not supervised by the higher centres. In ordinary dreams, on the other hand, we have a state comparable to that produced by brain lesions in what Pick terms motor apraxia, in which the higher centres are acting freely, but their plans are never carried into action owing to failure of the motor centres.

This characteristic of dreaming has seemed puzzling to some writers. They ask why, in our dreams, we should sometimes be so conscious of failure of movement, and why, when we strive to move in dreams, we do not always actually move.[1]

[1] This question is, for instance, asked by F. H. Bradley ('On the Failure of Movement in Dreams,' *Mind*, 1894, p. 373). The explanation he prefers is that the dream vision is out of relation to the very dimly conscious actual position of the body, so that the information necessary to complete the idea of the movement is wanting. Only as regards the less complicated movements of lips, tongue, or finger, when the motor idea is in harmony with the actual position of the body movements, does movement take

There scarcely seems to me to be any serious difficulty here; still, the question is one of considerable interest and importance. It is necessary to point out in the first place that, however complete the actual absence of movement, there is usually no failure of movement in the dream vision. We dream that we are talking, that we are moving from place to place, that we are performing various actions. We are conscious of no difficulty, even sometimes of a peculiar facility, in executing these movements. And in normal persons, under normal conditions, it would seem that the dream movements take place without even an incipient degree of corresponding actual movement perceptible to an observer. The efferent motor channels, and even to a large extent the afferent sensory channels, are asleep, and the whole representative circuit is completed within the brain, or, as we say, imaginatively.[1] Thus a middle-aged friend, whose habits are by no means athletic, dreams that, desiring to attract some one's

place. We have no means of distinguishing the real world from the world of our vision; 'our images thus move naturally to realise themselves in the world of our real limbs. But the world and its arrangement is for the moment out of connection with our ideas, and hence the attempt at motion for the most part must fail.' It is quite true that this conflict is an important factor in dreaming, but it fails to apply to the large number of movements which we dream of actually doing.

[1] The action of some drugs produces a state in this respect resembling that which prevails in dreams. 'Under the influence of a large dose of haschisch,' Professor Stout remarks (*Analytic Psychology*, vol. i. p. 14), 'I found myself totally unable to distinguish between what I actually did and saw, and what I merely thought about.' Not only are the motor and sensory activities relatively dormant, but the central activity is perfectly able, and content, to dispense with their services. 'Thought,' as Jastrow says (*Fact and Fable in Psychology*, p. 386), 'is but more or less successfully suppressed action.'

attention, he rests one knee on his wife's small worktable, and holding the foot of the other leg in one hand, he whirls rapidly and easily round and round on the pivot of the knee which rests on the table, the dream afterwards continuing without any awakening. A lady, again, who, when awake, is unable to swim, and knows no reason why she should think of swimming, vividly dreams that she jumps from a houseboat into the river, and proceeds to swim on her side with great ease, this dream also continuing without awakening. These dreamers were able to execute triumphantly the muscular feats they planned, because they had not really attempted to execute them at all, and, moreover, no sufficient sensory messages reached the brain to give information that the limbs were not actually obeying the orders of the brain. The dreamers were probably in a somewhat deep state of sleep.[1]

The dreams in which we seem to ourselves to be suffering from the difficulty or impossibility of movement thus constitute a special class. Jewell would apply to them the term 'nightmare,' which he regards as 'characterised by inability to move or speak.' When,

---

[1] This seems to me to be the answer to the question, asked by Freud, (*Die Traumdeutung*, p. 227), why we do not always dream of inhibited movement. Freud considers that the idea of inhibited movement, when it occurs in dreams, has no relation to the actual condition of the dreamer's nervous system, but is simply an ideatory symbol of an erotic wish that is no longer capable of fulfilment. But it is certain that sleep is not always at the same depth and that the various nervous groups are not always equally asleep. A dream arising on the basis of partial and imperfect sleep can scarcely fail to lead to the attempt at actual movement and the more or less complete inhibition of that movement, presenting a struggle which is often visible to the onlooker, and is not purely ideatory.

in dreams, we become conscious of difficult movement, it has frequently, and perhaps usually, happened that the motor channels are not entirely closed, the sensory channels unusually open, and very frequently, though not necessarily, this is associated with the approach of awakening. I dreamed that I was walking with a friend, that we quarrelled, and that thereupon I crossed the road, and walked on ahead of him. These actions seemed entirely effortless. Gradually, however, I became conscious of immense and ineffectual effort in keeping in front, and slowly began to experience, as I awakened, a feeling of lassitude in my actual and motionless limbs. In the process of awakening, I take it, the increased, but still defective, efflux of sensation from the legs, conveying the message of their real position, entered into conflict with the dream imagery, and produced a struggle in consciousness. It is by no means necessary to assume that there was a complete absence of sensory impressions from the legs during the earlier part of the dream; on the contrary, it is probable that the feeling of lassitude was itself the cause of the dream, the idea of walking being a theory to account for the lassitude; this seems more probable than that the actual lassitude was caused by the mental exertion in the dream.

In a dream which a friend tells me he has often had, and always finds painful, he imagines he is climbing a mountain, and at last reaches a point at which, notwithstanding all his efforts, further progress is impossible. It seems probable that this dream is also an

EMOTION IN DREAMS

example of the conflict due to the process of awakening. In this case, however, the solution is complicated by the fact that in earlier life the dreamer had really once found himself in the situation he now only experiences in dreams.

It is sometimes possible to prove, through the evidence of a witness, that in our dreams of movements executed with difficulty, we are really sufficiently awake on the motor side to be making actual movements, though these actual movements may only very roughly correspond to the movements we imagine we are trying to make. Very frequently, no doubt, dreams of difficult movement co-exist with, or are caused by, some degree of actual movement. In some such cases, indeed, the slight and imperfect actual movement may, in dream consciousness, be a complete and adequate movement. In these cases the imperfect sensory messages are not, it seems, sufficiently precise to reveal to sleeping consciousness the imperfection of the motor impulses.

Exactly the same thing occurs under the allied conditions of anaesthesia produced by drugs. Thus, on one occasion, when coming to consciousness after the administration of nitrous oxide gas, I had the sensation of crying out aloud, but in reality, as I was informed by a friend at my side, I merely made a slight guttural sound. In the same way we see sleeping dogs making slight movements of all their paws in succession, a faint and abortive movement of running, which in the sleeping dog's consciousness may, doubtless, be accompanied by the notion that he is dashing across a field after a rabbit.

In these dreams of failure of movement, it seems to me, the dream process, as the result of an approximation to the waking state, has become mixed with actual sensori-motor impulses, but the threshold of waking life is still too far off for actual movements to be completely and successfully accomplished, and in the case of the limbs the eye cannot be used to guide movements which the muscular and cutaneous sensations are still too dead to guide. It is important to remember that in waking life, under pathological conditions, we may have a precisely similar state of things. In some states of cerebro-spinal degeneration, resulting in defective sensibility of muscle and nerve, the subject sways unsteadily when he closes his eyes, and when there is loss of sensibility in the arm it is sometimes impossible to hold objects in the hand except with the guiding aid afforded by the eye.[1]

In a dream, dating from fifteen years back, that I now regard as conditioned by the approach of the moment of awakening, I imagined that I was making huge efforts to copy in a copy-book a capital H, engraved in a rather peculiar fashion, but really offering no difficulties to any waking schoolchild. By no means

[1] This explanation, based on the depth and kind of the sleep, is entirely distinct from the theory of Aliotta (*Il Pensiero e la Personalità nei Sogni*, 1905), who believes that dreamers differ according to their nervous type, the person of visual type assisting passively at the spectacle of his dreams, while the person of motor type takes actual part in them. I have no evidence of this, though I believe that dreams differ in accordance with the dreamer's personal type.

could I get the proportions right, if, indeed, I could make any stroke at all, and at the end of my painful and ineffectual efforts I seemed to be trying to write on sand, which was merely displaced by my hand. This final impression seems clearly to be that of a dreamer who is already sufficiently awake to be conscious of the bedclothes yielding to the touch.

The foregoing dream suggests that failure of movement in dreaming may tend to be associated with an accentuation of that shifting of imagery which is one of the most primary elements in dreaming, both failure of movement and accentuation of shifting imagery being, perhaps, alike due to the approach towards the waking state. Thus, if in a dream one is brushing one's coat, one finds, without any overwhelming surprise, that fresh patches of dust appear again and again, even when one's efforts in brushing them away are successful. Even when we feel able to effect movement in our dream, there may still be a failure of that movement to effect its object.

The question of movement in dreams, of the presence or absence of effort and inhibition, is thus seen to be explicable by reference to the depth of sleep and the particular groups of centres involved. In full normal sleep movements are purely ideatory, and no difficulty arises in executing any movement, for the reason that there really is no movement at all, or even any attempt at movement, while, even if slight movement occurs, no message of its actual defectiveness can reach the brain. Movement or attempt at movement, with more or less inhibition, tends to occur when the motor and sensory centres are in a partially aroused state ; it is a phenomenon which belongs to the period immediately before awakening.[1]

It is doubtless mainly due to the diffusion of inhibited nervous impulses through many channels, and the vague and massive character which they hence assume in consciousness, that we must attribute the magnification of dream imagery, and the exaggeration of dream feelings. This is not a constant tendency of our dreams ; sometimes, indeed, perhaps in special stages of sleep-consciousness, there is diminution, and people look no larger than dolls, and houses like doll's houses, while, on the emotional side, events which in real life would overwhelm us, may, in dreams, be accepted as matters of course. But the heightening of imagery and ideas and feelings is very common. There is a kind of normal megalomania in our dreams. We have already incidentally encountered many instances of this : a tooth

[1] Dugald Stewart argued that there is loss of control over the muscular system during sleep, and the body, therefore, is not subject to our command; volition is present but it cannot influence the limbs. Hammond argued, on the contrary, that Stewart was quite wrong ; the reason why voluntary movements are not performed during sleep is, he said, that volition is suspended. ' We do not will our actions when we are asleep. We imagine that we do, and that is all ' (*Treatise on Insanity*, p. 205). Dugald Stewart and Hammond, though their phraseology may have been too metaphysical, were, from the standpoint I have adopted, both maintaining tenable positions. In one type of dream, we imagine we easily achieve all sorts of difficult and complicated actions, but in reality we make no movement ; the ease and rapidity with which the mental machine moves is due to the fact that it is ungeared, and is effecting no work at all. In the other type of dream we make violent but inadequate efforts at movement and only partially succeed ; the machine is partially geared, in a state intermediate between deep sleep and the waking condition.

appears large enough for a mouse to play in, or like a great jagged rock ; the irritation of a mosquito evokes the image of a huge scarlet beetle ; in vesical dreams endless streams are seen to flow ; a canary's song is heard as Haydn's *Creation*, and the howling of the wind becomes a chanted Te Deum.

A French author has written an impressive literary description of his own purely visual dreams, with their magnificent exaggerations and joyous expansiveness, seeking to show that their chief character is their excessiveness ; ' the flowers are almost women.'[1] I cannot, however, recognise this as characteristic of normal dreaming. It bears more resemblance to De Quincey's opium dreams, or to the visions which came to Heine as he listened to Berlioz's music. In normal dreaming the imagery may, indeed, be stupendously vast, or fantastically absurd, or poignantly intense. But normal dreams are not built on a consistently colossal scale. The megalomania of dreaming is only accidental and occasional, not systematic.[2]

The heightening of dream experiences may, however, be very complete in, as it were, every direction : thus a botanical friend joined a large party for a pleasant country excursion, in the course of which, while sitting in a waggonette, an acquaintance, a miller, standing in the road, handed up to him a dog-rose. In the course of

---

[1] Jacques le Lorrain, *Revue Philosophique*, July 1895.
[2] The systematic megalomania of insanity can, however, have its rise in dreams ; Régis and Lalanne (*International Medical Congress*, 1900 ; *Proceedings, Section de Psychiatrie*, p. 227) met within a short period with four cases in which this had taken place.

a dream of agreeable emotional tone on the night following, this incident was reproduced, but the miller had become an angel, who handed down to him, instead of up from below, a flower which was a moss-rose.

Thus, not only do the actual stimuli taking place during sleep suggest to dream-consciousness imagery of a magnitude out of all proportion to their real intensity, but even the repercussion of the day's incidents in dreams under the influence of a favourable emotional tone may partake of the same heightening influence.

We may say, therefore, that while the excessiveness of dream imagery is mainly due to the conditions of the nervous sensory and motor channels, there is also probably a heightened affectability of the cerebral centres themselves—perhaps due to their state of dissociation or absence of apperception [1]—which leads us in our dreams to react extravagantly to the stimuli that reach the brain. A lady tells me that she often dreams of being very angry at things which, on awaking, she finds are mere trifles that would never make her angry when awake.[2] It is a common experience that

---

[1] This indeed seems to have been recognised by Wundt, who regards a functional rest of the sensory centres and of the apperception centre,' resulting in heightened latent energy which lends unusual strength to excitations, as a secondary condition of the dream state. Külpe (*Outline of Psychology*, p. 212) argues that the existence of vivid dreams shows that fatigue with its diminished associability fails to affect the central sensations themselves; this increased excitability resulting from dissociation may itself, however, be regarded as a symptom of fatigue; hyperaesthesia and anaesthesia are alike signs of exhaustion.

[2] The exhaustion sometimes felt on awaking from a dream perhaps testifies to its emotional potency. Delboeuf states that a friend of his experienced a dream so terrible in its emotional strain that on awaking his black hair was found to have turned completely white.

the things which, in our dreams, impress us as beautiful, eloquent, witty, profound, or amusing, no longer seem so, or only seem so in a much slighter degree, when we are able to recall them awake.

All these various considerations lead us up to a central fact in the psychology of dreaming : the controlling power of emotion on dream ideas. From our present point of view we are now able to say that the chief function of dreams is to supply adequate theories to account for the magnified emotional impulses which are borne in on sleeping consciousness. This is the key to imagination in dreams. From the first we have seen that in dream life the mind is always freely and actively reasoning ; we now see what is usually the real motive and aim of that reasoning. Sleeping consciousness is assailed by waves of emotion from various parts of the organism, but is entirely unable to detect their origin, and, therefore, invents an explanation of them. So that in sleep we have to weave theories concerning the unknowable origin of our emotions, just as when we are awake we weave theories concerning the ultimate origin of the totality of our experiences. The fundamental source of our dream life may thus be said to be emotion.[1]

---

[1] The fundamental character of emotion in dreams has been more or less clearly recognised by various investigators. Thus C. L. Herrick, who studied his own dreams for many months, found that the essential element is the emotional, and not the ideational, and that, indeed, when recalled *at once*, with closed eyes and before moving, they were nearly devoid of intellectual content (*Journal of Comparative Neurology*, vol. iii. p. 17, 1893). R. MacDougall considers that dreaming is ' a succession of intense states of feeling supported by a minimum of ideational content,' or, as he says

There is certainly no profounder emotional excitement during sleep than that which arises from a disturbed or distended stomach, and is reflected by the pneumogastric to the accelerated heart and the excited respiration.[1] We are thereby thrown into a state of emotional agitation, a state of agony and terror, such as we rarely or never attain during waking life. Sleeping consciousness, blindfolded and blundering, a prey to these massive waves from below, and fumbling about desperately for some explanation, jumps at the idea that only the attempt to escape some terrible danger or the guilty consciousness of some awful crime can account for this immense emotional uproar. Thus the

again, more accurately, 'the feeling is primary; the idea-content is the inferred thing' (*Psychological Review*, vol. v. p. 2). Grace Andrews, who kept a record of her dreams (*American Journal of Psychology*, October 1900), found that dream emotions are often stronger and more vivid than those of waking life; 'the dream emotion seems to me the most real element of the dream life.' P. Meunier, again ('Des Rêves Stéreotypés,' *Journal de Psychologie Normale et Pathologique*, September-October 1905), states that 'the substratum of a dream consists of a cœnæsthesia or an emotional state. The intellectual operation which translates to the sleeper's consciousness, while he is asleep, this cœnæsthesia or emotional state is what we call a dream.'

[1] The night-terrors of children have frequently been found to have their origin in gastric or intestinal disturbance. Graham Little brings together the opinions of various authorities on this point, though he is himself inclined to give chief importance to heart disease producing slight disturbances of breathing, since he has found that in nearly two-thirds of his cases (17 out of 30) night-terrors were associated with early heart disease (Graham Little, 'The Causation of Night-Terrors,' *British Medical Journal*, 19th August 1899). It should be added that night-terrors are more usually divided into two classes: (1) idiopathic (purely cerebral in origin), and (2) symptomatic (due to reflex disturbance caused by various local disorders); see *e.g.* Guthrie, 'On Night-Terrors,' *Clinical Journal*, 7th January 1899. J. A. Symonds has well described his own night-terrors as a child (Horatio Brown, *J. A. Symonds*, vol. i.). Lafcadio Hearn (in a paper on 'Nightmare-Touch' in *Shadowings*) also gives a vivid account of his own childish night-terrors.

dream is suffused by a conviction which the continued emotion serves to support. We do not—it seems most simple and reasonable to conclude—experience terror because we think we have committed a crime, but we think we have committed a crime because we experience terror. And the fact that in such dreams we are far more concerned with escape from the results of crime than with any agony of remorse is not, as some have thought, due to our innate indifference to crime, but simply to the fact that our emotional state suggests to us active escape from danger rather than the more passive grief of remorse. Thus our dreams bear witness to the fact that our intelligence is often but a tool in the hands of our emotions.[1]

In this tendency, it may be noted, we see the basis of the symbolism which plays so real a part in dreams. Such symbolism rests on the fact that we associate two things—even if the one happens to be physical and the other spiritual—which both happen to imply a similar state of feeling.[2] Symbolism of this kind is, indeed,

---

[1] It has not, I believe, been pointed out that such dreams might be invoked in support of the James-Lange or physiological theory of emotion, according to which the element of bodily change in emotion is the cause and not the result of the emotion.

[2] This physiological symbolism was clearly apprehended long ago by Hobbes: 'As anger causeth heat in some parts of the body when we are awake; so when we sleep the overheating of the same parts causeth anger, and raiseth up in the brain the imagination of an enemy. In the same manner as natural kindness, when we are awake, causeth desire and desire makes heat in certain other parts of the body; so also, too much heat in those parts, while we sleep, raiseth in the brain an imagination of some kindness shown. In sum, our dreams are the reverse of our waking imaginations; the motion, when we are awake, beginning at one end, and when we dream at another' (*Leviathan*, Part I. ch. 2).

characteristic of the human mind at all times, in all stages of its development. Thus the physical idea of *height* seems to express also a moral idea, which we feel to be correspondent, while wormwood and gall furnish a taste which enabled men to speak of what seemed to them the corresponding *bitterness* of death. In dreams this natural tendency of the mind is able to work unchecked and extravagantly. It acts with much facility on any impulse arising from the gastric region, because this region is the seat of various sensations and emotions, both physical and moral, which may thus act symbolically the one for the other.[1]

Even when we realise the process of transformation and irradiation, through which organic sensations can alone reach the brain in sleep, and the inevitable 'errors of judgment' thus produced, it may still seem strange and puzzling to observe how a stimulus which has its origin in the stomach will, by affecting the neighbouring viscera, in its circuitous course along the nerves and through the brain, be transformed, as it may be, into a tragic scene which has never been experienced, nor even deliberately imagined, as for instance—to cite a dream

---

[1] 'The pains of disappointment, of anxiety, of unsuccess, of all displeasing emotions,' remarks Mercier (art. 'Consciousness,' Tuke's *Dictionary of Psychological Medicine*), 'are attended by a definite feeling of misery which is referred in every case to the epigastrium.' He adds that the pleasures of success and good repute, aesthetic enjoyment, etc., are also attended by a definite feeling in the same region. This fact indicates the extreme vagueness of organic sensation. There is in fact much uncertainty and great difference of opinion as to the nature, and even the existence, of organic sensation; see *e.g.* a careful summary of the chief views by Dr. Elsie Murray, 'Organic Sensation,' *American Journal of Psychology*, July 1909.

of my own—in the fiery vision of following a leader, in real life a peaceful and inoffensive man, who, revolver in hand, dashes among foes, shooting and shot at, every moment in danger of life, and always miraculously escaping.

I may illustrate this transformation by the following example: A lady dreamed that her husband called her aside and said, 'Now, do not scream or make a fuss; I am going to tell you something. I have to kill a man. It is necessary, to put him out of his agony.' He then took her into his study, and showed her a young man lying on the floor, with a wound in his breast, and covered with blood. 'But how will you do it?' she asked. 'Never mind,' he replied; 'leave that to me.' He took something up and leaned over the man. She turned aside and heard a horrible gurgling sound. Then all was over. 'Now,' he said, 'we must get rid of the body. I want you to send for So-and-so's cart, and tell him I wish to drive it.' The cart came. 'You must help me to make the body into a parcel,' he said to his wife; 'give me plenty of brown paper.' They made it into a parcel, and with terrible difficulty and effort the wife assisted her husband to get the body downstairs, and lift it into the cart. At every stage, however, she presented to him the difficulties of the situation. But he carelessly answered all objections, said he would take the body up to the moor, among the stones, remove the brown paper, and people would think the murdered man had killed himself. He drove off, and soon returned with the empty cart. 'What's this blood in my cart ? ' asked the man to whom it belonged, looking inside. ' Oh, that's only paint,' replied the husband. But the dreamer had all along been full of apprehensions lest the deed should be discovered, and the last thing she could recall, before waking in terror, was looking out of the window at a large crowd which surrounded the house with shouts of ' Murder ! ' and threats.

This tragedy, with its almost Elizabethan air, was built up out of a few commonplace impressions received during the previous day, none of which impressions contained any suggestion of murder. The tragic element appears to have been altogether due to the psychic influences of indigestion arising from a supper of pheasant.[1] To account for our oppression during sleep, sleeping consciousness assumes moral causes, which alone appear to it of sufficient gravity to be adequate to the immense emotions we are experiencing. Even in our waking and fully conscious states we are inclined to give the preference to moral over physical causes, quite irrespective of the justice of our preferences ; in our sleeping states this tendency is exaggerated, and the reign of purely moral causes is not often disturbed by even a suggestion of physical causation.

In an emotional dream of similar visceral origin, I dreamed that I was to die—why or how I could not tell

[1] More than ten years later, the same dreamer, who had entirely forgotten the circumstances of this dream, again had a vivid dream of murder after eating pheasant at night ; this time it was she herself who was to be killed, and she awoke imagining that she was struggling with the would-be murderer.

on awakening. With the object of putting an end to my sufferings, I imagined that my wife administered to me some substance mixed in jam. I found the taste peculiar, not bitter, as I recalled on awaking, but warm and spicy, and I asked what she had put in it. She replied that it was strychnine. I remarked that that would be a very painful mode of death, and refused to take any more. I debated with myself whether I had probably taken a poisonous dose, and had not better resort to an antidote ; the only antidote that suggested itself to me was opium pills. Meanwhile the horror of impending death grew more and more acute until, at length, I awoke. I thereupon found that I had a headache, a faint taste in my mouth, and some general malaise evidently associated with a slightly disordered stomach. The definite images brought forward in the dream had all been fairly familiar during the previous day, but the idea of impending death which pervaded the whole dream so indefinitely and incoherently, yet so acutely, was entirely a theory to account for the massive and widely irradiated messages of discomfort which reached the sleeping brain.

Many people are unwilling to admit that psychic phenomena so tragical, poignant, or pathetic as these dreams may be, should receive their stimulus from a source which they regard as so humble as the stomach. Thus Frederick Greenwood, whose conception of the function of dreaming was very exalted, only admitted this association with reluctance, and was careful to point out that 'if an unwholesome supper produces such phenomena, it does so only in the sense that a bird singing in the air produced Shelley's "Ode to a Skylark."[1] That analogy really underestimates the distance of the physical stimulus of such dreams from its psychic concomitants. When we talk of dreams we must place ourselves at the dreamer's standpoint. The poet was conscious that his inspiration was stimulated by the bird's song, but the dreamer has no consciousness that the tragic experiences he passes through imaginatively are stimulated by the activity of his visceral organs. He is altogether unconscious of visceral disturbance; if he were conscious of any of these physical facts which occupy waking consciousness, he would no longer be a dreamer. He lives in a psychic world which physical facts, from within or from without, can never reach until they have been transformed. His position resembles, therefore, not that of the poet who deliberately seeks to interpret the song of the bird, but rather that of the bird itself, the poet 'hidden in the light of thought,' sublimely unconscious of the mechanism revealed in its own structure.

The explanations devised by sleeping consciousness to account for visceral discomfort of gastric origin are not necessarily tragic. Thus I dreamed, after a somewhat indigestible meal, that I was slowly and painfully eating bread mingled with cinders and mouse's excrement, trying in vain to avoid these impurities, and after the meal was over, finding my mouth full of cinders. On awaking there was no traceable taste or sensation

[1] F. Greenwood, *Imagination in Dreams*, p. 31.

EMOTION IN DREAMS

of any kind in the mouth, and the dream was apparently a theory to account for some gastric disturbance. Such a theory seems less far-fetched than that of murder, and probably indicates much less marked and diffused visceral disturbance. Occasionally the explanatory theories of actual sensations accepted by sleeping consciousness are plausible and ingenious, indeed entirely adequate and probable. Thus a lady dreamed that she was drinking glass after glass of champagne, saying to herself the while that she would have to pay for this afterwards. On awaking she found that she was feeling the slight rheumatic pains and discomfort that she was really liable to experience after taking a glass or two of champagne. She had not tasted champagne, or thought of it, for some time previously; the dream champagne was a theory invented to account for the sensations which were actually experienced, though those sensations remained outside dreaming consciousness.

Most of the examples I have presented of the influence of emotion of visceral origin in suggesting dream theories have had the stomach as their source. There can be no doubt that the stomach has enormous influence in this respect; its easily and constantly varying state of repletion, its central position and liability to press on other organs, its important nervous associations, together with the fact that sleep sometimes tends to impede its activity and initiate disturbance, combine to impart to it a manifold and extensive influence over the emotional state in sleep, and at the same time render the source of that emotional state peculiarly difficult for sleeping consciousness to detect.

It is, however, easy to show that any pronounced or massive feeling continuing or arising during sleep may similarly lead to an emotional state calling for explanation at the hands of sleeping consciousness. Thus, falling asleep with toothache during a singularly close night, I once dreamed that I had committed murder, having apparently killed several persons, and that I was occupied, after arrest, in considering whether my act was likely to be regarded as an unpremeditated act of manslaughter. A headache, again, may be a source of dreams. Thus, falling asleep with headache, I dream that I am waiting for an express train to London; an express comes up to the platform, and I cannot ascertain if it is the train I want. The explanation seems obvious ; railway travelling is a cause of headache, and it is therefore put forward in the dream, with accompanying imagery, to account for the sensations experienced. The actual sensation, as is always the case in dreams, that is, the headache, remains subconscious, and, indeed, totally unconscious; the imagery it suggests alone occupies the field of consciousness.[1] An entirely different type of dream may, however,

---

[1] Dreams of railway travelling, and especially of losing trains, are not always associated with headache or any other recognisable condition. They constitute a very common type of dream not quite easy to explain. Dr. Savage mentions, for instance, that in his own case scarcely a week passes without such a dream, though in real life he scarcely ever loses a train and never worries about it. Wundt considers that the dreams in which we seek something we cannot find or have left something behind are

be associated with headache. Thus I once dreamed that I was in a vast gloomy English cathedral, and on the wall I observed a notice to the effect that on such a day evensong would take place without illumination of the cathedral in order to avoid attracting moths. I awoke with slight headache. Here the cool, silent gloom of the cathedral is the symbol of what is desired to soothe the aching head, and the fantastic suggestion read on the notice is merely the theory of dreaming consciousness which knows nothing of the real reason of the wish.

Dreams of murder or impending death or the like tragic situations seem usually to be aroused by visceral stimuli. In some cases, however (as in Maury's famous dream of the guillotine), they are due to an external cutaneous sensation. When the stimulus thus comes from the periphery, the emotional element, even when the dreamed situation is tragic, seems usually (though this is not quite certain) to be less pronounced than when the stimulus is visceral. Thus in a dream of my own, which seemed to be due to a cramped position of the head and neck, I dreamed that I had died (though, somehow, I was not myself, but had become more or less identified with an ugly old woman), and was being autopsied. Then very gradually I became faintly and peacefully conscious of what was going on, though I remained motionless, and all the time believed that I was dead,

due to indefinite coenaesthesic disturbances involving feelings of the same emotional tone, such as an uncomfortable position or a slight irregularity of respiration. I have myself independently observed the same connection, though it is not invariably traceable.

and that my faint consciousness was merely a part of death. Preparations for the funeral were meanwhile being made, and I was about to be nailed down in my coffin. At this point I became horribly aware that these proceedings would cause suffocation, and, with great effort, I succeeded in moving my arms and speaking incoherently. Thereupon the funeral arrangements were discontinued, and very slowly I seemed to regain speech and the power of movement. But I felt that I must be extremely careful in making any movements, on account of the post-mortem wounds; especially I felt pain in my neck, and realised that it was necessary not to move my head, or the result might be instant death. In such a dream, it may be noted, and in some others I have recorded, we see very instructively the nature of the changes produced in the dream and in the dreamer's attitude by the approach of waking consciousness. The dreamer's relationship to his imagined situation becomes more and more what it would be if the situation occurred in real life, and as soon as there is painful effort and imperfect muscular movement, the coming of waking consciousness is imminent.

The visceral and emotional element in dreaming helps to explain the dreamer's moral attitude and the real significance of those criminal actions in dreams which have often been misinterpreted. Many writers on dreaming have referred, with profound concern, to the facility and prevalence of murder in dreams, sometimes as a proof of the innate wickedness of human nature made manifest in the unconstraint of sleep,

EMOTION IN DREAMS

sometimes as evidence of an atavistic return to the modes of feeling of our ancestors, the thin veneer of civilisation being removed during sleep. Maudsley and Mme. de Manacéïne, for example, find evidence in such dreams of a return to primitive modes of feeling. Clarke speaks of ' the entire absence of the moral sense ' from dreams.[1] Professor Näcke, who has given much attention to the phenomena of dreaming, writes in a private letter : ' What I am amazed at, having perceived it in myself, is the little known fact that a person's character becomes *worse* in dreaming. Not only the most secret thoughts, wishes, and aspirations become clear, but also qualities which have never been observed before, as, for instance, that one becomes a murderer, an adulterer, etc.' Freud, especially, has elaborated this aspect of dreams as representing the fulfilment of the dreamer's most secret desires.[2]

It may well be that there is an element of truth in the belief that in dreams we are brought back to mental conditions somewhat more closely approaching those of primitive times. It is the manifold variety and complexity of our mental representations which prevent us from responding immediately to impulse under civilised conditions, and when, by dissociation, only a few groups are present to consciousness, the inhibition on violent action tends to be removed. If, therefore, we

---

[1] E. H. Clarke, *Visions*, p. 294.
[2] An amusing, though solemn, interpretation of an ordinary dream of murder, railway travelling, and impending death, as experienced by Anna Kingsford, is furnished by her friend and biographer, Edward Maitland, *Anna Kingsford*, vol. i. p. 117.

are more violent, more immoral, more criminal, in our dreams than in waking life, this is by no means necessarily to be regarded as a revelation of our real nature, but is merely an inevitable result of the mental dissociation which prevents many important groups of mental representations from finding their way into consciousness, and at the same time brings all our mental possessions on to the same plane, so that the things we have merely thought or heard of have the same visual reality as our own actual experiences. The sleep of the real criminal, as Sante de Sanctis has shown on the basis of a wide experience, even of criminals guilty of serious acts of violence, tends to be peaceful and dreamless, and such dreams as they have are usually of a simple and innocent sort. If normal people often dream of crime, it is because they are more sensitive and imaginative, and because sleeping consciousness is strained to the utmost to invent a phantasmal tragedy adequate to account for the waves of emotion that beset it.[1]

There is another reason why, in dreams, we may find ourselves engaged in criminal operations. The purely automatic process by which the imagery of dreams is perpetually shifting in pursuit of associations of resemblance or contiguity, leads to confusions which are not rooted in any personal or primitive impulse, as in the example I have previously referred to, of a lady who had carved a duck at dinner, and a few hours later woke up

---

[1] Various opinions in regard to morality in dreams are brought together by Freud, *Die Traumdeutung*, pp. 45 *et seq.*

exhausted by the imaginary effort of cutting off her husband's head. Such a dream is merely a mechanical turn of the visionary kaleidoscope, bringing together two unrelated images.

The most potent cause of dream criminality, and especially of murders we have been guilty of before the dream commenced, seems clearly, however, to be that emotional factor of visceral origin which is well illustrated by one or two of the dreams already brought forward.[1] In these cases, again, we are not concerned with any primitive or personal impulse to crime, but we feel ourselves to be so possessed by all the physical symptoms of terror, that the only adequate explanation of our state seems to be the theory that we have committed murder. And if we are more concerned to flee from justice than to experience remorse, that is clearly because the really labouring and agitated heart suggests flight from pursuit far more than any passive emotion.[2] There is, moreover, no more fundamental and primitive emotion than fear.

While these considerations combine to deprive criminal dreams, when they occur, of any great significance as an index of the dreamer's latent morality, I must add that I am by no means prepared to agree that

[1] Head ('Mental Changes that Accompany Visceral Diseases,' *Brain*, 1902, p. 802) refers to the association between visceral pain and the anti-social impulses, and thinks that the viscera, being part of the oldest and most autonomic system of the body, appear in consciousness as 'an intrusion from without, an inexplicable obsession.'

[2] 'In my dreams,' W. D. Howells remarks, ' I am always less sorry for my misdeeds than for their possible discovery ' ('True I talk of Dreams,' *Harper's Magazine*, May 1895).

moral emotions are so absent from sleep as many writers have stated. There is often a diminished sense of morality, an easier yielding to temptation than would take place in real life, a diminished remorse—these tendencies being mainly due to the conditions of dream-life—but there is frequently a strong sense of morality in dreams, as well as a vivid perception of social proprieties. Those persons who have an unusually strong moral sense, when awake, frequently show, I think, a similar tendency when asleep, but in the dreams of most people moral and decorous considerations seem, as a rule, to make themselves more or less clearly felt, much as in waking life. It may be worth while to bring forward a few dreams which incidentally illustrate the moral attitude of the dreamer.

A lady narrated the following dream immediately on awakening : ' I had murdered a woman from some moral or political motive—I forget what—and had come in great agony to my husband with her shoes and watch-chain. He promised to help me, and while I was wondering what could be done for the benefit of the woman's family, some one came in and announced that a lecture was about to be given on the beauty of nakedness. I then went, with several prim and respectable ladies of my acquaintance [the names were given], into a crowded hall. The lecturer who—so far as appearance is concerned—was a well-known Member of Parliament, then entered and gave a most eloquent address on Whitman, nakedness, ugly figures, etc. He especially emphasised the fact that the reason

EMOTION IN DREAMS

people are shocked at nakedness is that they usually only see unbeautiful bodies which repel them because they are unlike their ideals. Then he put out his hand, and a naked woman entered the room. Her loveliness was extreme ; her form was perfectly rounded, but without suggestion of voluptuousness, though she was not an animated statue, but had all the characters of humanity ; she walked with undulating thighs, head slightly drooping, and hair falling down and framing a face that expressed wonderful spiritual beauty and innocence. The lecturer led her round, saying, " This is beauty ; now, if you can look at this and be ashamed—" and he waved his arm. She went away, and a beautiful Apollo-like youth, slender but athletic, entered the room, also completely naked. He walked round the room alone, with an air of majestic virility. I applauded, clapping my hands, but a shiver went through the ladies present ; their skin became like goose-flesh, and their lips quivered with horror as though they were about to be outraged. The youth went out, and the lecturer continued. At the climax of his oratory, the Apollo-like youth entered, dressed as a common soldier, with no appearance of beauty, and in a rough tone said : " 'Ere ! I want a shilling for this job." (And I sighed to myself: " It is always so.") No one had a shilling, and the lecturer proceeded to explain to the man that what he had done was for the sake of art and beauty, and for the moral good of the world. " What do I care for that ? " he returned, " I want a drink." Then a lady among the audience produced a collar, wrote on it a testimonial expressing the gratitude of those present for the man's services on this occasion, and handed it to me to present to him. "Damn it," he said, "this is only worth twopence halfpenny; I want my shilling!" Then I awoke.' The idea of murder with which this dream began seems to suggest that it may have had its origin in some slight visceral disturbance of which the subject was unconscious, but nothing had occurred to suggest the details of the episode. The interesting feature about it is the presence throughout of moral notions and sentiments substantially true to the dreamer's waking ideas.

In another dream of the same dreamer's the sense of responsibility is clearly present: 'Mrs. F. and Miss R. had called to see me, and I was sitting in my room talking to them, when a knock came at the door, and I found there a poor woman belonging to the neighbourhood, but who also combined in my dream the page-boy at a dear friend's house. From this friend, whom I had not heard from for some time, the woman bore a large letter. She tore it open in my presence, saying, "It says here that the bearer is to open this," and produced from it another letter, a large document of a legal character in my friend's handwriting. When the woman began to open the second letter I remonstrated; I was sure that there was some mistake, that that letter was private, and that no one else ought to see it. The woman, however, firmly insisted that she must carry out her instructions; so we had a long discussion. After a time I called Mrs. F. and appealed to her. She agreed with me that the instructions must only mean that the bearer was to open the outer envelope, not the inner letter. At last I took out five shillings and gave it to the woman, telling her that I would assume all the responsibility for opening the letter myself. With this she went away well satisfied, saying (as she would in real life), " All right, Mrs. ——, you're a lady, and you know. All right, my dear." Then at last I was able to tear open my letter and read these words: "*Always use Sunlight Soap.*" My vexation was extreme.'

On another occasion the same dreamer experienced remorse. She imagined she was in a restaurant, and the girl behind the counter pointed to a barrel of beer—a golden barrel, she said, with a magic key—which could only be opened by the owner. The dreamer declared, however, that she could open it, and, producing a key, proceeded to do so, handing round beer to the bystanders. Then she realised that she had been stealing, and was full of remorse. She asked a friend if she ought to tell the owner, but the friend replied, ' By no means.' This conclusion of the dream seems to indicate that the moral sense, though present in dreams, is apt to be impaired.

In yet another dream this dreamer exhibited a curious combination of moral sensibility and criminal indifference. She imagined that, while walking with a man, a friend, she revealed to him a secret of a woman friend's. Then, realising her betrayal of confidence, she decided that the best thing she could do would be to kill the man. On reflection, however, she thought that it would, after all, be unkind to do so since he was a friend, and so told him that if he ever repeated the secret she would have him torn to pieces. It will be seen that the betrayal of a secret was felt as a far more serious offence than murder. The facility with which, in such dreams as this, the suggestion of murder presents itself, even to dreamers who, when awake, cherish no bloodthirsty or revengeful ideas, is certainly remarkable.

It is often said that in dreams erotic suggestions present themselves with extreme facility, and are eagerly accepted by the dreamer. To some extent there is truth in this statement, but it is by no means always true. This may be illustrated by the following dream, the sources of which could be easily traced ; two days before I had seen the gambols of East Enders at Hampstead Heath on a Bank Holiday, and the day before I had visited a picture gallery, the two sets of impressions becoming ingeniously combined, according to the usual rule of dream confusion. I thought that when walking along a country lane a sudden turn brought me to a broader part of the road covered with grass, into the midst of a crowd of women, large and well-proportioned persons, mostly in a state of complete nudity, and engaged in romping together, more especially in tugs-of-war ; some of them were on horseback. My appearance slightly disturbed them, I heard one cry out my name, and to some extent they drew back, and partly desisted from their games, but only to a very slight degree, and with no overpowering embarrassment. I was myself rather embarrassed, and, glancing at them again, turned back. Afterwards my walk again brought me in view of them, and it occurred to me that women are somewhat changing their customs, a very wholesome change, it seemed to me. But I remonstrated with one or two of them that they ought to keep in constant movement to avoid catching cold. No erotic suggestions were present, although the dream might be said to lend itself to such suggestions.

The idea of moral retribution and eternal punishment may also be present in dreams. This may be illustrated by the dream of a lady who had an ill and restless girl companion sleeping with her, and was disturbed as well by a yelping and howling terrier outside. She had also lately heard that a friend had brought over a python from Africa. 'I dreamed last night I had a basket of cold squirming snakes beside me; they just touched me all over, but did not hurt; I felt mad with loathing and hate of them, and the beasts would not kill me. That, I thought, was my eternal punishment for my sins.' In her waking moments the dreamer was not apprehensive of eternal punishment, and it may be in such a case that, as Freud suggests, an unfamiliar moral idea emerges in sleep in much the same way as an unfamiliar or 'forgotten' fact may emerge.

On the whole, it may be said that while the moral attitude of the dreaming state is not usually identical with that of the waking state, there still nearly always is a moral attitude. It could not well be otherwise.

Our emotional states are intimately bound up with moral relationships ; we could not display such highly emotional states as we experience in dreams, with all their tragic accompaniments, in the absence of any sense of morality.

CHAPTER VI

AVIATION IN DREAMS

Dreams of Flying and Falling—Their Peculiar Vividness—Dreams of Flying an Alleged Survival of Primeval Experiences—Best explained as based on Respiratory Sensations combined with Cutaneous Anaesthesia—The Explanation of Dreams of Falling—The Sensation of Levitation sometimes experienced by Ecstatic Saints—Also experienced at the Moment of Death.

Dreams of flying, with the dreams of falling they are sometimes associated with, may fairly be considered the best known and most frequent type of dream. They were among the earliest dreams to attract attention. Ruths argues that the Greek conception of the flying Hermes, the god who possessed special authority over dreams, was based on such experiences. Lucretius, in his interesting passage on the psychology of dreaming, speaks of falling from heights in dreams;[1] Cicero appears to refer to dreams of flying; St. Jerome mentions that he was subject to them; Synesius remarked that in dreams we fly with wings and view the world from afar; Cervantes accurately described the dream of falling.[2] From the inventors of the legend

[1] Bk. IV. 1014-15:
'de montibus altis
Se quasi præcipitent ad terram corpore toto.'

[2] 'It has many times happened to me,' says the innkeeper's daughter in *Don Quixote* (Part I. ch. xvi.), 'to dream that I was falling down from a tower and never coming to the ground, and when I awoke from the dream to find myself as weak and shaken as if I had really fallen.'

of Icarus onwards, men have firmly cherished the belief that under some circumstances they could fly, and we may well suppose that that belief partly owes its conviction, and the resolve to make it practical, to the experiences that have been gained in dreams.

No dreams, indeed, are so vivid and so convincing as dreams of flying ; none leave behind them so strong a sense of the reality of the experience. Raffaelli, the eminent French painter, who is subject to the dreaming experience of floating in the air, confesses that it is so convincing that he has jumped out of bed on awaking and attempted to repeat it. 'I need not tell you,' he adds, 'that I have never been able to succeed.'[1] Herbert Spencer mentions that in a company of a dozen persons, three testified that in early life they had had such vivid dreams of flying downstairs, and were so strongly impressed by the reality of the experience, that they actually made the attempt, one of them suffering in consequence from an injured ankle.[2] The case is recorded of an old French lady who always maintained that on one occasion she actually had succeeded for a few instants in supporting herself on the air.[3] No one who is familiar with these dreaming experiences will be inclined to laugh at that old lady. It was during one of these dreams of levitation, in which one finds oneself leaping into the air and able to stay there, that it occurred to me that I would write a paper

---

[1] Chabaneix, *Le Subconscient*, p. 43.
[2] Herbert Spencer, *Principles of Sociology*, 3rd ed., vol. i. p. 773.
[3] *L'Intermédiaire des Chercheurs et des Curieux*, May 31, 1906.

AVIATION IN DREAMS

on the subject, for I thought in my dream that this power I found myself possessed of was probably much more widespread than was commonly supposed, and that in any case it ought to be generally known.

People who dabble in the occult have been so impressed by such dreams that they have sometimes believed that these flights represented a real excursion of the 'astral body.' This is the belief of Colonel de Rochas.[1] César de Vesme, the editor of the French edition of the *Annals of Psychical Research*, has thought it worth while to investigate the matter; and after summarising the results of a *questionnaire* concerning dreams of flying, he comes to the conclusion that ' the sensation of aerial flight in dreams is simply a hallucinatory phenomenon of an exclusively physiological [he means 'psychological'] kind,' and not evidence of the existence of the 'astral body.'[2] The fact, nevertheless, that so many people are found who believe such dreams to possess some kind of reality, clearly indicates the powerful impression they make.

All my life, it seems to me, certainly from an early age, until recently, I have at intervals had dreams in which I imagined myself rhythmically bounding into

[1] De Rochas describes the phenomenon as ' a property of the human organism, more or less developed in different individuals, when the soul, disengaging itself from the bonds of the body, enters the domain, still so mysterious, of dreams' (*L'Intermédiaire des Chercheurs et des Curieux*, May 10, 1906). In subsequent numbers of the *Intermédiaire* various correspondents describe their own experiences of such dreams. In *Luce e Ombra* for June 1906, and in the *Echo du Merveilleux* for the same date, neither of which I have seen, are given other experiences.

[2] *Annals of Psychical Research*, November 1896.

the air, and supported on the air, remaining there for a perceptible interval ; at other times I have felt myself gliding downstairs, but not supported by the stairs. In my case the experience is nearly always agreeable, involving a certain sense of power, and it usually evokes no marked surprise, occurring as a familiar and accustomed pleasure. On awaking I do not usually remember these dreams immediately, which seems to indicate that they are not due to causes specially operative at the end of sleep, or liable to bring sleep to a conclusion. But they leave behind them a vague yet profound sense of belief in their reality and reasonableness.

Dream-flight, it is necessary to note, is not usually the sustained flight of a bird or an insect, and the dreamer rarely or never imagines that he is borne high into the air. Hutchinson states that of all those whom he has asked about the matter ' hardly one has ever known himself to make any high flights in his dreams. One almost always flies low, with a skimming manner, slightly, but only slightly, above the heads of pedestrians.'[1]

Beaunis, from his own experience, describes what I should consider a typical kind of dream-flight as a series of light bounds, at one or two yards above the earth, each bound clearing from ten to twenty yards, the dream being accompanied by a delicious sensation of easy movement, as well as a lively satisfaction at being able to solve the problem of aerial locomotion by

[1] Horace Hutchinson, *Dreams and their Meanings*, p. 76.

AVIATION IN DREAMS

virtue of superior organisation alone.[1] Lafcadio Hearn, somewhat similarly, describes, in his *Shadowings*, a typical and frequent dream of his own as a series of bounds in long parabolic curves, rising to a height of some twenty-five feet, and always accompanied by the sense that a new power had been revealed which for the future would be a permanent possession.

The attempt to explain dreams of flying has led to some bold hypotheses. Freud characteristically affirms that the dream of flying is the bridge to a concealed wish.[2] I have already mentioned the notion that dreams of flight are excursions of the 'astral body.' Professor Stanley Hall, who has himself, from childhood, had dreams of flying, argues, with scarcely less boldness, that we have here 'some faint reminiscent atavistic echo from the primeval sea'; and that such dreams are really survivals—psychic vestigial remains comparable to the rudimentary gill-slits not uncommonly found in man and other mammals—taking us back to the far past when man's ancestors needed no feet to swim or float.[3] Such a theory may accord with the profound conviction of reality that accompanies these

---

[1] *American Journal of Psychology*, July-October 1903, p. 14.

[2] 'The wish to be able to fly,' he declares (*Eine Kindheitserinnerung des Leonardo da Vinci*, p. 59), 'signifies in dreaming nothing else but the desire to be capable of sexual activities. It is a wish of early childhood.'

[3] Stanley Hall, *American Journal of Psychology*, January 1879, p. 158; also F. E. Bolton, 'Hydro-Psychoses,' *ib.*, January 1899, p. 183; as regards rudimentary gill-slits, Bland Sutton, *Evolution and Disease*, pp. 48 *et seq.* Lafcadio Hearn travels still further along this road in search for an explanation of dreams of flight, and evokes a 'memory of vanished planets with fainter powers of gravitation,' but he fails to state when the ancestors of man inhabited these problematical planets.

dreams, though that may be more easily accounted for ; but it has the very serious weakness that it offers an explanation which will not fit the facts. Our dreams are of flying, not of swimming; but the ancestors of the mammals probably lived in the water, not in the air. In preference to so hazardous a theory, it seems infinitely more reasonable to regard these dreams as an interpretation—a misinterpretation from the standpoint of waking life—of actual internal sensations. If we can find the adequate explanation of a psychic state in conditions actually existing within the organism itself at the time, it is needless to seek an explanation in conditions that ceased to exist untold millenniums ago.

My own explanation was immediately suggested by the following dream. I dreamed that I was watching a girl acrobat, in appropriate costume, who was rhythmically rising to a great height in the air and then falling, without touching the floor, though each time she approached quite close to it. At last she ceased, exhausted and perspiring, and I had to lead her away. Her movements were not controlled by mechanism, and apparently I did not regard mechanism as necessary. It was a vivid dream, and I awoke with a distinct sensation of oppression in the chest. In trying to account for this dream, which was not founded on any memory, it occurred to me that probably I had here the key to a great group of dreams. The rhythmic rising and falling of the acrobat was simply the objectivation of the rhythmic rising and falling of my own respiratory muscles—in some dreams, perhaps, of the systole and diastole of the heart's muscles—under the influence of some slight and unknown physical oppression, and this oppression was further translated into a condition of perspiring exhaustion in the girl, just as men with heart disease may dream of sweating and panting horses climbing uphill, in accordance with that tendency to magnification which marks dreams generally.[1] We may recall also the curious sensation as of the body being transformed into a vast bellows or steam engine, which is often the last sensation felt before the unconsciousness produced by nitrous oxide gas.[2] When we are lying down there is a real rhythmic rising and falling of the chest and abdomen, centring in the diaphragm, a series of oscillations which at both extremes are only limited by the air. Moreover, in this position we have to recognise that the circulatory,

---

[1] I retain this statement of my explanation in almost the same words as first written down in 1895. I was not then aware that several psychologists had offered very similar explanations. Scherner (*Das Leben des Traumes*, 1861) seems to have been the first to connect the lungs with dreams of flying, though he put forward the explanation in too fanciful a form and failed to realise that other factors, notably a change in skin pressure, are also involved. Strümpell at a later date recognised this explanation, as well as Wundt.

[2] It is the same with chloroform. 'There are marked sensations in the vicinity of the heart,' says Elmer Jones ('The Waning of Consciousness under Chloroform,' *Psychological Review*, January 1909). 'The musculature of that organ seems thoroughly stimulated, and the contractions become violent and accelerated. The palpitations are as strong as would be experienced at the close of some violent bodily exertion.' It is significant, also, as bearing on the interpretation of the dream of flying, that under chloroform 'all movements made appeared to be much longer than they actually were. A slight movement of the tongue appeared to be magnified at least ten times. Clinching the fingers and opening them again produced the feeling of their moving through a space of several feet.'

nervous, and other systems of the whole internal organism, are differently balanced from what they are in the upright position, and that a disturbance of internal equilibrium always accompanies falling.

It is also noteworthy (as, indeed, Wundt has briefly remarked) that the modifications produced by sleep in the respiratory process itself tend to facilitate its interpretation as a process of flying. Mosso showed that respiration in sleep is more thoracic than when awake, that it is lengthened, and that the respiratory pause is less marked.[1] That is to say that both the aerial element and the actual rhythmic movement of the ribs become accentuated during sleep.

That the respiratory element is the chief factor in dreams of flying is clearly indicated by the fact that many persons subject to such dreams are conscious on awaking from them of a sense of respiratory or cardiac disturbance. I am acquainted with a psychologist who, though not a frequent dreamer, is subject to dreams of flying, which do not affect him disagreeably, but on awaking from them he always perceives a slight flutter of the heart. Any such sensation is by no means constant with me, but I have occasionally noted it down in exactly the same words after this kind of dream.[2] It is worth while to observe, in this connection, how large a number of people, and especially very young

---

[1] See *e.g.* Marie de Manacéïne, *Sleep*, p. 7.

[2] Horace Hutchinson, who in his *Dreams and their Meanings* (1901), has independently suggested that 'this flying dream is caused by some action of the breathing organs,' mentions the significant fact (p. 128) that the idea of filling the lungs as a help in levitation occurs in the flying dreams of many persons.

people, associate their dreams of flying with staircases. The most frequent cause of cardiac and respiratory stimulation, especially in children, who constantly run up and down them, is furnished by staircases, and though in health this fact may not be obvious, it is undoubtedly registered unconsciously, and may thus be utilised by dreaming intelligence.

There is, however, another element entering into the problem of nocturnal aviation: the state of the skin sensations. Respiratory activity alone would scarcely suffice to produce the imagery of flight if sensations of tactile pressure remained to suggest contact with the earth. In dreams, however, the sense of movement suggested by respiratory activity is unaccompanied by the tactile pressure produced by boots or the contact of the ground with the soles of the feet. In addition, also, there is probably, as Bergson also has suggested, a numbness due to pressure on the parts supporting the weight of the body. Sleep is not a constant and uniform state of consciousness; a heightened consciousness of respiration may easily co-exist with a diminished consciousness of tactile pressure due to anaesthesia of the skin.[1] In normal sleep it may, indeed, be said that the conditions are probably often favourable to the production of this combination, and any slight thoracic disturbance even in healthy persons,

[1] We have an analogous state of tactile anaesthesia in the early stages of chloroform intoxication. Thus Elmer Jones found that this sense is, after hearing, the first to disappear. 'With the disappearance of the tactile sense and hearing,' he remarks, 'the body has completely lost its orientation It appears to be nowhere, simply floating in space. It is a most ecstatic feeling.'

arising from heart or stomach, and acting on the respiration, serves to bring these conditions to sleeping consciousness and to determine the dream of flying.

Dreams of flying are sometimes associated with dreams of falling, the falling sensation occurring either at the beginning or at the end of the dream; such a dream may be said to be of the Icarus type.[1] Jewell considers that the two kinds of dream have the same causation, the difference being merely a difference of apperception. The frequent connection between the two dreams indicates that the causation is allied, but it scarcely seems to be identical. If it were identical, we should scarcely find that while the emotional tone of the dream of flying is usually agreeable, that of the dream of falling is usually disagreeable.[2]

I have no personal experience of the sensation of falling in normal dreaming, although Jewell and Hutchinson have found that it is more common than flying, the latter

---

[1] Lafcadio Hearn describes the fall as coming at the beginning of the dream. Dr. Guthrie (*Clinical Journal*, June 7, 1899), in his own case, describes the flying sensations as coming first and the falling as coming afterwards, and apparently due to sudden failure of the power of flight; the first part of the dream is agreeable but after the fall the dreamer awakes shaken, shocked, and breathless.

[2] The disagreeable nature of falling in dreams may probably be connected with the absence of rhythm usually present in dreams of flying. Most of the psychologists who have occupied themselves with rhythm have insisted on its pleasurable emotional tone, as leading to a state bordering on ecstasy (see *e.g.* J. B. Miner, 'Motor, Visual, and Applied Rhythms,' Monograph Supplement to *Psychological Review*, June 1903). The pleasure is especially marked, as MacDougall remarks, when there is 'a coincidence of subjective and objective change.' In dreams of flying we have this coincidence, the real subjective rhythm being transformed in consciousness to an objective rhythm.

AVIATION IN DREAMS

regarding it, indeed, as the most common kind of dream, the dream of flying coming next in frequency. A friend who has no dreams of flying, but has experienced dreams of falling from his earliest years, tells me that they are always associated with feelings of terror. This suggests an organic cause, and the fact that the sensation of falling may occur in epileptic fits during sleep,[1] seems further to suggest the presence of circulatory and nervous disturbance. It would seem probable that while the same two factors—respiratory and tactile— are operative in both types of dream, they are not of equal force in each. In the dream of flying, respiratory activity is excited, and in response to excitation it works at a high level adequate to the needs of the organism. In the dream of falling it may be that respiratory activity is depressed, while concomitantly, perhaps, the anaesthetic state of the skin is increased. In the first state the abnormal activity of respiration triumphs in consciousness over the accompanying dulness of tactile sensation ; in the second state the respiratory breathlessness is less influential than a numbness of the skin unconscious of any external pressure. This difference is rendered possible by the fact that in dreams of flying we are not usually far from the earth, and seem able to touch it lightly at intervals ; that is to say that tactile sensitiveness is impaired, but is not entirely absent as it is in a dream of falling.[2]

[1] Féré, 'Note sur les Rêves Epileptiques,' *Revue de Médecine*, September 10, 1905.
[2] Sir W. R. Gowers has on several occasions (*e.g.* 'The Borderland of Epilepsy,' *British Medical Journal*, July 21, 1906) argued that dreams of

In my own experience the sensation of falling only occurs in illness or under the influence of drugs, sometimes when sleep seems incomplete, and it is an unpleasant, though not terrifying, sensation. I once experienced it in the most marked and persistent manner after taking a large dose of chlorodyne to subdue pain. Under such circumstances the sensation is probably due to the fact that the morphia in chlorodyne both weakens respiratory action and produces anaesthesia of the peripheral nerves, so that the skin becomes abnormally insensitive to the contact and pressure of the bed, and the sensation of descent is necessarily aroused.[1] It is possible that persons liable to the dream of falling are predisposed to a stage of sleep unconsciousness, in which cutaneous insensibility is marked. It is also possible that there is a contributory element of slight cardiac or respiratory disturbance.[2]

In a dream belonging to this group, I imagined I was being rhythmically swung up and down in the air by a young woman, my feet never touching the ground; and then that I was swinging her similarly. At one

---

falling have an aural origin, and are caused by contraction of the stapedius muscle, leading to a change in the ampullae which might suggest descent; he has himself suddenly awakened from such a dream and caught the sound of the muscular contraction. The opinion of so acute an investigator deserves consideration.

[1] Such sensations are, indeed, a recognised result of morphia. Morphinomaniacs, Goron remarks (*Les Parias de l'Amour*, p. 125), are apt to feel that they are flying or floating over the world.

[2] Jewell states that 'certain observers, peculiarly liable to dreams of falling or flying, ascribe these distinctly to faulty circulation, and say their physicians, to regulate the heart's action, have given them medicines which always relieve them and prevent such dreams' (*American Journal of Psychology*, January 1905, p. 8).

time she seemed to be swinging me in too jerky and hurried a manner, and I explained to her that it must be done in a slower and more regular manner, though I was not conscious of the precise words I used. There had been some dyspepsia on the previous day, and on awaking I felt slight discomfort in the region of the heart. The symbolism into which slightly disturbed respiratory or cardiac action is here transformed seems very clear in this dream, because it shows the actual transition from the subjective sensation to the objective imagery of flying. By means of this symbolic imagery we find sleeping consciousness commanding the hurried heart to beat in a more healthy manner.

Although, in youth, my dreams of flying were of what may be considered normal type, after the age of about thirty-five they tended, as illustrated by the example I have given, to take on a somewhat objective form. A further stage in this direction, the swinging movement being transformed to an inanimate object, is illustrated by a dream of comparatively recent date, in which I seemed to see an athlete of the music-hall, a graceful and muscular man, who was manipulating a large elastic ball, making it bound up from the floor. On awaking, there was a distinct sensation of cardiac tremor and nervousness.[1]

It may seem strange that dreams of flying, if so often

[1] Interesting evidence in favour of the respiratory origin of such visions is furnished by Silberer's observations on his own symbolic hypnagogic visions which are certainly allied to dream visions. He found (*Jahrbuch für Psychoanalytische Forschungen*, Bd. i., 1909, p. 523) that on drawing a deep breath, and so raising the chest wall, the representation came to him of attempting with another person to raise a table in the air.

due to organic disturbances, should usually be agreeable in character. It is not, however, necessary to assume that they are caused by serious interference with physiological functions; often, indeed, they may simply be due to the presence of a stage of consciousness in which respiration has become unduly prominent, as it is apt to be in the early stage of nitrous oxide anaesthesia, that is to say, to a relative wakefulness of the respiratory centres. It would seem that the disturbance is frequently almost, or quite, imperceptible on waking, and by no means to be compared with the more acute organic disturbances which result in dreams of murder, although it may be of nervous origin.[1] In some cases, however, it appears that dreams of flying are accompanied by circumstances of terror. Thus a medical correspondent, who describes his health as fairly good, writes in regard to dreams of flying: 'I have often had such dreams, and have wondered if others have them. Mine, however, are not so much dreams of flying, as dreams of being entirely devoid of weight, and of rising and falling at will. A singular feature of these levitation dreams is that they are always accompanied by an intense and agonising fear of an evil presence, a presence that I do not see but seem to feel, and my greatest terror is that I *shall* see it. The presence is ill-defined, but very real, and it seems to suggest the potentiality of all possible moral, mental,

---

[1] J. de Goncourt (*Journal des Goncourt*, vol. iii. p. 3) mentions that after drinking port wine, to which he was unaccustomed, he had a dream in which he observed on his counterpane grotesque images in relief which rose and fell.

AVIATION IN DREAMS

and physical evil. In these dreams it always occurs to me that if this evil presence shall ever become embodied into a something that I could *see*, the sight of it would be so ineffably horrible as to drive me mad. So vivid has this fear been that on several occasions I have awakened in a cold sweat or a nameless fear that would persist for some minutes after I realised that I had only been dreaming.' This seems to be an abnormal type of the dream of flight.

It is somewhat surprising that while dreams of floating in the air are so common and clearly indicate the respiratory source of the dream, dreams of floating on water seem to be rare, for as the actual experience of floating on water is fairly familiar, we might have expected that sleeping consciousness would have found here rather than in the never experienced idea of floating in air the explanation of its sensations. The dream of floating on water is, however, by no means unknown; thus Rachilde (Mme. Vallette), the French novelist and critic, whose dream life is vivid and remarkable, states that her most agreeable dream is that of floating on the surface of warm and transparent lakes or rivers.[1] One of the correspondents of *L'Intermédiaire des Chercheurs et des Curieux* [2] also states that he has often dreamed of walking on the water.

It is not only in sleep that the sensation of flying is experienced. In hysteria a sense of peculiar lightness of the body, and the idea of the soul's power to fly, may

---

[1] Chabaneix, *Le Subconscient*, p. 43.
[2] May 30, 1906.

occur incidentally,[1] and may certainly be connected both with the vigilambulism, as Sollier terms the sleep-like tendencies of such cases, and the anaesthetic conditions found in the hysterical. It is noteworthy that Janet found that in an ecstatic person who experienced the sensation of rising in the air there was anaesthesia of the soles of the feet. In such hysterical ecstasy, which has always played so large a part in religious manifestations, it is well known that the sense of rising and floating in the air has often prominently appeared. St. Theresa occasionally felt herself lifted above the ground, and was fearful that this sign of divine favour would attract attention (though we are not told that that was the case), while St. Joseph of Cupertino, Christina the Wonderful, St. Ida of Louvain, with many another saint enshrined in the *Acta Sanctorum*, were permitted to experience this sensation; and since its reality is as convincing in the ecstatic state as it is in dreams, the saints have often been able to declare, in perfect good faith, that their levitation was real.[2] In all great religious movements among primitive peoples, similar phenomena occur, together with other nervous and hallucinatory manifestations. They occurred, for instance, in the great Russian religious movement which took place among the peasants in

---

[1] L. Binswanger, 'Versuch einer Hysterieanalyse,' *Jahrbuch für Psychoanalytische Forschungen*, Bd. I. 1909.

[2] Their word has often been accepted. Levitation as experienced by the saints has been studied by Colonel A. de Rochas, *Les Frontières de la Science*, 1904; also in *Annales des Sciences Psychiques*, January-February 1901. 'Levitation is a perfectly real phenomena,' he concludes, 'and much more common than we might at first be tempted to believe.'

AVIATION IN DREAMS

the province of Kief during the winter of 1891-2. The leader of the movement, a devout member of the Stundist sect, a man with alcoholic heredity, who had received the revelation that he was saviour of the world, used not only to perceive perfumes so exquisite that they could only, as he was convinced, emanate from the Holy Ghost, but during prayer, together with a feeling of joy, he also had a sensation of bodily lightness and of floating in the air. His followers in many cases had the same experiences, and they delighted in jumping up into the air and shouting. In these cases the reality of the sensory obtuseness of the skin as an element in the manifestations was demonstrated, for Ssikorski, who had an opportunity of investigating these people, found that many of them, when in the ecstatic condition, were completely insensible to pain.

The sensation of flying is one of the earliest to appear in the dreams of childhood.[1] It is sometimes the last sensation at the moment of death. To rise, to fall, to glide away, has often been the last conscious sensation recalled by those who seemed to be dying, but have afterwards been brought back to life. Those rescued from drowning, for instance, have sometimes found that the last conscious sensation was a beatific feeling of being borne upwards. Piéron has also noted this sensation at the moment of death from disease in a number of cases, usually accompanied by a sense of

---

[1] It seems to become less frequent after middle age. Beaunis states that in his case it ceased at the age of fifty. I found it disappear, or become rare, at a somewhat earlier age.

well-being.[1] The cases he describes were mostly tuberculous, and included individuals of both sexes, and of atheistic as well as religious belief. In all, the last sensation to which expression was given was one of flying, of moving upwards. In some death was peaceful, in others painful. In one case a girl died clasping the iron bars of the bed, in horror of being borne upwards. Piéron, no doubt rightly, associates this sensation with the similar sensation of rising and floating common in dreams, and with the feeling of moving upwards and resting on the air experienced by persons in the ecstatic state. In all these cases alike life is being concentrated in the brain and central organs, while the outlying districts of the body are becoming numb and dead.

In this way it comes about that out of dreams and of dream-like waking states, one of the most permanent of human spiritual conceptions has been evolved. To float, to rise into the air, to fly up to heaven, has always seemed to man to be the final climax of spiritual activity. The angel is the most ethereal creature the human imagination can conceive. Browning's cry to his 'lyric love, half angel and half bird,' pathetically crude as poetry, is sound as psychology. The prophets and divine heroes of the race have constantly seemed to their devout followers to disappear at last by floating up into the sky, like Elijah, who went up 'by a whirlwind into heaven.' St. Peter once thought he saw his Master walking on the waves, and the last vision of

---

[1] H. Piéron, 'Contribution à la Psychologie des Mourants,' *Revue Philosophique*, December 1902.

Jesus in the Gospels reveals him rising into the air. For it is in the world of dreams that the human soul has its indestructible home, and in the attempt to realise these dreams lies a large part of our business in life.

CHAPTER VII

SYMBOLISM IN DREAMS

The Dramatisation of Subjective Feelings Based on Dissociation—Analogies in Waking Life—The Synaesthesias and Number-forms—Symbolism in Language—In Music—The Organic Basis of Dream Symbolism—The Omnipotence of Symbolism—Oneiromancy—The Scientific Interpretation of Dreams—Why Symbolism prevails in Dreaming—Freud's Theory of Dreaming—Dreams as Fulfilled Wishes—Why this Theory cannot be applied to all Dreaming—The Complete Form of Symbolism in Dreams—Splitting up of Personality — Self-objectivation in Imaginary Personalities—The Dramatic Element in Dreams—Hallucinations—Multiple Personality— Insanity — Self-objectivation a Primitive Tendency—Its Survival in Civilisation.

In discussing dreams of flying I have referred to a dream in which a slight disturbance of the heart's action was transformed by sleeping consciousness into the image of an athlete manipulating an elastic ball. This objectivation of what are really the dreamer's subjective sensations, although he is not conscious of them as subjective, is, indeed, a phenomenon which we have encountered many times. It is, however, so important a feature of dream psychology, and probably of such significant weight in its influence on waking life, that it is worth while to deal with it separately.

The dramatisation of subjective elements of the personality, which contributes so largely to render our dreams vivid and interesting, rests on that dissociation,

SYMBOLISM IN DREAMS

or falling apart of the constituent groups of psychic centres, which is so fundamental a fact of dream life. That is to say, that the usually coherent elements of our mental life are split up, and some of them—often, it is curious to note, precisely those which are at that very moment the most prominent and poignant—are reconstituted into what seems to us an outside and objective world, of which we are the interested or the merely curious spectators, but in neither case realise that we are ourselves the origin of.

An elementary source of this tendency to objectivation is to be found, it may be noted, in the automatic impulse towards symbolism by which all sorts of feelings experienced by the dreamer become transformed into concrete visible images. When objectivation is thus attained, dissociation may be said to be secondary. So far indeed as I am able to dissect the dream-process, the tendency to symbolism seems nearly always to precede the dissociation in consciousness, though it may well be that the dissociation of the mental elements is a necessary subconscious condition for the symbolism.

Sensory symbolism rests on a very fundamental psychic tendency. On the abnormal side we find it in the synaesthesias which, since Galton first drew attention to them in 1883, in his *Inquiries into Human Faculty*, have become well known, and are found among between six to over twelve per cent. of people. Galton investigated chiefly those kinds of synaesthesias which he called 'number-forms' and 'colour associations.' The number-form is characteristic of those people who almost invariably think of numerals in some more or less constant form of visual imagery, the number instantaneously calling up the picture. In persons who experience colour-associations, or coloured-hearing, there is a similar instantaneous manifestation of particular colours in connection with particular sounds, the different vowel sounds, for instance, each constantly and persistently evolving a definite tint, as *a* white, *e* vermilion, *i* yellow, etc., no two persons, however, having exactly the same colour scheme of sounds.[1] These phenomena are not so very rare, and, though they must be regarded as abnormal, they occur in persons who are perfectly healthy and sane.

It will be seen that a synaesthesia—which may involve taste, smell, and other senses besides hearing and sight—causes an impression of one sensory order to be automatically and involuntarily linked on to an impression of another totally different order. In other words, we may say that the one impression becomes the *symbol* of the other impression, for a symbol—which is literally a throwing together—means that two things of different orders have become so associated that one

---

[1] See *e.g.* Galton, *Inquiries* (Everyman's Library edition), pp. 79-112. Among more recent writings on this subject may be mentioned Bleuler, art. 'Secondary Sensations,' Tuke's *Dictionary of Psychological Medicine*; Suarez de Mendoza, *L'Audition Colorée*; Jules Millet, *Audition Colorée*, and especially a useful summary by Clavière, 'L'Audition Colorée,' *L'Année Psychologique*, fifth year, 1899. A case of auditory gustation is recorded by A. M. Pierce, *American Journal of Psychology*, 1907. It may be noted that Boris Sidis has argued (*Psychological Review*, January 1904) that all hallucinations are of the nature of secondary sensations.

of them may be regarded as the sign and representative of the other.

There is, however, another still more natural and fundamental form of symbolism which is entirely normal, and almost, indeed, physiological. This is the tendency by which qualities of one order become symbols of qualities of a totally different order, because they instinctively seem to have a similar effect on us. In this way, things in the physical order become symbols of things in the spiritual order. This symbolism penetrates indeed the whole of language; we cannot escape from it. The sea is *deep*, and so also may thoughts be; ice is *cold*, and we say the same of some hearts; sugar is *sweet*, as the lover finds also the presence of the beloved; quinine is *bitter*, and so is remorse. Not only our adjectives, but our substantives and our verbs are equally symbolical. To the etymological eye every sentence is full of metaphor, of symbol, of images that, strictly and originally, express sensory impressions of one order, but, as we use them to-day, express impressions of a totally different order. Language is largely the utilisation of symbols. This is a well-recognised fact which it is unnecessary to elaborate.[1]

An interesting example of the natural tendency to symbolism, which may be compared to the allied tendency in dreaming, is furnished by another language, the language of music. Music is a representation of

---

[1] Ferrero, in his *Lois Psychologiques du Symbolisme* (1895), deals broadly with symbolism in human thought and life.

the world—the internal or the external world—which, except in so far as it may seek to reproduce the actual sounds of the world, can only be expressive by its symbolism. And the symbolism of music is so pronounced that it is even expressed in the elementary fact of musical pitch. Our minds are so constructed that the bass always seems *deep* to us and the treble *high*. We feel it incongruous to speak of a *high* bass voice or a *deep* soprano. It is difficult to avoid the conclusion that this and the like associations are fundamentally based, that there are, as an acute French philosophic student of music, Dauriac (in an essay ' Des Images Suggérées par l'Audition musicale ' [1]), has expressed it, ' sensorial correspondences,' as, indeed, Baudelaire had long since divined [2]; that the motor image is that which demands from the listener the minimum of effort ; and that music almost constantly evokes motor imagery.[3]

[1] *Revue Philosophique*, November 1902.
[2] ' Richard Wagner et Tannhauser ' in *L'Art Romantique*.
[3] The motor imagery suggested by music is in some persons profuse and apparently capricious, and may be regarded as an anomaly comparable to a synaesthesia. Heine was an example of this, and he has described in *Florentine Nights* the visions aroused by the playing of Paganini, and elsewhere the visions evoked in him by the music of Berlioz. Though I do not myself experience this phenomenon, I have found that there is sometimes a tendency for music to arouse ideas of motor imagery; thus some melodies of Handel suggest a giant painting frescoes on a vast wall space. The most elementary motor relationship of music is seen in the tendency of many people to sway portions of their body—to ' beat time '—in sympathy with the music. (This phenomenon has been experimentally studied by J. B. Miner, ' Motor, Visual, and Applied Rhythms,' Monograph Supplement to the *Psychological Review*, vol. v., No. 4, June 1903). Music is fundamentally an audible dance, and the most primitive music is dance music.

SYMBOLISM IN DREAMS

The association between high notes and physical ascent, between low notes and physical descent, is certainly in any case very fixed.[1] In Wagner's *Lohengrin*, the ascent and descent of the angelic chorus is thus indicated. Even if we go back to the early composers, the same correspondence is found. In Purcell it is very definite. In Bach—pure and abstract as his music is generally considered—not only this elementary association, but an immense amount of motor imagery is to be found ; Bach shows, indeed, a curious preoccupation in translating the definite sense of the words he is musically illustrating into corresponding musical terms ; the skill and subtlety with which he accomplishes this, can often, as Pirro and Schweitzer have shown, be appreciated only by musicians.[2] It is

---

[1] The instinctive nature of this tendency is shown by the fact that it persists even in sleep. Thus Weygandt relates that he once fell asleep in the theatre during one of the last scenes of *Cavalleria Rusticana*, when the tenor was singing in ever higher and higher tones, and dreamed that in order to reach the notes the performer was climbing up ladders and stairs on the stage.

[2] See, especially the attractive book of André Pirro, *L'Esthétique de J. S. Bach* (1907), and also Albert Schweitzer, *J. S. Bach* (1908), especially chapters xix.-xxiii. 'Concrete things,' says Ernest Newman, summarising some of these results (*Nation*, December 25, 1909), 'incessantly suggested abstract ideas or inward moods to Bach, and *vice versâ*. He would time after time use the same musical formula for the same word or idea. He first suggests the external concepts of "high" and "low," as other composers have done, by high or low notes, and motion up or down by ascending or descending themes. But Bach correlates with the outward, objective thing a whole series of things that are purely subjective. Thus moods of elation or of depression are to him the mental equivalents of the physical acts of going up or down. So he gives us a whole series of ascending themes to words that express "mounting" states of mind, as it were—such as pride, courage, strength, resolution—and descending themes to words that express "declining" states of mind—such as prostration, adoration, depression, discouragement, grief at sin, humility, poverty,

sometimes said that this is 'realism' in music. That is a mistake. When the impressions derived from one sense are translated into those of another sense, there can be no question of realism. A composer may attempt a realistic representation of thunder, but his representation of lightning can only be symbolical; audible lightning can never be realistic.

Not only is there an instinctive and direct association between sounds and motor imagery, but there is an indirect but equally instinctive association between sounds and visual imagery which, though not itself motor, has motor associations. Thus Bleuler considers it well established that among colour-hearers there is a tendency for photisms that are light in colour (and belonging, we may say, to the 'high' part of the spectrum) to be produced by sounds of high quality, and dark photisms by sounds of low quality; and, in the same way, sharply-defined pains or tactile sensations, as well as pointed forms, produce light photisms. Simil-

fatigue, and illness. For the two sets of concepts, internal and external, he will use the same musical symbols. To represent the physical concept of "surrounding," again, he adopts the device of a circling or undulating theme. A crown or a garland suggests the same idea to him, so for this, too, he uses the same kind of theme. But the correspondence goes still further; for when he comes to the word "considering," he uses the same curving musical symbol once more—his notion of "considering" being that of looking round on all sides. Again, a word of purely external signification that suggests something twisted will have an appropriately twisted theme. Then come the subjective applications of the theme—the same disordered melodic outline is used to express a frame of mind like anxiety or confusion, or to depict the wiles of Satan. Careful study of the vocal works of Bach, and especially of the cantatas, has revealed a host of these curious symbols.' The whole subject, it may be added, has been briefly and suggestively discussed by Goblot, 'La Musique Descriptive,' *Revue Philosophique*, July 1901.

arly, bright lights and pointed forms produce high photisms, whole low photisms are produced by opposite conditions. Urbantschitsch, again, by examining a large number of people who were not colour-hearers, found that a high note of a tuning-fork seems higher when looking at red, yellow, green, or blue, but lower if looking at violet. Thus two sensory qualities that are both symbolic of a third quality are symbolic to each other.

This symbolism, we are justified in believing, is based on fundamental organic tendencies. Piderit, nearly half a century ago, forcibly argued that there is a real relationship of our most spiritual feelings and ideas to particular bodily movements and facial expressions. In a similar manner, he pointed out that bitter tastes and bitter thoughts tend to produce the same physical expression.[1] He also argued that the character of a man's looks—his *fixed* or *dreamy* eyes, his *lively* or *stiff* movements—correspond to real psychic characters. If this is so we have a physiological, almost anatomical, basis for symbolism. Cleland,[2] again, in an essay, 'On the Element of Symbolic Correlation in Expression,' argued that the key to a great part of expression is the correlation of movements and positions with ideas, so that there are, for instance, a host of associations in the human mind by which 'upward' represents the good, the great, and the living, while 'downward' represents the evil and the dead. Such

---

[1] T. Piderit, *Mimik und Physiognomik*, 1867, p. 73.
[2] J. Cleland, *Evolution, Expression and Sensation*, 1881.

associations are so fundamental that they are found even in animals, whose gestures are, as Féré[1] remarked, often metaphorical, so that a cat, for instance, will shake its paw, as if in contact with water, after any disagreeable experiences.

The symbolism that to-day interpenetrates our language, and indeed our life generally, has mostly been inherited by us, with the traditions of civilisation, from an antiquity so primitive that we usually fail to interpret it. The rare additions we make to it in our ordinary normal life are for the most part deliberately conscious. But so soon as we fall below, or rise above, that ordinary normal level—to insanity and hallucination, to childhood, to savagery, to folk-lore and legend, to poetry and religion—we are at once plunged into a sea of symbolism.[2] There is even a normal sphere in which symbolism has free scope, and that is in the world of dreams.

Oneiromancy, the symbolical interpretation of dreams, more especially as a method of divining the future, is a widespread art in early stages of culture. The discerning of dreams is represented in the Old Testament as a very serious and anxious matter (as in regard to Pharaoh's dream of the fat and lean cattle), and, nearer to our time, the dreams of great heroes, especially Charlemagne, are represented as highly important

---

[1] Féré, 'La Physiologie dans les Métaphores,' *Revue Philosophique*, October 1895.

Maeder discusses symbolism in some of these fields in his ' Die Symbolik in den Legenden, Märchen, Gebräuchen und Träumen,' *Psychiatrisch-Neurologische Wochenschrift*, Nos. 6 and 7, May 1908.

SYMBOLISM IN DREAMS

events in the mediæval European epics. Little manuals on the interpretation of dreams have always been much valued by the uncultured classes, and among our current popular sayings there are many dicta concerning the significance, or the good or ill luck, of particular kinds of dreams.

Oneiromancy has thus slowly degenerated to folk-lore and superstition. But at the outset it possessed something of the combined dignities of religion and of science. Not only were the old dream interpreters careful of the significance and results of individual dreams, in order to build up a body of doctrine, but they held that not every dream contained in it a divine message ; thus they would not condescend to interpret dreams following on the drinking of wine, for only to the temperate, they declared, do the gods reveal their secrets.[1] The serious and elaborate way in which the interpretation of dreams was dealt with is well seen in the treatise on this subject by Artemidorus of Daldi, a native of Ephesus, and contemporary of Marcus Aurelius.[2] He divided dreams into two classes : *theorematic* dreams, which come literally true, and *allegorical* dreams. The first group may be said to correspond to the modern groups of prophetic and proleptic or prodromic dreams, while the second group includes the symbolical dreams which have of recent years again attracted attention. Synesius, who lived

---

[1] So Philostratus, and Pliny (*Natural History*, Bk. x. ch. ccxi.) puts the same point on somewhat more natural grounds.
[2] It has been translated by F. S. Krauss, *Symbolik der Traume*, 1881.

in the fourth century, and eventually became a Christian bishop without altogether ceasing to be a Greek pagan, wrote a very notable treatise on dreaming, in which, with a genuinely Greek alertness of mind, he contrived to rationalise and almost to modernise the ancient doctrine of dream symbolism. He admits that it is in their obscurity that the truth of dreams resides, and that we must not expect to find any general rules in regard to dreams; no two people are alike, so that the same dream cannot have the same significance for every one, and we have to find out the rules of our own dreams. He had himself (like Galen) often been aided in his writings by his dreams, in this way getting his ideas into order, improving his style, and receiving criticisms of extravagant phrases. Once, too, in the days when he hunted, he invented a trap as a result of a dream. Synesius declares that attention to divination by dreams is good on moral grounds alone. For he who makes his bed a Delphian tripod will be careful to live a pure and noble life. In that way he will reach an end higher than that he aimed at.[1]

It seems to-day by no means improbable that, amid the absurdities of this popular oneiromancy, there are some items of real significance. Until recent years,

[1] A translation of Synesius's 'Treatise on Dreams' is included in Druon's *Œuvres de Synésius*, pp. 347 *et seq.* Synesius is probably best known to modern English readers through Charles Kingsley's novel, *Hypatia*. His treatise on dreams has been unduly neglected, though it commended itself mightily to the pioneering mind of Lord Monboddo, who even says (*Ancient Metaphysics*, vol. ii., 1782, p. 217) in reference to this treatise: 'Indeed it appears to me that since the days of Plato and Aristotle there has not been a philosopher of greater depth than Synesius.'

however, the absurdities have frightened away the scientific investigator. Almost the only investigator of the psychology of dreaming who ventured to admit a real symbolism in the dream world was Scherner,[1] and his arguments were not usually accepted nor even easy to accept. When we are faced by the question of definite and constant symbols it still remains true that scepticism is often called for. But there can be no manner of doubt that our dreams are full of symbolism.[2]

The conditions of dream life, indeed, lend themselves with a peculiar facility to the formation of symbolism, that is to say, of images which, while evoked by a definite stimulus, are themselves of a totally different order from that stimulus. The very fact that we *sleep*, that is to say, that the avenues of sense which would normally supply the real image of corresponding

---

[1] K. A. Scherner, *Das Leben des Traumes*, 1861. In France Hervey de Saint-Denis, in a remarkable anonymous work which I have not seen (*Les Rêves et les Moyens de les Diriger*, p. 356, quoted by Vaschide and Piéron, *Psychologie du Rêve*, p. 26), tentatively put forward a symbolic theory of dreams, as a possible rival to the theory that permanent associations are set up as the result of a first chance coincidence. ' Do there exist,' he asked, ' bizarre analogies of internal sensations in virtue of which certain vibrations of the nerves, certain instinctive movements of our viscera, correspond to sensations apparently quite different ? According to this hypothesis experience would bring to light mysterious affinities, the knowledge of which might become a genuine science ; . . . and a real key to dreams would not be an unrealisable achievement if we could bring together and compare a sufficient number of observations.'

[2] It is interesting to note that hallucinations may also be symbolic. Thus the Psychical Research Society's Committee on Hallucinations recognised a symbolic group, and recorded, for instance, the case of a man who, when his child lies dying, sees a blue flame in the air and hears a voice say, ' That's his soul' (*Proceedings Society for Psychical Research*, August 1894, p. 125).

order to the stimulus are more or less closed, renders symbolism inevitable.[1] The direct channels being thus largely choked, other allied and parallel associations come into play, and since the control of attention and apperception is diminished, such play is often unimpeded. Symbolism is the natural and inevitable result of these conditions.[2]

It might still be asked why we do not in dreams more often recognise the actual source of the stimuli applied to us. If a dreamer's feet are in contact with something hot, it might seem more natural that he should think of the actual hot-water bottle, rather than of an imaginary Etna, and that, if he hears a singing in his ears, he should argue the presence of the real bird he has often heard rather than a performance of Haydn's *Creation*, which he has never heard. Here, however, we have to remember the tendency to magnification in dream imagery, a tendency which rests on the emotionality of dreams. Emotion is normally heightened in dreams. Every impression reaches sleeping consciousness through this emotional atmosphere, in an

---

[1] Maeder states that the tendency to symbolism in dreams and similar modes of psychic activity is due to 'vague thinking in a condition of diminished attention.' This is, however, an inadequate statement and misses the central point.

[2] In the other spheres in which symbolism most tends to appear, the same or allied conditions exist. In hallucinations, which (as Parish and others have shown) tend to occur in hypnagogic or sleep-like states, the conditions are clearly the same. The symbolism of an art, and notably music, is due to the very conditions of the art, which exclude any appeal to other senses. The primitive mind reaches symbolism through a similar condition of things, coming as the result of ignorance and undeveloped powers of apperception. In insanity these powers are morbidly disturbed or destroyed, with the same result.

enlarged form, vaguer it may be, but more massive. The sleeping brain is thus not dealing with actual impressions—if we are justified in speaking of the impressions of waking life as 'actual'—even when actual impressions are being made upon it, but with transformed impressions. The problem before it is to find an adequate cause, not for the actual impression, but for the transformed and enlarged impression. Under these circumstances symbolism is quite inevitable. Even when the nature of an excitation is rightly perceived its quality cannot be rightly perceived. The dreamer may be able to perceive that he is being bitten, but the massive and profound impression of a bite which reaches his dreaming consciousness would not be adequately accounted for by the supposition of the real mosquito that is the cause of it; the only adequate explanation of the transformed impression received is to be found (as in a dream already narrated) in a creature as large as a lobster. This creature is the symbol of the real mosquito.[1] We have the same phenomenon under somewhat similar conditions in the intoxication of chloroform and nitrous oxide.

The obscuration during sleep of the external sensory

---

[1] The magnification we experience in dreams is manifested in their emotional aspects and in the emotional transformation of actual sensory stimuli, from without or from within the organism. The size of objects recalled by dreaming memory usually remains unchanged, and if changed it seems to be more usually diminished. 'Lilliputian hallucinations,' as they are termed by Leroy, who has studied them (*Revue de Psychiatrie*, 1909, No. 8), in which diminutive, and frequently coloured, people are observed, may also occasionally occur in alcoholic and chloral intoxication, in circular insanity, and in various other morbid mental conditions. They are usually agreeable in character.

L

channels, with the checks on false conclusions they furnish, is not alone sufficient to explain the symbolism of dreams. The dissociation of thought during sleep, with the diminished attention and apperception involved, is also a factor. The magnification of special isolated sensory impressions in dreaming consciousness is associated with a general bluntness, even an absolute quiescence, of the external sensory mechanism. One part of the organism, and it seems usually a visceral part, is thus apt to magnify its place in consciousness at the expense of the rest. As Vaschide and Piéron say, during sleep 'the internal sensations develop at the expense of the peripheral sensations.' That indeed seems to be the secret of the immense emotional turmoil of our dreams. Yet it is very rare for these internal sensations to reach the sleeping brain as what they are. They become conscious, not as literal messages, but as symbolical transformations. The excited or labouring heart recalls to the brain no memory of itself, but some symbolical image of excitement or labour. There is association, indeed, but it is association not along the matter-of-fact lines of our ordinary waking civilised life, but along much more fundamental and primitive channels, which in waking life we have now abandoned or never knew.

There is another consideration which may be put forward to account for one group of dream-symbolisms. It has been found that certain hysterical subjects of old standing when in the hypnotic state are able to receive mental pictures of their own viscera, even though they may be quite ignorant of any knowledge of the shape of these viscera. This *autoscopy*, as it has been called, has been specially studied by Féré, Comar, and Sollier.[1] Hysteria is a condition which is in many respects closely allied to sleep, and if it is to be accepted as a real fact that autoscopy occasionally occurs in the abnormal psychic state of hypnotic sleep in hysterical persons, it is possible to ask whether it may not sometimes occur normally in the allied state of sleep. In the hypnotic state it is known that parts of the organism normally involuntary may become subject to the will; it is not incredible that similarly parts normally insensitive may become sufficiently sensitive to reveal their own shape or condition. We may thus, indeed, the more easily understand those premonitory dreams in which the dreamer becomes conscious of morbid conditions which are not perceptible to waking consciousness until they have attained a greater degree of intensity.[2]

[1] Sollier, 'L'Autoscopie Interne,' *Revue Philosophique*, January 1903. Sollier deals with the objections made to the reality of the phenomenon.

[2] 'Many people,' writes Dr. Marie de Manacéïne (*Sleep*, 1897, p. 294), 'when threatened by a gastric or intestinal attack dream of seeing fish. The late Professor Sergius Botkine told me that he had found this coincidence in his own case, and I have myself several times found it in the case of a young girl who is well known to me. Some have supposed that the sleeping consciousness receives an impression of the elongated shape of the stomach or intestine; but such a supposition is easier to make than to prove.' Scherner associated dreams of fish with sensations arising from the bladder, and here also it may be said that we are concerned with a fish-like viscus. Greenwood (*Imagination in Dreams*, p. 195) stated that he had always been subject, at intervals of months or years, to a recurrent dream in which he would see a river swarming with fish that were finally piled in a horrible sweltering mass; this dream always left a feeling of 'squalid horror,' but he was never able to ascertain its cause and significance.

The recognition of the transformation in dream life of internal sensations into symbolic motor imagery is ancient. Hippocrates said that to dream, for instance, of springs and wells denoted some disturbance of the bladder. In such a case a disturbed bladder sends to the brain, not the naked message of its own needs, but a symbolic message of those needs in motor imagery, as (in one case known to me) of a large cistern with a stream of water flowing from it.[1] Sometimes the symbolism aroused by visceral processes remains physiological; thus indigestion frequently leads to dreams of eating, as of chewing all sorts of inedible and repulsive substances, and occasionally—it would seem more abnormally—to agreeable dreams of food.

It is due to the genius of Professor Sigmund Freud, of Vienna—to-day the most daring and original psychologist in the field of morbid psychic phenomena—that we owe the long-neglected recognition of the large place of symbolism in dreaming. Scherner had argued in favour of this aspect of dreams, but he was an undistinguished and unreliable psychologist, and his arguments failed to be influential. Freud avows himself a partisan of Scherner's theory of dreaming and opponent of all other theories,[2] but his treatment of

---

[1] Freud states (*Die Traumdeutung*, p. 233) that he knows a case in which (as in the *Song of Songs*) columns and pillars appear in dreams as symbols of the legs, and doors as symbols of the openings of the body.

[2] Freud, *Die Traumdeutung*, p. 66. This work, published in 1900, is the chief and most extensive statement of Freud's views. A shorter statement is embodied in a little volume of the 'Grenzfrägen' Series, *Ueber den Traum*, 1901. A brief exposition of Freud's position is given by Dr. A. Maeder of Zurich in 'Essai d'Interprétation de Quelques Rêves,'

SYMBOLISM IN DREAMS

the matter is incomparably more searching and profound. Freud, however, goes far beyond the fundamental—and, as I believe, undeniable—proposition that dream-imagery is largely symbolic. He holds that behind the symbolism of dreams there lies ultimately a *wish*; he believes, moreover, that this wish tends to be really of more or less sexual character, and, further, that it is tinged by elements that go back to the dreamer's infantile days. As Freud views the mechanism of dreams, it is far from exhibiting mere disordered mental activity, but is (much as he has also argued hysteria to be [1]) the outcome of a desire, which is driven back by a kind of inhibition or censure (*i.e.*, that kind of moral check which is still more alert in the waking state), and is seeking new forms of expression. There is first in the dream the process of what Freud calls condensation (*Verdichtung*), a process which is that fusion of separate elements which must be recognised at the outset of every discussion of dreaming, but Freud maintains that in this fusion all the elements have a point in common,

Archives de Psychologie, April 1907 ; as also by Ernest Jones ('Freud's Theory of Dreams,' *Review of Neurology and Psychiatry,* March 1910, and *American Journal of Psychology,* April 1910). For Freud's general psychological doctrine, see Brill's translation of 'Freud's Selected Papers on Hysteria,' 1909. There have been many serious criticisms of Freud's methods. As an example of such criticism, accompanying an exposition of the methods, reference may be made to Max Isserlin's ' Die Psychoanalytische Methode Freuds,' *Zeitschrift für die Gesamte Neurologie und Psychiatrie,* Bd. 1. Heft 1. 1910. A judicious and qualified criticism of Freud's psychotherapeutic methods is given by Löwenfeld ('Zum gegenwärtigen Stande der Psychotherapeutie,' *Münchener medizinische Wochenschrift,* Nos. 3 and 4, 1910).

[1] I have set forth Freud's views of hysteria, now regarded as almost epoch-making in character, in *Studies of the Psychology of Sex,* vol. i. 3rd ed. pp. 219 *et seq.*

and overlie one another like the pictures in a Galtonian composite photograph. Then there comes the process of displacement or transference (*Verschiebung*), a process by which the really central and emotional basis of the dream is concealed beneath trifles. Then there is the process of dramatisation or transformation into a concrete situation of which the elements have a symbolic value. Thus, as Maeder puts it, summarising Freud's views, 'behind the apparently insignificant events of the day utilised in the dream there is always an important idea or event hidden. We only dream of things that are worth while. What at first sight seems to be a trifle is a grey wall which hides a great palace. The significance of the dream is not so much held in the dream itself as in that substratum of it which has not passed the threshold and which analysis alone can bring to light.'

'We only dream of things that are worth while.' That is the point at which many of us are no longer able to follow Freud. That dreams of the type studied by Freud do actually occur may be accepted; it may even be considered proved. But to assert that all dreams must be made to fit into this one formula is to make far too large a demand. As regards the presentative element in dreams—the element that is based on actual sensory stimulation—it is in most cases unreasonable to invoke Freud's formula at all. If, when I am asleep, the actual song of a bird causes me to dream that I am at a concert, that picture may be regarded as a natural symbol of the actual sensation, and it is unreasonable to expect that psycho-analysis could reveal any hidden personal reason why the symbol should take the form of a concert. And, if so, then Freud's formula fails to hold good for phenomena which cover one of the two main divisions of dreams, even on a superficial classification, and perhaps enter into all dreams.

But even if we take dreams of the remaining or representative class—the dreams made up of images not directly dependent on actual sensation—we still have to maintain a cautious attitude. A very large proportion of the dreams in this class seem to be, so far as the personal life is concerned, in no sense 'worth while.' It would, indeed, be surprising if they were. It seems to be fairly clear that in sleep, as certainly in the hypnagogic state, attention is diminished, and apperceptive power weakened. That alone seems to involve a relaxation of the tension by which we will and desire our personal ends. At the same time, by no longer concentrating our psychic activities at the focus of desire it enables indifferent images to enter more easily the field of sleeping consciousness. It might even be argued that the activity of desire, when it manifests itself in sleep and follows the course indicated by Freud, corresponds to a special form of sleep in which attention and apperception, though in modified forms, are more active than in ordinary sleep.[1] Such dreams

[1] This is supported by the fact that in waking reverie, or day-dreams, wishes are obviously the motor force in building up visionary structures. Freud attaches great importance to reverie, for he considers that it furnishes the key to the comprehension of dreams (*e.g. Sammlung Kleiner*

seem to occur with special frequency, or in more definitely marked forms, in the neurotic and especially the hysterical, and if it is true that the hysterical are to some extent asleep even when they are awake, it may also be said that they are to some extent awake even when they are asleep. Freud certainly holds, probably with truth, that there is no fundamental distinction between normal people and psychoneurotic people, and that there is, for instance, as Ferenczi says, emphasising this point, ' a streak of hysterical disposition in everybody.' Freud has, indeed, made interesting analytic studies of his own dreams, but the great body of material accumulated by him and his school is derived from the dreams of the neurotic. Thus Stekel states that he has analysed many thousand dreams, but his lengthy study on the interpretation of dreams deals exclusively with the dreams of the neurotic.[1] Stekel believes, moreover, that from the structure of the dream life conclusions may be drawn, not only as to the life and character of the dreamer, but also as to his neurosis, the hysterical person dreaming differently from the obsessed person, and so on. If that is the case we are certainly justified in doubting whether conclusions

Schriften zur Neurosenlehre, 2nd series, pp. 138 *et seq.*, 197 *et seq.*). But it must be remembered that day-dreaming is not real dreaming, which takes place under altogether different physiological conditions, although it may quite fairly be claimed that day-dreaming represents a state intermediate between ordinary waking consciousness and consciousness during sleep.

[1] The special characteristics of dreaming in the hysterical were studied, before Freud turned his attention to the question, by Sante de Sanctis (*I Sogni e il Sonno nell' Isterismo*, 1896). See also Havelock Ellis, *Studies in the Psychology of Sex*, vol. i. 3rd ed., 1910, ' Auto-erotism.'

SYMBOLISM IN DREAMS 169

drawn from the study of the dreams of neurotic people can be safely held to represent the normal dream life, even though it may be true that there is no definite frontier between them. Whatever may be the case among the neurotic, in ordinary normal sleep the images that drift across the field of consciousness, though they have a logic of their own, seem in a large proportion of cases to be quite explicable without resort to the theory that they stand in vital but concealed relationship to our most intimate self.

Even in waking life, and at normal moments which are not those of reverie, it seems possible to trace the appearance in the field of consciousness of images which are evoked neither by any known mental or physical circumstance of the moment, or any hidden desire, images that are as disconnected from the immediate claims of desire and even of association as those of dreams seem so largely to be. It sometimes occurs to me—as doubtless it occurs to other people—that at some moment when my thoughts are normally occupied with the work immediately before me, there suddenly appears on the surface of consciousness a totally unrelated picture. A scene arises, vague but usually recognisable, of some city or landscape—Australian, Russian, Spanish, it matters not what—seen casually long years ago, and possibly never thought of since, and possessing no kind of known association either with the matter in hand or with my personal life generally. It comes to the surface of consciousness as softly, as unexpectedly, as disconnectedly, as a minute bubble might arise and break on the surface of an actual stream from ancient organic material silently disintegrating in the depths beneath.[1] Every one who has travelled much cannot fail to possess, hidden in his psychic depths, a practically infinite number of such forgotten pictures, devoid of all personal emotion. It is possible to maintain, as a matter of theory, that when they come up to consciousness, they are evoked by some real, though untraceable, resemblance which they possess to the psychic or physical state existing when they reappear. But that theory cannot be demonstrated. Nor, it may be added, is it more plausible than the simple but equally unprovable theory that such scenes do really come to the surface of consciousness as the result of some slight spontaneous disintegration in a minute cerebral centre, and have no more immediately preceding psychic cause than my psychic realisation of the emergence of the sun from behind a cloud has any psychic preceding cause.

Similarly, in insanity, Liepmann, in his study *Ueber Ideenflucht*, has forcibly argued that ordinary logorrhœa —the incontinence of ideas linked together by super-

---

[1] Gissing, the novelist, an acute observer of psychic states, in the most personal of his books, *The Private Papers of Henry Ryecroft*, has described this phenomenon : ' Every one, I suppose, is subject to a trick of mind which often puzzles me. I am reading or thinking, and at a moment, without any association or suggestion that I can discover, there rises before me the vision of a place I know. Impossible to explain why that particular spot should show itself to my mind's eye ; the cerebral impulse is so subtle that no search may trace its origin.' Gissing proceeds to say that a thought, a phrase, an odour, a touch, a posture of the body, may possibly have furnished the link of association, but he knows no evidence for this theory.

SYMBOLISM IN DREAMS

ficial associations of resemblance or contiguity—is a linking *without direction*, that is, corresponding to no interest, either practical or theoretical, of the individual. Or, as Claparède puts it, logorrhœa is a trouble in the reaction of *interest* in life. It seems most reasonable to believe that in ordinary sleep the flow of imagery follows, for the most part, the same easy course. That course may to waking consciousness often seem peculiar, but to waking consciousness the conditions of dreaming life are peculiar. Under these conditions, however, we may well believe that the tendency to movement in the direction of least resistance still prevails. And as attention and will are weakened and loosened during sleep, the tense concentration on personal ends must also be relaxed. We become more disinterested. Personal desire tends for the most part rather to fall into the background than to become more prominent. If it were not a period in which desire were ordinarily relaxed, sleep would cease to be a period of rest and recuperation.

Sleeping consciousness is a vast world, a world scarcely less vast than that of waking consciousness. It is futile to imagine that a single formula can cover all its manifold varieties and all its degrees of depth. Those who imagine that all dreaming is a symbolism which a single cypher will serve to interpret must not be surprised if, however unjustly, they are thought to resemble those persons who claim to find on every page of Shakespeare a cypher revealing the authorship of Bacon. In the case of Freud's theory of dream interpretation, I hold the cypher to be real, but I believe that it is impossible to regard so narrow and exclusive an interpretation as adequate to explain the whole world of dreams. It would, *a priori*, be incomprehensible that sleeping consciousness should exert so extraordinary a selective power among the variegated elements of waking life, and, experientially, there seems no adequate ground to suppose that it does exert such selective action. On the contrary, it is, for the most part, supremely impartial in bringing forward and combining all the manifestations, the most trivial as well as the most intimate, of our waking life. There is a symptom of mental disorder called *extrospection*, in which the patient fastens his attention so minutely on events that he comes to interpret the most trifling signs and incidents as full of hidden significance, and may so build up a systematised delusion.[1] The investigator of dreams must always bear in mind the risk of falling into morbid extrospection.

Such considerations seem to indicate that it is not true that every dream, every mental image, is ' worth while,' though at the same time they by no means diminish the validity of special and purposive methods of investigating dream consciousness. Freud and those who are following him have shown, by the expenditure of much patience and skill, that his method of dream-interpretation may in many cases yield coherent results which it is not easy to account for by chance. It is quite possible, however, to recognise Freud's service

[1] Extrospection has been specially studied by Vaschide and Vurpas in *La Logique Morbide*.

in vindicating the large place of symbolism in dreams, and to welcome the application of his psycho-analytic method to dreams, while yet denying that this is the only method of interpreting dreams. Freud argues that all dreaming is purposive and significant, and that we must put aside the belief that dreams are the mere trivial outcome of the dissociated activity of brain centres. It remains true, however, that, while reason plays a larger part in dreams than most people realise, the activity of dissociated brain centres furnishes one of the best keys to the explanation of psychic phenomena during sleep. It would be difficult to believe in any case that in the relaxation of sleep our thoughts are still pursuing a deliberately purposeful direction under the control of our waking impulses. Many facts indicate—though Freud's school may certainly claim that such facts have not been thoroughly interpreted—that, as a matter of fact, this control is often conspicuously lacking. There is, for instance, the well-known fact that our most recent and acute emotional experiences—precisely those which might most ardently formulate themselves in a wish—are rarely mirrored in our dreams, though recent occurrences of more trivial nature, as well as older events of more serious import, easily find place there. That is easily accounted for by the supposition—not quite in a line with a generalised wish-theory—that the exhausted emotions of the day find rest at night.

It must also be said that even when we admit that a strong emotion may symbolically construct an elaborate dream edifice which needs analysis to be interpreted, we narrow the process unduly if we assert that the emotion is necessarily a wish. Desire is certainly very fundamental in life and very primitive. But there is another equally fundamental and primitive emotion—fear.[1] We may very well expect to find this emotion, as well as desire, subjacent to dream phenomena.[2]

The infantile form of the wish-dream, alike in adults and children, is thus, there can be little doubt, extremely common, and, even in its symbolic forms, it is a real and not rare phenomenon. But it is impossible to follow Freud when he declares that all dreams fall into the group of wish-dreams. The world of psychic life during sleep is, like the waking world, rich and varied ; it cannot be covered by a single formula. Freud's subtle and searching analytic genius has greatly contributed to enlarge our knowledge of this world of sleep. We may recognise the value of

---

[1] On the psychic importance of fears, see G. Stanley Hall, 'A Study of Fears,' *American Journal of Psychology*, 1897, p. 183. Metchnikoff (*Essais Optimistes*, pp. 247 *et seq*.) insists on the mingled fear and strength of the anthropoid apes.

[2] Foucault has pointed this out, and Morton Prince, and Giessler (who admits that the wish-dream is common in children), and Flournoy (who remarks that not only a fear but any emotion can be equally effective), as well as Claparède. The last remarks that Freud might regard a fear as a suppressed desire, but it may equally be said that a desire involves, on its reverse side, a fear. Freud has indeed himself pointed out (*e.g. Jahrbuch für Psychoanalytische Forschungen*, Bd. 1., 1909, p. 362) that fears may be instinctively combined with wishes ; he regards the association with a wish of an opposing fear as one of the components of some morbid psychic states. But he holds that the wish is the positive and fundamental element : ' The unconscious can only wish ' (' Das Unbewusste kann nichts als wünschen '), a statement that seems somewhat too metaphysical for the psychologist.

SYMBOLISM IN DREAMS

his contribution to the psychology of dreams while refusing to accept a premature and narrow generalisation.

The wish-dream of the kind elaborately investigated by Freud may be accepted as one type of dreaming, and a very interesting type, but it seems evident that it is only one type. There are even other types which seem closely related to it, and yet are quite distinct. This is, for instance, the case with the contrast-dream. The contrast-dream of Näcke's type represents the emergence of characteristics which are distinctly opposed to the dreamer's character and habits. Thus, in the course of four consecutive nights, I have dreamed in much detail that (1) I was the mayor of a large northern city about to take the chair at a local meeting of the Bible Society ; (2) that I was a soldier in the heat of battle ; and (3) that I was meditating the step of going on the stage as a comedian—the only rôle of the three which seemed to cause me any nervousness or misgiving. In contrast-dreams of this type we are not concerned with the eruption of concealed and repressed wishes. They are merely based on vestigial possibilities, entirely alien to our temperament as it has developed in life, and only a part of our complex personalities in the sense that, as Schopenhauer said, whatever path we take in life there are latent germs within us which could only have developed in an exactly opposite path. Even the very same dream may be due to quite different causes. To take a very simple dream, for we may best argue on the simplest facts : the dream of eating. We dream of eating when we are hungry, but sometimes we also dream of eating when the stomach is suffering from repletion. The dream is the same, but the psychological mechanism is entirely different, in the one case emotional, in the other intellectual. In the first case the picture of eating is built up in response to an organic visceral craving, and we have an elementary wish-dream of what Freud would call infantile type ; in the second case the same dream is a theory, embodied in a concrete picture, to account for the existence of the repletion experienced.

There cannot be the slightest doubt that the wish-dream, in its simple or what Freud calls its infantile form, represents an extremely common type of dream.[1] A large number of the dreams of children are concerned with wishes and their fulfilments. Those dreams of adults which are aroused by actual organic sensations also tend to fall, though not invariably, into the same form. Again, we chance to want a thing when we are awake; when we are asleep we dream we have found it. It may also be said, almost with certainty, that in some cases our dreams are the fulfilment of unexpressed and unconscious waking wishes. Even the best people, it is probable, may occasionally dream of events which represent the fulfilment of wishes they have never consciously formulated. Archbishop Laud was accustomed to note down his dreams in his Diary. On one

---

[1] Thus A. Wiggam (' A Contribution to the Data of Dream Psychology,' *Pedagogical Seminary*, June 1909) records a great many wish-dreams, mostly in the young.

SYMBOLISM IN DREAMS

occasion we find him setting down a disturbing dream, in which he saw the Lord Keeper dead, and 'rotten already.' A little later we find that Laud is 'much concerned at the envy and undeserved hatred borne to me by the Lord Keeper.'[1] It is not difficult to see in the Archbishop's relations to the Lord Keeper an explanation of his dream.

If, however, wishes, conscious or unconscious, are often fulfilled in dreams, and if, as we have seen reason to conclude, symbolism is a fundamental tendency of dreaming activity, it is inevitable that wish-dreams should sometimes take on a symbolic form. It is thus, for instance, that I interpret my dream of being in an English cathedral and seeing on the wall a notice to the effect that at evensong on such a day the edifice will not be illuminated, in order to avoid attracting moths ; I awake with a slight headache, and the un-illuminated cathedral was the symbol of the coolness and absence of glare which one desires when suffering from headache.

There cannot, also, be any doubt that erotic wishes frequently make themselves felt as dreams, both in the infantile and the symbolic form. It is sufficient to bring forward one illustration. It is furnished by a young lady of somewhat neurotic tendencies and heredity, aged twenty-three, musical and intelligent, who was in love with her music-master, the organist at her church. The dream was written down at the time. 'I was at the school of my childhood, and I was

---

[1] Laud, *Works*, vol. iii. p. 144.

told that I was St. Agnes Virgin and Martyr, and in five minutes' time I was to be beheaded with a large knife. The sheen of the blade frightened me so much that I asked if instead I might be strangled by the man I was in love with. Permission was given if I could induce him to come in time. I ran to our church (saying to myself that I knew it was a dream, but that I *must* see what he would say) over huge stones that cut my bare feet, and wondered what age I was living in, longing to meet some women in order to find out. When I did, they all wore crinolines. I rushed up the central aisle, which was full of people, thinking that, as I was going to be killed, nothing could matter. Mr. T. (the organist) was giving a choir practice in the vestry. I ran up to him and said : " Come at once, I am going to be killed." He became very angry, and said : " Do go away ; you are always interrupting my choir practice." I said : " Don't you understand ? I am going to be killed at once ; there is a knife hanging over my head, but I would rather be strangled by you, and they said I could if I fetched you in time." As soon as he understood that he came at once. Then it seemed in the dream that we were married, and had a son, who was to be a musical composer. I said I must say good-bye to this son first, and told the nurse to bring him to me. When he came I said : " Good-bye, I am going to be killed." He said, " Mother, am I a boy or a girl ? When I am with boys I don't seem like them, and they call me a girl, and yet I don't look like a girl." I replied : " You are both in one, because you are going

SYMBOLISM IN DREAMS 179

to be a perfect musical genius."' In this dream, which represents the fulfilment in sleep of an affection unsatisfied in life, we see side by side the infantile and the symbolic fulfilments of the erotic wish, culminating in a gifted musical child. The wish to be strangled is an undoubted erotic symbol,[1] and it is significant that in the course of the dream the accepted death by strangulation became fused with marriage, although the idea of death still inconsistently survives, doubtless because dream consciousness failed to realise that the accepted form of death was a subconsciously furnished symbol of the consummation of marriage.

The wish-dream of Freud's type has presented itself for consideration here, because it is a special and elaborate illustration of symbolism in dreaming. The important place of symbols in dreaming is by no means dependent on the validity of this particular type of dream, and we may now proceed to continue the discussion of the significance of the symbolic tendency during sleep in its most important form.

The symbols we have so far been mainly concerned with have been the result of a tendency of dreaming consciousness to objectify feelings and affections within the organism in concrete objects or processes outside the organism. In its complete form this symbolic tendency becomes the objectivation of part of the dreamer's feelings or personality in a distinct imaginary

[1] Havelock Ellis, *Studies in the Psychology of Sex*, vol. iii., 'Love and Pain.'

personality. A process of dramatisation occurs, and the dreamer finds himself in action and reaction, friendly or hostile or indifferent, with seemingly external personalities which, by the light of the analysis possible on awakening, are demonstrably created out of split-off portions of his own personality.[1] A common and simple form of such objectivation, closely allied to some of the symbolisms already brought forward, occurs when the dreamer sees the image of a person suffering from some affection of a part of the body and finds on awakening that he is himself experiencing pain or discomfort in that part. Thus a medical man dreams he is examining a tumour in a patient's groin, and on awakening finds slight irritation in the same region of his own body. And similarly, just as our bodily needs, when experienced during sleep, may be symbolised by inanimate natural objects and processes, so they may also become objective in the image of another person who is occupied in gratifying the need which we are ourselves unconsciously experiencing.

An interesting and significant group of cases is furnished by those dreams in which—as the result of some compression or effort—the tactile and muscular sensations of our own limbs are split off from sleeping consciousness and built up into an imaginary personality. Thus a medical friend, shortly after an attack of influenza, dreamed that in conversation with a lady patient his hand rested on her knee ; she requested him

---

[1] The dramatic element in dreaming was dealt with at length by Carl du Prel (*Philosophy of Mysticism*, vol. i. ch. iii.), but he threw little light on it.

to remove it, but his efforts to do so were fruitless, and he awoke in horror from this unprofessional situation to find that his hand was firmly clasped between his own knees. His body had thus been divided in dreaming consciousness between himself and an imaginary other person; the knee had become the other person's, while the hand remained his own, the hand being claimed in preference to the knee no doubt on account of its greater tactile sensibility and more complexly intimate association with the brain. In the hypnagogic (or hypnopompic) state such dream sensations may almost reach the intensity of hallucination. Thus, after an indigestible supper, I awake with the vivid feeling that some one is lying on me and attempting to drag off the bedclothes, and I find myself violently attempting, but apparently in vain, to articulate: 'Who is there?' In a dream of similar type, which occurred when lying on my back (and possibly with slight indigestion due to an unusually late dinner), I awoke making a kind of inarticulate exclamation which awakened my wife. I had dreamed that I was lying in bed, and that some unseen creature—more supernatural than human, it seemed—was violently dragging the bedclothes off me, while I shouted to it, very distinctly it seemed to me, 'Avaunt, avaunt!'

It is evident that my own sense of oppression, my own unconscious and involuntary movements in disturbing the bedclothes, were reconstructed by sleeping consciousness as the actions of an external person, in the second case, a supernatural creature, which, it is interesting to note, I duly accepted as such and addressed in the conventionally appropriate manner of old romance. The illusion may persist for some moments after waking. A lady, after breathing rather loudly and convulsively for a few seconds, wakes up, saying 'There is a rat or a mouse on the bed, shaking it up and down.' 'You were asleep,' her husband replied, 'as I knew by your breathing.' 'Oh, I was breathing like that,' she said, 'to make it jump off.' Here we see that, somewhat as in the previous cases, the dreamer's own muscular activity is, during sleep, reconstructed into the image of an external force ; but when she is in the semi-waking hypnagogic stage, she recognises that the activity was her own, though still unable to dismiss the delusion based on the theory formed during sleep.

At this point we reach the threshold of hallucination, and the next case to be brought forward may be said to lie on the threshold, for an impression received in the hypnagogic (or hypnopompic) stage is accepted in its illusional form, even when the dreamer is fully awake. A farmer's daughter—a bright girl of twenty-one, with quick nervous reactions, but untrained mind—dreamed that she saw her brother (dead some years previously) with blood streaming from his fingers. She awoke in a fright, and was comforting herself with the thought that it was only a dream when she felt a hand grip her shoulder three times in succession. There was no one in the room, the door was locked, and no explanation seemed possible to her. She was very frightened, got

SYMBOLISM IN DREAMS

up at once, dressed, and spent the rest of the night downstairs working. She was so convinced that a real hand had touched her that, although it seemed impossible, she asked her brothers if they had not been playing a trick on her. The nervous shock was considerable, and she was unable to sleep well for some weeks afterwards. She naturally knew nothing about abnormal psychic phenomena, and was utterly puzzled to explain the experience, except by supposing that it may have been a ghost. The explanation is really very simple. It is well recognised that involuntary muscular twitches may occur in the shoulder, especially after it has been subjected to pressure, and that in some cases such contractions may simulate a touch.[1] The dream of a bleeding hand indicates, when we bear in mind the tendency to objectify sensations symbolically, now familiar to us in dreaming, that the dreamer's arm was probably pressed beneath her in a cramped position.[2] This pressure would account, not only for the dream, but

[1] Thus in the Psychical Research Society's 'Report on the *Census of Hallucinations*,' the case is given of an over-worked and worried man who, a few moments after leaving a tram car, had the vivid feeling that some one touched him on the shoulder, though on turning round he found no one near. He then remembered that on the car he had been leaning against an iron bolt, and that, therefore, what he had experienced was doubtless a spontaneous muscular contraction excited by the pressure (*Proceedings, Society for Psychical Research*, August 1894, p. 3). Touches felt on awakening, in correspondence with a dream, are not so very uncommon. Thus Wagner, when in love with Mathilde Wesendonk, wrote, in the private diary he kept for her, how, after a dream, 'as I awoke I distinctly felt a kiss on my brow.'

[2] Various pressures lead to dreams of blood. Thus a friend with a weak heart tells me that when he sleeps on his left side he dreams of blood. In some of these cases it is possible that there are retinal sensations of red.

for the muscular twitches occurring on awakening. The nature of the dream, the terrified emotional state it produced, and the mental obscurity of the hypnagogic state, naturally combined, in a subject unaccustomed to self-analysis, to create an illusion which reflection is unable to dispel, though in the normal waking state she would probably have given no attention at all to such muscular twitches. Strictly speaking, such an experience is an illusion—that is to say, a misinterpretation of a real sensation—and not a hallucination—or perception without known objective causation—but there is no clear line of demarcation. In any case it may now be taken as proved that hallucinations tend to occur in the neighbourhood of sleep, and therefore to partake of the nature of dreams.[1]

So far we have been concerned with the tendency in dreams to objectify portions of the body by constructing out of them new personalities. But precisely the same process goes on in sleep with regard to our thoughts and feelings. We split off portions of these also and construct other personalities out of them, and sometimes even endow the persons thus formed with thoughts and feelings more native to our own normal personality than those which we reserve for ourselves. Thus a lady who dreamed that when walking with a friend she discovered a species of animal fruit, a kind of

[1] In the *Census of Hallucinations* (chapter ix.) it was pointed out by the Psychical Research Society's Committee that hallucinations are specially apt to occur on awakening, or in the state between sleeping and waking; and Parish in his very searching study, *Hallucinations and Illusions* (Contemporary Science Series), has further developed this fact and insisted on its significance.

SYMBOLISM IN DREAMS

damson containing a snail, expressed her delight at finding a combination so admirably adapted to culinary purposes ; it was the friend who, retaining the attitude of her own waking moments, uttered an exclamation of disgust. Most of the dreams in which there is any dramatic element are due to this splitting up of personality ; in our dreams we may experience shame or confusion from the rebukes or the arguments of other persons, but the persons who administer the rebuke or apply the argument are still ourselves.[1]

Some writers on dreaming have marvelled greatly at this tendency of the sleeping mind to objectify portions of itself, and so to create imaginary personalities and evolve dramatic situations. It has seemed to them quite unaccountable except as the outcome of a special gift of imagination appertaining to sleep. Yet, remarkable as it is, this process is simply the inevitable outcome of the conditions under which psychic life exists during sleep. If we realise that a more or less pronounced degree of dissociation of the contents of the mind occurs during sleep, and if we also realise that, sleeping fully as much as waking, mind is a thing that instinctively reasons, and cannot refrain from building up hypotheses, then we may easily see how the personages and situations of dreams develop. Much the

---

[1] Dr. Johnson's remark on this point has often been quoted. He dreamed that he had been worsted in a verbal argument, and was thereby much mortified. 'Had not my judgment failed me,' he said, 'I should have seen that the wit of this supposed antagonist, by whose superiority I felt myself depressed, was as much furnished by me as that which I thought I had been uttering in my own character' (Boswell's *Johnson*, ed. by Hill, vol. iv. p. 5).

same process might, under some circumstances, occur in waking life. If, for instance, we heard an unknown voice speaking behind a curtain, we could not fail to build up an imaginary person in connection with that voice, the characteristics of the imaginary person being largely determined by the nature of the voice and of the things it uttered ; it would, further, be quite easy to enter into conversation with the person we had thus constructed. That is what seems to occur in dreams. We hear a voice behind the curtain of darkness, and to fit that voice and the things it utters we instinctively form a picture which, in virtue of the hallucinatory aptitude of sleep, is thrown against the curtain ; it is then quite easy to enter into conversation with the person we have thus constructed. It no more occurs to us during sleep to suppose that the voice we hear is only a voice and nothing more, than it would occur to us awake to suppose that the voice behind the curtain is only a voice and nothing more. The process is the same ; the difference is that in dreams we are, without knowing it, living among what from the waking point of view are called hallucinations.

This process by which dreams are formed in sleeping consciousness through the splitting of the dreamer's personality for the construction of other personalities has been recognised ever since dreams began to be seriously studied. Maury referred to the scission of personality in dreams.[1] Delboeuf dealt with what he termed the altruising by the dreamer of part of his

[1] Maury, *Le Sommeil et les Rêves*, 1861, p. 118.

representations.[1] Foucault terms the same process personalisation.[2] Giessler attempts elaborately to explain the enigma of self-diremption—the formation of a secondary self—in dreams; if, he argues, a touch or other sensation exceeds the dream-body's capacity of adaptation—*i.e.*, if the state of stimulus is above the apperceptive threshold—only one part of the perception is referred to the dream-body and the other is transferred to a secondary self.[3] This explanation, while it very fairly covers the presentative class of dreams, directly connected with sensory stimuli, cannot so easily be applied to the dramatisation of our representative dreams, which are not obviously traceable to direct bodily stimulation.

The splitting up of personality is indeed a very pronounced and widely extended tendency of the mind, and has, during recent years, been elaborately studied. We thus have the basis of that psychic phenomenon which is variously termed secondary personality, double personality, duplex personality, multiple personality, alternation of personality, etc.,[4] and in earlier ages was regarded as due to possession by demons. Such conditions seem to be usually associated with hysteria.

[1] Delbœuf, *Le Sommeil et les Rêves*, pp. 24, *et seq.*
[2] Foucault, *Le Rêve*, p. 137.
[3] Giessler, 'Das Ich im Träume,' *Zeitschrift für Psychologie und Physiologie der Sinnesorgane*, 1905, Heft 4 and 5, pp. 300 *et seq.*
[4] See especially Pierre Janet's works, and also those of Morton Prince, Albert Wilson, etc. Flournoy's very elaborate study of Mlle. Helène Smith (*Des Indes à la Planète Mars*, 1900) is noteworthy. A summary of some important cases of multiple personality will be found in Marie de Manacéïne's *Sleep*, pp. 127 *et seq.*, and some bibliographical references, *ib.* p. 151.

The essential fact about hysteria is, according to Janet, its lack of synthetising power, which is at the same time a lack of attention and of apperception, and has as its result a disintegration of the field of consciousness into mutually exclusive parts; that is to say, there is a process of dissociation. Now that is a condition resembling, as we have seen, the condition found in dreaming. It is not, therefore, difficult to accept the view of Sollier and others, that hysteria is a condition allied to sleep, a condition of vigilambulism in which the patients are often unable to obtain normal sleep, simply because they are all the time in a state of abnormal sleep; as one said to Sollier : ' I cannot sleep because I am asleep all the time.' It may thus be the case that hysterical multiple personalities[1] furnish a pathological analogue of that tendency to the dramatic objectivation of portions of our personality which is normal and healthy in dreams.

Similarly in insanity we have an even more constant and pronounced tendency for the subject to attribute his own sensations to imaginary individuals, and to create personalities out of portions of the real personality. All the illusions, delusions, and hallucinations of the insane are merely the manifold manifestations of this tendency. Without it the insanity would not exist. It is not because he is subjected to unusual sensations — visionary, auditory, tactile, olfactory, visceral, etc.—that a man is insane. It is because he

---

[1] J. Milne Bramwell argues ('Secondary and Multiple Personalities,' *Brain*, 1900) that such cases are not invariably hysterical.

SYMBOLISM IN DREAMS

creates imaginary personalities to account for these sensations; if his food tastes strange some one has given him posion; if he hears a strange voice it is some one communicating with him by telephones or microphones or hypnotism; if he feels a strange internal sensation it is perhaps because he has another person inside him. The case has even been recorded of a man who attributed any feeling he experienced, even the most normal sensations of hunger and thirst, to the people around him. It is exactly the same process as goes on in our dreams. The sane man, the normal waking man, may experience all these strange sensations, but he recognises that they are the spontaneous outcome of his own organisation.

We may, however, advance a step beyond this position. This self-objectivation, this dramatisation of our experiences, is not confined to sleep and to pathological conditions which resemble sleep. It is natural and primitive in a far wider sense. The infant will gaze inquisitively at its own feet, watch their movements, play with them, ' punish ' them; consciousness has not absorbed them as part of the self.[1] The infant really acts and feels towards the remote parts of his own body as the adult acts and feels in dreaming. We are reminded of the generalisation of Giessler that dream consciousness corresponds to the

---

[1] See G. Stanley Hall, ' The Early Sense of Self,' *American Journal of Psychology*, April 1898. Cooley ('The Early Use of Self-Words by a Child,' *Psychological Review*, 1909, p. 94) finds that the child distinguishes between itself as (1) body and as (2) self-assertion united with action; it refers to the former as ' Baby,' and to the latter as ' I.'

normal psychic state in childhood, while sleeping subconsciousness corresponds to the embryonic psychic state ; so that the dream state represents the renascence of the ego disentangling itself from the impersonal sensations and indistinct images of the embryonic stage of life. That sleeping consciousness is the primitive embryonic consciousness is, indeed, indicated, it has often seemed to me, by the fact that in many animals the embryonic position is the position of rest and sleep. Ducklings and chicks in the shell have their heads beneath their wing. The dog lies with his feet together, head flexed, and hind-quarters drawn up. Man, alike in the womb and asleep, tends to be curled up, with the flexors predominating over the extensors.

The savage has gone beyond the infant in ability to assimilate the impressions of his own limbs, but on the psychic side he still constantly tends to objectify his own feelings and ideas, re-creating them as external beings. Primitive man has done so from the first, and this impulse has struck its roots into all our most fundamental human traditions even as they survive in civilisation to-day. The man of the early world moves, like the dreamer, among a sea of emotions and ideas which he cannot recognise the origin of, and, like the dreamer, he instinctively dramatises them. But, unlike the dreamer, he gives stability to the images he has thus created and in good faith mistaken for independent beings. Thus we have the animistic stages of culture, and early man peoples his world with gods and spirits and demons and fairies and ghosts

SYMBOLISM IN DREAMS

which enter into the traditions of his race, and are more or less accepted even by a later race which no longer creates them for itself.

In our more advanced civilisations we are still struggling with later forms of that Protean tendency to objectify the self and to animate the things and even the people around us with our own spirit. The impatient and imperfectly bred child, or even man, kicks viciously the object he stumbles against, animate or inanimate, in order to revenge a wrong which exists only in himself. On a slightly higher plane, the men of mediæval times brought actions in the law courts against offending animals and solemnly pronounced sentence against them as 'criminals,'[1] while even to-day society still 'punishes' the human criminal because it has imaginatively re-created him in the image of an ordinary normal person, and lacks the intelligence to perceive that he has been moulded by the laws of his nature and environment into a creature which we do well to protect ourselves against, but have no right to 'punish.'[2] Everywhere we still see around us the

[1] See, *e.g.*, Havelock Ellis, *The Criminal*, 4th ed., 1910, p. 367.
[2] In the existing traditions of law and police, it is still possible to find many survivals of this tendency to objectify subjective impressions. Thus Mr. Theodore Schroeder has shown (*Free Press Anthology*, 1909, pp. 171 *et seq.*) that the prosecutions which have in various so-called civilised countries pursued many estimable and even noble works of literature, science, and art are based on the primitive notion that 'indecency' resides in the object and not in the person who experiences the feeling, and who ought, therefore, alone to be suppressed, if suppression is called for. This psychological fallacy continues to subsist, though it was unmasked in the clearest manner even by St. Paul (*e.g.* Romans xiv. 14). It is somewhat analogous to the mediæval conception of the criminality of animals.

surviving relics of this primitive tendency of men to project their own personalities into external objects. A fine civilisation lies largely in the due subordination of this tendency, in the realisation and control of our own emotional possibilities, and in the resultant growth of personal responsibility.

It is thus impossible to over-estimate the immense importance of the primitive symbolic tendency to objectify the subjective. Men have taken out of their own hearts their best feelings and their worst feelings, and have personalised and dramatised them, bowed down to them or stamped on them, unable to hear the voice with which each of their images spoke : ' I am thyself.' Our conceptions of religion, of morals, of many of the mightiest phenomena of life, especially the more exceptional phenomena, have grown up under this influence, which still serves to support many movements of to-day by some people imagined to be modern.

Dreaming, as we have seen, is not tne sole source of such conceptions. But they could scarcely have been found convincing, and possibly could not even have arisen, among races which were wholly devoid of dream experiences. A large part of all progress in psychological knowledge, and, indeed, a large part of civilisation itself, lies in realising that the apparently objective is really subjective, that the angels and demons and geniuses of all sorts that once seemed to be external forces taking possession of feeble and vacant individualities are themselves but modes of action of marvellously rich and varied personalities. In our dreams we are brought back into the magic circle of early culture, and we shrink and shudder in the presence of imaginative phantoms that are built up of our own thoughts and emotions, and are really our own flesh.

CHAPTER VIII

DREAMS OF THE DEAD

Mental Dissociation during Sleep—Illustrated by the Dream of Returning to School Life—The Typical Dream of a Dead Friend—Examples — Early Records of this Type of Dream — Analysis of such Dreams—Atypical Forms—The Consolation sometimes afforded by Dreams of the Dead—Ancient Legends of this Dream Type—The Influence of Dreams on the Belief of Primitive Man in the Survival of the Dead.

OUR memories tend to fall into groups or systems. We all possess a great number of such systematised groups of impressions. Every period of life, every subject we have occupied ourselves with, every intimate friend we have had, each represents a more or less separate mass of ideas and feelings. Within each system one idea or feeling easily calls up another belonging to the same system. Moreover, in full and alert waking life, each system is in touch with the systems related to it. If there crowd into the field of consciousness the memories belonging to one period of life, or one country we have lived in, we can control and criticise those memories by reference to others belonging to another period or another country. If we are overwhelmed by the thoughts and emotions associated with the memory of one friend we can restore our mental balance by evoking the thoughts and emotions associated with another friend. The various systems are in this way co-ordinated in apperception.[1]

In sleep, however, these groups are not usually so firmly held together by the cords along which we can move in our waking moments from one to the other. They are, as it were, loosened from their moorings, and on the sea of sleeping consciousness they drift apart or jostle together in new and what seem to be random associations. This is that process of dissociation which we find so marked in dreaming, and in all those psychic phenomena—hallucinations, hysteria, multiple personality, insanity—which are allied to dreaming.

A simple illustration of the clash and confusion of two opposing systems of memories in dreams, when due apperceptive control is lacking, is supplied by a common and well-recognised type of dream, the dream of returning to the school of youth.[2] Many people are occasionally liable to this dream, which is often vivid and disturbing. We may have left the schoolroom thirty years or more ago, and never seen it since; it may have vanished from our waking thoughts. Yet from time to time we find ourselves there in our dreams,

---

[1] I may refer to the very interesting discussion by Professor G. F. Stout (*Analytic Psychology*, vol. ii. p. 145) of the conflict of systems in apperception, and of the suspense and deadlock which occur when two or more systems come into conflict in such a way that the success of one is the defeat of the other. The discussion is full of interest from its undesigned bearing on the phenomena of dreaming.

[2] Foucault, for instance (*Le Rêve*, p. 25), discusses and illustrates dreams of this type. I am not here concerned with the causation of this type of dream. Perhaps, as Wundt believes, it is due to some physical discomfort of the sleeper, such as a cramped position, expressing itself symbolically.

and called upon to take our old place, always with a sense of conflict, a vague discomfort, a feeling of something incongruous and humiliating, for we realise that we are now too old. Here is a dream in illustration : I find myself back at my old school, but my old schoolmaster is not there ; he is away ill, as I am told by his substitute, whose face somehow seems familiar, though I cannot recall where I have seen it. I do not know any of the boys ; I am returning after an absence of some months. I realise that I am to take my old place again, and yet I feel a profound repulsion to do so, a sense that it is somehow incongruous. This latter feeling seems to prevail, for I finally assume the part of a visitor, and remark, insincerely, to the master that it is pleasant to see the old place again.

In such a case as this it seems that a picture from an ancient system of memories floats across the field of sleeping consciousness, and the dreamer is naturally drawn into that system and begins to adapt himself to its demands. But, as he does so, the influence of other later and incompatible systems of memories begins unconsciously to affect the dreamer.[1] The cords of connection, however, which when awake would enable him to adjust critically the opposing systems, are not acting ; apperception is defective. Yet the opposing systems are there, outside the immediate

---

[1] It may be added that dreams of returning to the school scenes of early life are not necessarily always of the type here described, as may be illustrated by the dream already brought forward on p. 83, which, it is worth while noticing, occurred after a day on which I had been thinking over the dreams of this class.

field of consciousness, and jostling the ancient system which has come into the central focus. Finally this jostling of the ancient system by more recent systems causes a harmonising modification in consciousness. The dreamer ceases to be a boy in his old school, and assumes the part of a visitor.

Dreams of our recently dead friends furnish a type of dream which is formed in exactly the same way as these dreams of a return to school life. The only difference is that they often present it in a more vivid, pronounced, and poignantly emotional shape. This is so, partly from the very subject of such dreams, and partly because the fact of death definitely divides our impressions of our dead friends into two groups, which are intimately allied to each other by their subject, and yet absolutely opposed by the fact that in the one group the friend is alive, and in the other dead.

I proceed to present two series of dreams—one in a man, the other in a woman—illustrating this type of dream.[1]

Observation I.—Mr. C., age about twenty-eight, a man of scientific training and aptitudes. Shortly after his mother's death he repeatedly dreamed that she had come to life again. She had been buried, but it was somehow found out that she was not really dead. Mr. C. describes the painful intellectual struggles that went on in these dreams, the arguments in favour of

[1] I reproduce these two series in the same form as first published (Havelock Ellis, 'On Dreaming of the Dead,' *Psychological Review*, September 1895) since they have formed the starting point of my own and others' investigation into this type of dream.

death from the impossibility of prolonged life in the grave, and how these doubts were finally swallowed up in a sense of wonder and joy because his mother was actually there, alive, in his dream.

These dreams became less frequent as time went on, but some years later occurred an isolated dream which clearly shows a further stage in the same process. Mr. C. dreamed that his father had just returned home, and that he (the dreamer) was puzzled to make out where his mother was. After puzzling a long time he asked his sister, but at the very moment he asked it flashed upon him—more, he thinks, with a feeling of relief at the solution of a painful difficulty than with grief—that his mother was dead.

Observation II.—Mrs. F., age about thirty, highly intelligent but of somewhat emotional temperament. A week after the death of a lifelong friend to whom she was greatly attached, Mrs. F. dreamed for the first time of her friend, finding that she was alive, and then in the course of the dream discovering that she had been buried alive.

A second dream occurred on the following night. Mrs. F. imagined that she went to see her friend, whom she found in bed, and to whom she told the strange things that she had heard (*i.e.*, that the friend was dead). Her friend then gave Mrs. F. a few things as souvenirs. But on leaving the room Mrs. F. was told that her friend was really dead, and had spoken to her after death.

In a fourth dream, at a subsequent date, Mrs. F. imagined that her friend came to her, saying that she had returned to earth for a few minutes to give her messages and to assure her that she was happy in another world and in the enjoyment of the fullest life.

Another dream occurred more than a year later. Some one brought to Mrs. F., in her dream, the news that her friend was still alive; she was taken to her and found her as in life. The friend said she had been away, but did not explain where or why she had been supposed dead. Mrs. F. asked no questions and felt no curiosity, being absorbed in the joy of finding her friend still alive, and they proceeded to talk over the things that had happened since they last met. It was a very vivid, natural, and detailed dream, and on awaking Mrs. F. felt somewhat exhausted. Although not superstitious, the dream gave her a feeling of consolation.

The next series has been observed more recently. I include all the dreams and the intervals at which they occurred. The somewhat unexpected news reached me of the death of a near and lifelong friend when I was myself recovering from an attack of influenza. No dream which could be connected with this event occurred until about a fortnight later[1] (16th January).

---

[1] It is well known, and has often been pointed out (by Weygandt, Sante de Sanctis, Jewell, etc., and perhaps first by T. Beddoes in his *Hygeia*, 1803, vol. iii. p. 88), that while in childhood all the emotions of the past day are at once echoed in dreams, after adolescence, this is not so in the case of intense emotions, which do not emerge in dreams until after a more or less considerable interval. Marie de Manacéïne and Sante de Sanctis attribute this to exhaustion of the emotion which needs a period of repair and organic synthesis before it can repeat itself. Vaschide believed that we dream of recent events in shallow sleep and of remote events in deep sleep; this sounds plausible, but will scarcely account for all the phenomena.

I then dreamed that I was with my friend and asking him (he had been a clergyman and Biblical scholar) whether, in his opinion, Jesus had been able to speak Greek. I awoke before I received his answer, but no sort of doubt, hesitation, or surprise was aroused by his appearance alive.

Nineteen days later (4th February) occurred the next dream. This time I dreamed that my friend was just dead, and that I was gazing at a postcard of good wishes, written partly in Latin, which he had sent me a few days before (on the actual date of my birthday), and regretting that I had not answered it. There was no doubt in my mind as to the fact of his death. (I may remark that the last letter I had written to my friend was on his birthday, and he had been unable to reply, so that there was here one of those reversals which Freud and others have noted as not uncommon in dreams.)

The next dream occurred thirty-four days later (10th March). I thought that I met my friend, and at once realised that it was not he but his wife who had died, and I clasped his hand sympathetically.

Some months later (27th July) I again dreamed that I was walking with my friend and talking, as we might have talked, on topics of common interest. But at the same time I knew, and he knew that I knew, that he was to die on the morrow.

Once more, a fortnight later (10th August), I dreamed that I had an appointment to meet my friend in a certain road, but he failed to appear. I began to wonder whether he had forgotten the appointment, or I had made a mistake, and I was seeking for the letter making the appointment when I awoke.

It would appear that the dreams of this type are less pronounced in the ratio of the less pronounced affectional intensity of the relationship which unites the friends. The next dream concerned a man for whom I had the highest esteem and regard, but had not been intimately associated with. I dreamed that I saw this friend, who was the editor of a psychological journal, alive and well in his room, together with two foreign psychologists also known to me, who had apparently succeeded him in the editorship of the journal, for I saw their names on the title-page of a number of it which was put in my hands. It surprised me that, though alive and well, he should have ceased to edit the journal ; the theory by which I satisfactorily accounted to myself for his appearance was that, though he had been so near death that his life was despaired of, he had not actually died ; his death had been prematurely reported. It flashed across my dream consciousness, indeed, that I had read obituaries of my friend in the papers, but this reminiscence merely suggested the reflection that some one had been guilty of a grave indiscretion.[1]

[1] Since the publication of my paper 'On Dreaming of the Dead,' several psychologists have returned to the subject. Thus Binet (*L'Année Psychologique*, 2nd year, issued in 1896, p. 848) gave a dream of his own, very similar to mine of the editor, in which a doctor, dead a month previously, is talking to him in his room. On Binet expressing surprise at seeing him, the doctor explains that he had only sent news of his death in order to see how many people would come to his funeral. Binet has also had

Although no attempt had been made to analyse this type of dream before 1895, the dream itself had often been noted down, as from its poignant and affecting character it could not fail to be. An early example is furnished by the philosopher Gassendi, who states that he dreamed he met a friend, that he greeted him as one returned from the dead, and that then, saying to himself in his dream that this was impossible, he concluded that he must be dreaming.[1] Pepys, again, in his *Diary*, on the 29th June 1667, a few months after his mother's death, dreamed that ' my mother told me she lacked a pair of gloves, and I remembered a pair of my wife's in my chamber, and resolved she should have them, but then recollected [reflected] how my mother came to be here when I was in mourning for her, and so thinking it to be a mistake in our thinking her all this while dead, I did contrive that it should be said to any that in-

two dreams, similar to that described on p. 200, in which he is walking in the country with a dead friend, who seems in good health, though the dreamer knows he will soon die. Foucault (*Le Rêve*, p. 128), who, in accordance with his own theory, regards my dream of the editor as belonging to the period of awakening, brings forward a dream of his own in which he saw his father, dead six months before, sitting in a chair; at first this seems to him a hallucination, but he finally accepts the vision as real. I have had a number of letters from people who have had dreams of this type. One correspondent, an anthropologist and folk-lorist of note, says that his dreams of dead friends are of the type of Mrs. F.'s. Professor Näcke writes that he has had such dreams (and see also his articles in the *Archiv für Kriminalanthropologie*, 1903, p. 307, and the *Neurologisches Centralblatt*, 1910, No. 13). One young lady states that, thirteen years after her mother's death, she still dreams of her as coming to life again or never having really died. I may add that this type of dream is admirably illustrated in a series of dreams concerning a dead friend, published in a letter from a lady to *Borderland*, January 1896, p. 51.

[1] Gassendi, *Syntagma Philosophicum*, 1658, pars. 71, lib. viii. (*Opera Omnia*, vol. i.).

quired that it was my mother-in-law, my wife's mother, that was dead, and we in mourning for.' This dream, Pepys adds, 'did trouble me mightily.' Edmond de Goncourt, in his *Journal* (27th July 1870), well describes how in the first dream of the dead brother to whom he was so tenderly attached, the two streams of memories appeared. He dreamed he was walking with his brother, but at the same time he knew he was in mourning for him, and friends were coming up to offer condolences; the emotions caused by the conflict of these two certainties — his brother's life affirmed by his presence and his death affirmed by all the other circumstances of the dream—was profoundly distressing. A few years earlier Renan, when his dearly loved sister Henrietta died by his side in the Lebanon, also had dreams of this type, which deeply affected even his cautious and sceptical nature. She had died of Syrian fever, from which he also was suffering, and shortly afterwards he wrote in a letter that 'in feverish dreams a terrible doubt has risen up before me; I have fancied I heard her voice calling to me from the vault where she was laid.' He comforted himself, however, with the thought that this horrible supposition was unjustified, since French doctors had been present at her death. Maury also mentions that he had often had dreams of this type in which the dead appeared as living, though the sight of them always produced astonishment and doubt which the sleeping brain endeavoured to allay by some kind of explanation. Beaunis also describes

[1] Maury, *Le Sommeil et les Rêves*, p. 145.

how he has dreamed with surprise of meeting a friend whom even in his dream he knew to be dead.[1]

It is not difficult, in the light of all that we have been able to learn regarding the psychology of the world of dreams, to account for the process here described, for its frequency, and for its poignant emotional effects. This dream type is only a special variety of the commonest species of dream, in which two or more groups of reminiscences flow together and form a single bizarre congruity, a *confusion* in the strict sense of the word. The death of a friend sets up a barrier which cuts into two the stream of impressions concerning that friend. Thus, two streams of images flow into sleeping consciousness, one representing the friend as alive, the other as dead. The first stream comes from older and richer sources; the second is more poignant, but also more recent and more easily exhausted. The two streams break against each other in restless conflict, both, from the inevitable conditions of dream life, being accepted as true, and they eventually mix to form an absurd harmony, in which the older and stronger images (in accordance with that recognised tendency for old psychic impressions generally to be most stable) predominate over those that are more recent. Thus, in the first observation the dreamer seems to have begun his dream by imagining that his mother was alive as of old; then his more recent experiences interfered with the assertion of her death. This resulted in a struggle between the old-established

[1] *American Journal of Psychology*, July–October, 1903, p. 18.

images representing her as alive and the later ones representing her as dead. The idea that she had come to life again was evidently a theory that had arisen in his brain to harmonise these two opposing currents. The theory was not accepted easily; all sorts of scientific objections arose to oppose it, but there could be no doubt, for his mother was there. The dreamer is in the same position as a paranoiac who constantly seems to hear threatening voices; henceforth he is absorbed in inventing a theory (electricity, hypnotism, or whatever it may be) to account for his hallucinations, and his whole view of life is modified accordingly. The dreamer, in the cases I am here concerned with, sees an image of the dead person as alive, and is therefore compelled to invent a theory to account for this image; the theories that most easily suggest themselves are either that the dead person has never really died, or else that he has come back from the dead for a brief space. The mental and emotional conflict which such dreams involve renders them very vivid. They make a profound impression even after awakening, and for some sensitive persons are almost too sacred to speak of.

When a series of these dreams occurs concerning the same dead friend the tendency seems to be, on the whole—though there are certainly many exceptions—for the living reality of the vision of the dead friend to be more and more positively affirmed. Whether awake or asleep, it is very difficult for us to resist the evidence of our senses. It is even more difficult asleep than awake, for, as we have seen reason to believe, apperception, with the critical control it involves, is weakened. Just as the savage or the child accepts as a reality the illusion of the sun traversing the sky, just as the paranoiac accepts the reality of the hallucinations he is subjected to, and gradually weaves them into a more or less plausible theory, so the dreamer seems to employ all the acutest powers of sleeping reason available to construct a theory in support of the reality of the visions of his dead friend.

Sometimes atypical dreams of the dead occur in which even from the first there appears little clash or doubt. When the vision can thus easily be accepted, it is sometimes a source of consolation, joy, and even religious faith which may still persist in the waking state. Chabaneix has, for instance, recorded the dream experiences of a poet and philosopher who had been deeply attached to a woman with whom his relations were both passionate and intellectual. From the night after her death onwards, at intervals, he had dreams of the beloved woman, at first appearing as a floating vision, later as a vividly seen and tangible person; these dreams caused refreshment and mental invigoration, and seemed to bring the dreamer into renewed communication with his dead friend.[1]

I am indebted to a clergyman for the record of a

---

[1] Chabaneix, *Le Subconscient chez les Artistes, les Savants et les Ecrivains*, 1897, pp. 45-8. Chabaneix was in touch with various persons of distinction, and one is inclined to identify the poet-philosopher with Sully-Prudhomme, at that time still living. Du Maurier's remarkable novel, *Peter Ibbetson*—which records similar serial dreams of union with a beloved woman after death, and seems to be based on real experience—may also be mentioned in this connection.

somewhat similar experience. 'A close friendship,' he writes, 'once existed between myself and a lady, somewhat older, and of a religious temperament. We often discussed the life beyond the grave, and agreed that if she died first, and this appeared more than probable, as she was the victim of a mortal disease, she would appear to me. I may add that she was of a highly-strung and nervous nature, and though purely English had many of the psychic characteristics of the Celt. After her death, I looked for some appearance or manifestation, and about three days after dreamed that she had come back to me, and was discussing with me a matter which I much wished to speak about before her death, but was unable to, owing to her weakness and the presence of strangers. In the dream it was perfectly clear to me that she was a dead woman back from another sphere of existence. For some weeks after this I had similar experiences. They were never dreams of the old life and friendship before death, but always reappearances from the other world. Of course it may be said of this experience of mine, that it was merely the result of expectation. But I have found that the things most on my mind are rarely the subject of my dreams. Moreover, these dreams formed a series, lasting for weeks, and all of the same character, though the conversations differed.'

When a dreamer awakes in an emotional state which corresponds to a dream he has just experienced, it is usually a safe assumption that the dream was the result, and not the cause, of the emotional state. That is by no means always the case, however, and in the type of dream we are here concerned with it is rarely the case. Even though it may be quite true that an emotional state evoked the dream, it is equally true that in its turn the dream itself may arouse an emotional state. The dream of encountering a celestial visitant, especially if the visitant is a beloved friend, cannot fail to produce an especial effect of this kind. It is noteworthy that the emotional influence may be present even when the fact of dreaming has not been recalled. Thus a lady who, on waking in the morning could not remember having dreamed, realised during the day that she was feeling as she was accustomed to feel after dreaming of a beloved friend, and was ultimately able to recall fragments of the dream.[1] A man of so great an intellect as Goethe has borne witness to the consoling influence of dreams. 'I have had times in my life,' he said, in old age, to Eckermann, ' when I have fallen asleep in tears, but in my dreams the loveliest figures come to give me comfort and happiness, and I awake next morning once more fresh and cheerful.' [2]

[1] Unconscious dream suggestions of this kind resemble, as R. MacDougall has remarked (*Psychological Review*, March 1898, p. 167), post-hypnotic suggestions.

[2] This type of dream—in which the emotion of the day is inverted in sleep, depressing emotions giving place to exalting emotions, and so on— is by some (Griesinger, Lombroso, Sante de Sanctis, etc.), termed the contrast-dream. The dream is in such a case, Sante de Sanctis remarks, complementary, having the same significance as a complementary after-image and indicating a phase of anabolic repair. Thus A. Wiggam (*Pedagogical Seminary*, June 1909), gives the case of a girl of twenty, who when tired and restless always has good dreams, while her dreams are bad when she is well and free from care. It should be added that, as understood by Näcke (' Ueber Kontrast-Träume' *Archiv für Kriminalanthropologie*,

If we take a wide sweep we shall find in many parts of the world stories and legends concerning the relationship of the living with the dead which have a singular resemblance with the typical dream of the dead here investigated. Thus, in Japan, it appears that stories of the returning of the dead are very common. Lafcadio Hearn reproduces one, as told by a Japanese, which closely resembles some of the dreams we have met with. 'A lover resolved to commit suicide on the grave of his sweetheart. He found her tomb and knelt before it, and prayed and wept, and whispered to her that which he was about to do. And suddenly he heard her voice cry to him "Anata!" and felt her hand upon his hand: and he turned and saw her kneeling beside him, smiling and beautiful as he remembered her, only a little pale. Then his heart leaped so that he could not speak for the wonder and the doubt and the joy of that moment. But she said, "Do not doubt; it is really I. I am not dead. It was all a mistake. I was buried because my parents thought me dead—buried too soon. Yet you see I am not dead, not a ghost. It is I; do not doubt it!"' It is perhaps worth mentioning that the incident told in the Fourth Gospel (xx. 11-18) as

---

1907), a contrast-dream is one that is in striking contrast to the dreamer's ordinary character. In this type of contrast-dream it is not quite clear that the mechanism is the same, and the contrast may sometimes be accidental. Thus a dream of being a soldier on a battlefield, with shells bursting around me, was merely suggested by a passage of Nietzsche, read in the evening, which contained the words 'the thunders of the battle of Wörth,' and the question of contrast or resemblance to my character and habits was irrelevant.

occurring to Mary Magdalene when at the tomb of Jesus, recalls the dream process of fusion of images. She turns and sees, as she thinks, the gardener, but in the course of conversation it flashes on her that he is Jesus, risen from the tomb. In quite another part of the world the Salish Indians of British Columbia have a story of a man who goes back to the spirit-world to reclaim his lost wife ; this can only be done under special conditions, and for some time refraining to touch her ; if he breaks these conditions she vanishes in his arms, and he is left alone.[1] That story, again, cannot fail to remind us of the almost identical Greek legend of the return of Orpheus to the under-world to reclaim his dead wife Eurydice. If these myths and legends were not directly based on the dream-process, it can only be on the ground, alleged with some force by Freud's school, that myths and legends themselves develop by means of the same mechanism as dreams.

The probable influence of dreams in originating or confirming the primitive belief of men in a spirit world has often been set forth. Herbert Spencer attached great importance to this factor in the constitution of the belief in another world, in spirits and in gods.[2] Wundt even considers that such dreams furnish the whole origin of animism. Other writers, less closely associ-

[1] *Journal of the Anthropological Institute*, July–December 1904, p. 339.
[2] See Herbert Spencer, *Principles of Sociology*, 3rd ed., 1885, vol. i. ch. x., especially pp. 140, 182, 201, 772. Spencer believed that Lubbock was the first to point out this factor in primitive beliefs, which has been chiefly developed by Tylor. It is, of course, by no means the only factor. See *post*, p. 266.

DREAMS OF THE DEAD

ated with anthropological psychology, have argued in the same sense.[1]

But while these thinkers have in some cases specifically referred to dreams of the dead, and not merely to the widespread belief of savages that in sleep the soul leaves the body to wander over the earth, they have never realised that there is a special mechanism in the typical dream of a dead friend, due to mental dissociation during sleep, which powerfully suggests to us that death sets up no fatal barrier to the return of the dead. In dreams the dead are thus rendered indestructible ; they cannot be finally killed, but rather tend to reappear in ever more clearly affirmed vitality. Dreams of this sort must certainly have come to men ever since men began to be. If their emotional effects are great to-day, we can well believe that they were much greater in the early days when dream life and what we call real life were less easily distinguished. The repercussion of this kind of dream through unmeasured ages cannot fail to have told at last on the traditions of the race.

[1] Thus Professor Beaunis (*loc. cit.*) considers that dreams furnish the only rational explanation of the belief in survival after death. Jewell, again (*American Journal of Psychology*, January 1905), also considers that dreams are responsible for primitive man's inability to conceive of death as ending our association with our friends ; he brings forward evidence, highly significant in this connection, to show that children, on dreaming of the dead as alive, are influenced in waking life to doubt the reality of their death. Ruths, also writing since the publication of my first paper (*Experimental-Untersuchungen über Musikphantome*, 1898, pp. 438 *et seq.*), considers that the conception of an under-world is founded on dreams of the dead coming to life.

CHAPTER IX

MEMORY IN DREAMS

The Apparent Rapidity of Thought in Dreams—This Phenomenon largely due to the Dream being a Description of a Picture—The Experience of Drowning Persons—The Sense of Time in Dreams—The Crumpling of Consciousness in Dreams—The Recovery of Lost Memories through the Relaxation of Attention — The Emergence in Dreams of Memories not known to Waking Life—The Recollection of Forgotten Languages in Sleep — The Perversions of Memory in Dreams—Paramnesic False Recollections—Hypnagogic Paramnesia—Dreams mistaken for Actual Events—The Phenomenon of Pseudo-Reminiscence—Its Relationship to Epilepsy—Its Prevalence especially among Imaginative and Nervously Exhausted Persons—The Theories put forward to Explain it—A Fatigue Product—Conditioned by Defective Attention and Apperception — Pseudo-Reminiscence a reversed Hallucination.

THE peculiarities of memory in dreams—its defects, its aberrations, its excesses—have attracted attention ever since dreams began to be studied at all. It is not enough to assure ourselves that on awakening from a dream our memory of that dream may fairly be regarded as trustworthy so far as it extends. The characteristics of memory revealed within the reproduced dream have sometimes seemed so extraordinary as to be only explicable by the theory of supernatural intervention.

A problem which at one time greatly puzzled the scientific students of dreaming is furnished at the outset

MEMORY IN DREAMS

by the apparent abnormal rapidity of the dream process, the piling together in a brief space of time of a great number of combined memories. Stories were told of people who, when awakened by sounds or contacts which must have aroused them almost immediately, had yet experienced elaborate visions which could only have been excited by the stimulus which caused the awakening. The dream of Maury — who, when awakened by a portion of the bed cornice falling on his neck, imagined that he was living in the days of the Reign of Terror, and, after many adventures, was being guillotined—has become famous.[1]

It is unquestionably true that dreams are sometimes evoked by sensory stimuli which almost immediately awake the dreamer. But the supposition that this fairly common fact involves an extraordinary acceleration of the rapidity with which mental images are formed is due to a failure to comprehend the conditions under which psychic activity in sleep takes place. If the sleeper were wide awake, and were suddenly startled by a mysterious voice at the window or the door, he would arrive at a theory of the sound, and even form a plan of action, with at least as much rapidity as when the stimulus occurs during sleep. The difference is that in sleep the ordinary mental associations are more or less in abeyance, and the way is therefore easily open to new associations. These new associations, when we

---

[1] It is as well to bear in mind that this dream occurred when Maury was a student, long before he began to study dreaming, and (as Egger has pointed out) was probably not written down until thirteen years later. On these grounds alone it is not entitled to serious consideration.

look back at them from the standpoint of waking life, seem to us so bizarre, so far-fetched, that we think it must have required a long time to imagine them. We fail to realise that, under the conditions of dream thought, they have come about as automatically and as instantaneously as the ordinary psychic concommitants of external stimulation in waking life. It must also be remembered that in all the cases in which the rapidity of the dream process has seemed so extraordinary, it has merely been a question of visual imagery, and it is obviously quite easy to see in an instant an elaborate picture or series of pictures which would take a long time to describe.[1] At the most the dreamer has merely seen a kind of cinematographic drama which has been condensed and run together in very much the way practised by the cinematographic artist, so that although the whole story seems to be shown in constant movement, in reality the action of hours is condensed into moments. Further, it has always to be borne in mind that, asleep as well as awake, intense emotion involves a loss of the sense of time. We say in a terrible crisis that moments seemed years, and when sleeping consciousness magnifies a trivial stimulation into the occasion of a great crisis the same effect is necessarily produced.

Exactly the same illusion is experienced by persons who are rescued from drowning, or other dangerous

---

[1] As Sir Samuel Wilks once remarked ('On the Nature of Dreams, *Medical Magazine*, Feb. 1894), 'The dreamer merely forms a mental picture, and the *description* of it he calls his dream.'

MEMORY IN DREAMS

situations. It sometimes seems to them that their whole life has passed before them in vision during those brief moments. But careful investigation of some of these cases, notably by Piéron, has shown that what really happened was that a scene from childhood, perhaps of some rather similar accident, came before the drowning man's mind and was followed by five, six, perhaps even ten or twelve momentary scenes from later life. When the time during which these scenes flashed through the mind was taken into account it was found that there had by no means been any remarkable mental rapidity.

Such considerations have now led most scientific investigators of dreaming to regard these problems of dream memory as settled. Woodworth's observations on the hypnagogic or half-waking state revealed no remarkable rapidity of mental processes. Clavière showed by experiments with an alarum clock which struck twice with an interval of twenty-two seconds that speech dreams at all events take place merely with normal rapidity, or are even slightly slower than under waking conditions. The imagery of sleep, Clavière concluded, is not more rapid than the imagery of waking life, though to the dreamer it may seem to last for hours or days. It is often slackened rather than accelerated, says Piéron, who refers to the corresponding illusion under the influence of drugs like hashisch, though in some cases he finds that there is really a slight acceleration. The illusion is simply due, Foucault thinks, to the dreamer's belief that the events of his dream occupy the same time as real events. This illusion of time, concludes Dr. Justine Tobolowska, in her Paris thesis on this subject, is simply the necessary and constant result of the form assumed by psychic life during sleep.[1]

If this peculiarity of memory in dreaming is not difficult to explain as a natural illusion, there are other and rarer characteristics of dream memory which are much more puzzling.

In attempting to unravel these, it is probable that, as in explaining the illusion of rapidity, we must always bear in mind the tendency of memory-groups in dreams to fall apart from their waking links of association, so well as the complementary tendency to form associations which in waking life would only be attained by a strained effort. Apperception, with the power it involves of combining and bringing to a focus all the various groups of memories bearing on the point in hand, is defective. The focus of conscious attention is contracted, and there is the curious and significant phenomenon that sleeping consciousness is occasionally unconscious of psychic elements which yet are present just outside it and thrusting imagery into its focus. The imagery becomes conscious, but its relation to the existing focus of consciousness is not consciously perceived. Such a psychic mechanism, as Freud and his

[1] Egger, 'La Durée apparente des Rêves,' *Revue Philosophique*, Jan. 1895, pp. 41-59; Clavière, 'La Rapidité de la Pensée dans le Rêve,' *ib.* May 1897, p. 509; Piéron, 'La Rapidité des Processes Psychiques,' *ib.* Jan. 1903, pp. 89-95; Foucault, *Le Rêve*, pp. 158 *et seq.*; Tobolowska, *Etude sur les Illusions du Temps dans les Rêves du Sommeil Normal* : Thèse de Paris, 1900.

disciples have shown, quite commonly appears in hysteria and obsessional neuroses when healthy normal consciousness is degraded to a pathological level resembling that which is normal in dreams.[1] In such a case the surface of sleeping consciousness is, as it were, crumpled up, and the concealed portion appears only at the end of the dream or not at all. A simple example may make this clear. In a dream I ask a lady if she knows the work of the poet Bau; she replies that she does not; then I see before me a paper having on it the name Baudelaire, clearly the name which should have been contained in my query.[2] In such a dream the crumpling and breaking of consciousness, at its very focus, is shown in the most unmistakable manner.[3] But many of the most remarkable dreams of dramatic dreamers are due to the same phenomenon, which in an intellectual form is exactly the phenomenon which always makes a dramatic situation effective. Robert Louis Stevenson was an abnormally vivid dreamer, and found the germ of some of the plots of his stories in his dreams; he has described one of his dreams in

[1] Thus Freud tells (*Jahrbuch für Psychoanalytische Forschungen*, vol. i. part ii. p. 387) of a man who was obsessed by the idea that he should never pass money until he had carefully cleaned it, for fear he might be infecting other people, but was quite unaware that this obsession sprang from remorse due to his own sins of sexual impurity. In such a case there is, of course, not only a crumpling of consciousness, but a definite dislocation and transference of the parts.

[2] We also see here an interesting dissociation of the motor (speech) centre from the visual centre; it is the latter which is in this instance most closely in touch with facts.

[3] The 'selvdrolla' dream, recorded in a previous chapter (p. 43), illustrates the same point with the difference that the crumpled up portion of consciousness never became visible in the dream.

which the dreamer imagines he has committed a murder ; the crime becomes known to a woman who, however, never denounces it ; the murderer lives in terror, and cannot conceive why the woman prolongs his torture by this delay in giving him up to justice ; only at the end of the dream comes the clue to the mystery, and the explanation of the woman's attitude, as she falls on her knees and cries : ' Do you not understand ? I love you.'[1]

There is another and very interesting class of dreams in which we find not merely that some memory-groups disappear from consciousness or become merely latent, but also that other memory-groups, latent or even lost to waking consciousness, float into the focus of sleeping consciousness. In other words, we can remember in sleep what we have forgotten awake. We then have what is called the *hypermnesia*, the excessive or abnormal memory, of sleep.

There can be little doubt that the two processes—the sinking of some memory-groups and the emergence on the surface of other memory-groups which, so far as waking life is concerned, had apparently fallen to the depths and been drowned—are complementarily related to one another. We remember what we have forgotten because we forget what we remembered. The order of our waking impressions involves a certain tension, that is to say a certain attention, which holds them in our consciousness, and excludes any other order which might serve to bring lost memory-groups

[1] R. L. Stevenson, ' A Chapter on Dreams,' in *Across the Plains*, 1892.

MEMORY IN DREAMS

to sight. Sometimes we are conscious of a lost memory which is just outside consciousness, but which, with the existing order of our memory-groups, we cannot bring into consciousness. We have the missing name, the missing memory, at the tip of our tongue, we say, but we cannot quite catch it.[1] In dreams apperception is defective, the strain of conscious attention is relaxed, and the conditions are furnished under which new clues and strains may come into action and the missing name glide spontaneously into consciousness. Even the mere approach of sleep, with its accompanying relaxation of attention, may effect this end. Thus I was trying one day to recall the name of the unpleasant Chinese scent, patchouli. The name, though not usually unfamiliar, escaped me. At night, however, just before falling asleep, it spontaneously occurred to me. In the morning, when fully awake, I was again unable to recall it.

In such a case we see how waking consciousness is tense in a certain direction, which happens not to be that in which the desired thing is to be found. Attention under such circumstances impedes rather than aids recollection. In this particular case, I felt con-

---

[1] In most cases the missing memory, after making itself felt outside the conscious area, seems to reach that area, not so much by its own spontaneous unconscious movement as by a tentative search for clues. Thus I read one day the words 'the breaking of a goblet by a little black imp,' and immediately became conscious that I was reminded of something similar in recent experience, but could not tell what. I asked myself if it could have been in a dream. In a few moments, however, the memory recurred to me that two hours previously I had noticed a broken vase, and casually wondered how it had become broken. Under such circumstances we are for a time thinking of something, and yet have no conscious knowledge as to what we are thinking of.

vinced that the name I wanted began with *h*, and thus my mind was intently directed towards a wrong quarter. But on the approach of sleep attention is automatically relaxed, and it is then possible for the forgotten word to slip in from its unexpected quarter. On these occasions it is by indirection that direction is found.[1]

It is interesting to observe that this same process of discovery due to the wider outlook of relaxed attention can take place, not only in sleep and the hypnagogic state, but also, subconsciously, in the fully waking state when the mind is occupied with some other subject. Thus in reading a MS., I came upon an illegible word which I was unable to identify, notwithstanding several guesses and careful scrutiny through a magnifying glass. I passed on, dismissing the subject from my mind. A quarter of an hour afterwards, when walking, and thinking of quite a different subject, I became conscious that the word 'ceremonial' had floated into the field of mental vision, and I at once realised that this was the unidentified word. The instance may be trivial, but no example could better show how the

[1] Jastrow remarks, somewhat in the same way (*The Subconscious*, p. 93), that 'a letting down of the effort, a focusing of the mind upon a point a little or a good deal to one side of the fixation point, distinctly aids the mental vision.' The process seems, however, to be most effective when it is automatic, for attention cannot easily relax its own tension. A large number of the discoveries and solutions of difficulties effected in dreams are due to this dispersal of attention over a wider field, so enabling the missing relationship to be detected. See, for instance, some cases recorded by Newbold (*Psychological Review*, March 1896, p. 132), as of Dr. Hilprecht, the Assyriologist, who discovered in a dream that two fragments of tablets he had vainly been endeavouring to decipher, were really parts of the same tablet.

mind may continue to work subconsciously in one direction while consciously working in an entirely different direction.

In dreams, however, we can effect more than a mere recovery of memories which have temporarily escaped us, or the discovery of relationships which have eluded us. The dissociation of familiar memory-groups becomes so complete, the appearance of unfamiliar groups so eruptive, that we can remember things that have entirely and permanently sunk below the surface of waking consciousness, or even things which are so insignificant that they have never made any mark on waking consciousness at all. In this way, we may be said, in a certain sense, to remember things we never knew. The first dream which enabled me, some twenty years ago, to realise this hypermnesia of the mind in dreams [1] was the following unimportant but instructive case. I woke up recalling the chief items of a rather vivid dream : I had imagined myself in a large old house, where the furniture, though of good quality, was ancient, and the chairs threatened to give way as one sat on them. The place belonged to one Sir

[1] Hypermnesia, or excessive memory, is found in waking life in various abnormal conditions. It is not uncommon in men of genius; Macaulay is a well-known example. It scarcely seems, however, an especially favourable condition for keen intellectual power; the mental machine that is clogged with unnecessary and unimportant facts can scarcely fail to work under difficulties. 'Hypermnesia,' remarks Stoddart ('Early Symptoms of Mental Disease,' *British Medical Journal*, 11th May 1907), 'occurs most frequently in certain cases of idiocy, and in some cases of chronic mania. One such patient could enumerate all the occasions when any given medical officer had played tennis since he entered the institution.' Hypermnesia in dreams has been dealt with by Carl du Prel, *Philosophy of Mysticism*, vol. ii. ch. i.

Peter Bryan, a hale old gentleman, who was accompanied by his son and grandson. There was a question of my buying the place from him, and I was very complimentary to the old gentleman's appearance of youthfulness, absurdly affecting not to know which was the grandfather and which the grandson. On awaking I said to myself that here was a purely imaginative dream, quite unsuggested by any definite experiences. But when I began to recall the trifling incidents of the previous day, and the things I had seen and read, I realised that that was far from being the case. So far from the dream having been a pure effort of imagination, I found that every minute item could be traced to some separate source, though none of them had the slightest resemblance to the dream as a whole. The name of Sir Peter Bryan alone completely baffled me ; I could not even recall that I had at that time ever heard of any one called Bryan. I abandoned the search and made my notes of the dream and its sources. I had scarcely done so when I chanced to take up a volume of biographies of eccentric personages, which I had glanced through carelessly the day before. I found that it contained, among others, the lives of Lord *Peter*borough and George *Bryan* Brummel. I had certainly seen those names the day before ; yet before I took up the book once again it would have been impossible for me to recall the exact name of Beau Brummel. It so happened that the forgotten memory which in this case re-emerged to sleeping consciousness, was a fact of no consequence to myself or any one else. But it furnishes the key to many dreams which have been of more serious import to the dreamers.

Since then I have been able to observe among my friends several instances of dreams containing veracious though often trivial circumstances unknown to the dreamer when awake, though on consideration it was found to be in the highest degree probable that they had come under his notice, and been forgotten, or not consciously observed. Thus a musical correspondent tells me he once dreamed of playing a piece of Rubinstein's in the presence of a friend who told him he had made a mistake in re-striking a tied note. In the morning he found the dream friend was correct. But up to then he had always repeated the note. Usually when the forgotten or unnoticed circumstance is trivial, it is of quite recent date. That it is not always very recent may be illustrated by a dream of my own. I dreamed that I was in Spain and about to rejoin some friends at a place which was called, I thought, Daraus, but on reaching the booking-office I could not remember whether the place I wanted to go to was called Daraus, Varaus, or Zaraus, all which places, it seemed to me, really existed. On awaking, I made a note of the dream, exactly as reproduced here, but was unable to recall any place, in Spain or elsewhere, corresponding to any of these names. The dream seemed merely to illustrate the familiar way in which a dream image perpetually shifts in a meaningless fashion at the focus of sleeping consciousness. The note was put away, and a few months later taken out again.[1] It was still equally impossible to me to recall any real name corresponding to the dream names. But on consulting the Spanish guide-books and railway time-tables, I found that, on the line between San Sebastian and Bilbao, there really is a little seaside resort, in a beautiful situation, called Zarauz, and I realised, moreover, that I had actually passed that station in the train two hundred and fifty days before the date of my dream.[2] I had no associations with this place, though I may have admired it at the time ; in any case it vanished permanently from conscious memory, perhaps aided by the fatigue of a long night journey before entering Spain. Even sleeping memory, I may remark, only recovered it with an effort, for it is notable that the name was gradually approached by three successive attempts.[3]

[1] This delay is worth mentioning, for it is conceivable that, in the case of a weak recollection, transference to the subconscious sphere of sleep might involve a temporary disappearance from the conscious waking sphere.

[2] There is a possible interest in the exact length of the interval. Swoboda (*Die Perioden des Menschlichen Organismus in ihrer psychologischen und biologischen Bedeutung*, 1904) believes that the recurrence of memories tends to obey a law of periodicity, so that, for instance, a melody heard at a concert may recur at a regular interval. I cannot say that I have myself found evidence of such periodicity, though I have made several observations on the recurrence of such memories.

[3] Similarly, Foucault (*Le Rêve*, p. 79) records the dream of a lady concerning a place called Brétigny, near Dijon, though when awake she was not aware there is such a place there. Elsewhere (p. 214) Foucault also gives examples of sensations, not consciously perceived in the waking state, but revived in dream. Beaunis, in his interesting ' Contribution à la Psychologie du Rêve' (*American Journal of Psychology*, July-Oct. 1903) narrates a dream of his own in which a forgotten or unconscious memory revived. Many such dreams could easily be brought together. An often-quoted dream, apparently of this kind (see *e.g.*, *British Medical Journal*, 7th April 1900, p. 850), is that of Archbishop Benson who, like

MEMORY IN DREAMS

A special form of lost or unconscious memories recurring in sleep is constituted by the cases in which people when asleep, or in a somnambulistic state, can speak languages which they have forgotten, or never consciously known, when awake. A simple instance, known to me, is furnished by a servant who had been taken to Paris for a few weeks six months before, but had never learned to speak a word of French, and whose mistress overheard her talking in her sleep, and repeating various French phrases, like ' Je ne sais pas, Monsieur ' ; she had certainly heard these phrases, though she maintained, when awake, that she was ignorant of them. Speaking in a language not consciously known, or xenoglossia, as it is now termed, occurs under various abnormal conditions, as well as in sleep, and is sometimes classed with the tendency which is found, especially under great religious excitement, to ' speak with tongues,' or to utter gibberish.[1] But in various sleep-like states it occurs as a true revival of forgotten

his predecessor, Laud, took an interest in his dreams. He dreamed that he was suffering severely in his chest, and that his doctor, on being called in, told him that he had angīna pectoris. The archbishop in his dream exclaimed with indignation: ' Angīna, angīna!' The dream made such an impression on him that he looked the matter up, but only found the ordinary pronunciation, angĭna, recorded. A week later he was at Cambridge, dining in hall at Trinity, and seated next to Munro, the Professor of Latin, who happened to ask him about the death of Thomas Arnold. ' He died of angīna pectoris,' said Benson. Munro smiled grimly and said softly : ' Of angĭna, as we now call it.' There can be no doubt that Benson, who was closely in touch with the academic world, had met with this correction, which is accepted by all modern Latinists, and ' forgotten ' it.

[1] Xenoglossia, as well as the tendency to utter gibberish, are both classed under glossolalia. See *e.g.* E. Lombard, ' Phénomènes de Glossolalie,' *Archives de Psychologie*, July 1907.

P

memories, sometimes of memories which belong to childhood and in normal consciousness have been long overlaid and lost. On one occasion, by the bedside of a lady who was kept for a considerable period in a light condition of chloroform anaesthesia, the patient began to talk in an unfamiliar language which one of us recognised as Welsh ; as a child, she afterwards owned, she had known Welsh, but had long since forgotten it.[1] A similar reproduction of lost memories occurs in the hypnotic state.

This psychic process, by which unconscious memories become conscious in dreams, is of considerable interest and importance because it lends itself to many delusions. Not only the ignorant and uncultured, but even well-trained and acute minds, are often so unskilled in mental analysis that they are quite unable to pierce beneath the phenomenon of conscious ignorance to the deeper fact of unconscious memory ; they are completely baffled, or else they resort to the wildest hypotheses. This is illustrated by the following narrative received twelve years ago from a medical correspondent in Baltimore. ' Several years ago,' he writes, ' a friend made a social call at my house and in the course of conversation spoke very enthusiastically of Mascagni's *Cavalleria Rusticana*, the first performance of which in the United States he had attended a few nights previously. I had never even heard of

[1] In the eighteenth century Lord Monboddo (*Ancient Metaphysics*, vol. iii., 1782, p. 217) referred to a Countess of Laval who, during the delirium of illness, spoke the Breton tongue which she had known as a child, but long since forgotten.

the opera before, but that night I dreamed that I heard it performed. The dream was a very vivid one, so vivid that several times during the next day I found myself humming airs from the dream opera. Several evenings later I went to the theatre to see a comedy, and before the curtain rose the orchestra played a selection which I instantly recognised as part of my dream opera. I exclaimed to a lady who was with me : " That selection is from *Cavalleria Rusticana*." On inquiring of the leader of the orchestra such proved to be the case.' Now, at that period, shortly after the first appearance of *Cavalleria Rusticana*, portions of it had become extremely popular and were heard everywhere, by no means merely on the operatic stage. It was difficult not to have heard something of it. There cannot be the slightest doubt that my correspondent had heard not only the name but the music, though, writing at an interval of some years, he probably exaggerated the extent of his unconscious recollections. This seems the simple explanation of what to my correspondent was an inexplicable mystery. Other people, like the late Frederick Greenwood, not content to remain baffled, go further and regard such dreams as ' dreams of revelation,' as they also consider that class of dreams in which the dreamer works out the solution of a difficulty which he had vainly grappled with when awake.

This is a kind of dream which has occurred in all ages, and has at times been put down to divine interposition. Sixteen centuries ago Bishop Synesius of Ptolemais wrote that in his hunting days a dream revealed to him an idea for a trap which he successfully employed in snaring animals, and at the present time inventions made in dreams have been successfully patented. The Rev. Nehemiah Curnock, who lately succeeded in deciphering Wesley's *Journal*, has stated that an important missing clue to the cypher came to him in a dream. A friend of my own, an expert in chemistry, was not long since in frequent communication with a practical manufacturer, assisting him in his inventions by scientific advice. One day the manufacturer wrote to my friend asking if the latter had been thinking of him during the night, for he had been much puzzled by a difficulty, and during the night had seen a vision of my friend who explained the solution of the difficulty ; in the morning the proposed solution proved successful. There was, however, no telepathic element in the case ; the dreamer's solution was his own.

An interesting group of cases in this class is furnished by the dreams in which the dreamer, in opposition to his waking judgment, sees an acquaintance in whom he reposes trust acting in a manner unworthy of that trust, subsequent events proving that the estimate formed during sleep was sounder than that of waking life. Hawthorne (in his *American Notebooks*), Greenwood, Jewell, and others have recorded cases of this kind.

Various as these phenomena are, they fall into the same scheme. They all help to illustrate the fact that

MEMORY IN DREAMS

though on one side mental life in sleep is feeble and defective, on the other side it shows a tendency to vigorous excess. Sleep, as we know, involves a relaxation of tension, both physical and psychic; attention is no longer focused at a deliberately selected spot.[1] The voluntary field becomes narrower, but the involuntary field becomes extended. Thus it happens that the contents of our minds fall into a new order, an order which is often fantastic but, on the other hand, is sometimes a more natural and even a more rational order than that we attain in waking life. Our eyes close, our muscles grow slack, the reins fall from our hands. But it sometimes happens that the

[1] In a somewhat similar manner the muscular contractions of the hysterical may disappear during sleep, as may their paralyses and their anaesthesias, as well as their losses of memory. (These phenomena have been especially observed and studied by Raymond and Janet, *Névroses et Idées Fixes*, vol. ii.) Such characteristics of the sleep of the hysterical may well be a manifestation of the same tendency which in the sleep of normal people leads to hypermnesia. In this connection reference may be made to the interesting opposition between attention and memory developed by Dr. Marie de Manacéine ('De l'antagonisme qui existe entre chaque effort de l'attention et des innervations motrices,' *Atti dell' XI. Congresso Internazionale Medico*, 1894, Rome, vol. ii., 'Fisiologia,' p. 48). Concentrated attention, she argues, paralyses memory, and there is an absolute antagonism between motor innervation, or real movement, which favours memory, and the concentrated effort which favours attention. 'In psychological researches we must always separate the phenomena of memory from the phenomena of attention, for memory is only possible through muscular movement, and attention, on the contrary, is only active through the suppression of movement.' In sleep, it is true, there may be no actual movement, but there is relaxation of muscular tension and freedom of motor ideas. It should be added that not all investigators confirm Manacéine's conclusion as to the antagonism between the conditions for memory and attention. Thus R. MacDougall ('The Physical Characteristics of Attention,' *Psychological Review*, March 1895), while finding that muscular relaxation accompanies the recall of memories, finds also, though not so markedly and constantly, a similar relaxation accompanying both voluntary and spontaneous attention.

horse knows the road home even better than we know it ourselves.

Hypermnesia, or abnormally wide range of recollection, is not the only or the most common modification of memory during sleep. We find much more commonly, and indeed as one of the chief characteristics of sleep, an abnormally narrow range of recollection. We find, also, and perhaps as a result of that narrow range, paramnesia or perversion of memory. The best known form of paramnesia is that in which we have the illusion that the event which is at the moment happening to us has happened to us before.[1]

This form of paramnesia is common in dreams, though it is often so slightly pronounced that we either fail to recall it on awakening or attach no significance to it.[2] I dream, for instance, that I am walking along a path, along which, it seems to me, I have often walked before, and that the path skirts the lawn of a house by which stands a policeman whom, also, it seems to me, I have often seen there before ; the policeman approaches me and says, ' You have come to see Mr. So-and-so, sir ? '

[1] The term ' paramnesia ' was devised by Kraepelin, who wrote the first comprehensive study of the subject, though he offered no explanatory theory of it (' Ueber Erinnerungsfälschungen,' *Archiv für Psychiatrie*, Bd. xvii. and xviii.). A very clear and comprehensive account of the subject, up to the date of the article, was given by W. H. Burnham ('Paramnesia,' *American Journal of Psychology*, May 1889). In the following pages, together with much new matter, I have made use of my paper entitled ' A Note on Hypnagogic Paramnesia,' published in *Mind*, vol. vi. No. 22, in 1896.

[2] It has long been recognised by psychologists that paramnesia occurs in dreams. Thus Burnham refers to it as frequent, and Kraepelin mentions that he once dreamed of smoking a cigar for the fourth or fifth time, though he had never smoked in his life.

MEMORY IN DREAMS

and thereupon I suddenly recollect, with some confusion, that I have come to see Mr. So-and-so, and I walk up to the door. Again, an author dreams that he sees a list of his own books with, at the head of them, one entitled 'The Book of Glory.' He could not recall writing it (and to waking consciousness the name was entirely unknown), but the only reflection he made in his dream was 'How stupid to have forgotten!' In this case there was evidently some resistance to the suggestion, which yet was quickly accepted. In all such dreams it seems that we are in a state of mental weakness associated with defective apperceptual control and undue suggestibility, very similar to the state found in some forms of confusional insanity or of precocious dementia.[1] Consciousness feebly slides down the path of least resistance; it accepts every suggestion; the objects presented to it seem things that it knew before, the things that are suggested to it to do seem things that it already wanted to do before. Paramnesia, thus regarded, seems simply a natural outcome of a state of consciousness temporarily depressed below its normal standard of vigour.

It must be remembered that the suggestibility of sleeping consciousness varies in degree, and in the face of serious improbabilities there is often a considerable amount of resistance, just as the hypnotised person

[1] In alcholic insanity, for instance, especially when it leads to the occurrence of Korsakoff's syndrome, there is a notable degree of mental weakness with a tendency to form false memories, both in the form of confabulation (or the filling by imagination of lacunae in memory) and pseudo-reminiscence. (See *e.g.* John Turner, 'Alcoholic Insanity,' *Journal of Mental Science*, Jan. 1910, p. 41.)

seriously resists the suggestions that fundamentally outrage his nature. But some degree of suggestibility, some tendency to regard the things that come before us in dreams as familiar—in other words, as things that have happened to us before—is not merely a natural result of defective apperception, but one of the very conditions of dreaming. It enables us to carry on our dreams; without it their progress would be fatally inhibited by doubt, uncertainty, and struggle. So it is, perhaps, that in all dreaming, or at all events in certain stages of sleeping consciousness, we are liable to fall into a state of pseudo-reminiscence.

It is an interesting and highly significant fact that this paramnesic delusion of our dreams—the feeling that the thing that is happening to us is the thing that has happened to us before or that might happen to us again—tends to persist in the hypnagogic (or hypnopompic) stage immediately following sleep. When we have half awakened from a dream and are just able to realise that it was a dream, that dream constantly tends to appear in a more plausible or probable light than is possible a few moments later when we are fully awake.[1]

The first experience which enabled me clearly to

[1] Dr. Marie de Manacéïne, who has studied the phenomena of the hypnagogic state experimentally in much detail (*Sleep*, pp. 195-220), finds that in its deepest stage it is marked by echolalia, or the tendency to repeat automatically what is said, and in a less deep stage by abnormal suggestibility or the tendency to accept ideas and especially emotions. She considers that the hypnagogic state becomes abnormal when it lasts for more than fifteen seconds. It may last for more than six minutes, and is then of serious import. She shows reason to believe that the hypna-

MEMORY IN DREAMS

realise this phenomenon, and its probable explanation, occurred many years ago. About the middle of the night I had a very vivid dream, in which I imagined that two friends—a gentleman and his daughter—with a certain Lord Chesterfield (I had lately been reading the *Letters* of the famous Lord Chesterfield), were together at a hotel, that they were playing with weapons, that the lady accidentally killed or wounded Lord Chesterfield, and that she then changed clothes with him with the object of escaping, and avoiding discovery which would somehow be dangerous. I was informed of the matter, and was much concerned. I awoke, and my first thought was that I had just had a curious dream which I must not forget in the morning. But then I seemed to remember that it was a real and familiar event. This second thought lulled my mental activity, and I went to sleep again. In the morning I was able to recall the main points in my dream, and my thoughts on awaking from it.

Since then I have given attention to the point, and I have found on recalling my half-waking consciousness after dreams that, while it is doubtless rare to catch the assertion 'That really occurred,' it is less rare to catch the vague assertion, 'That is the kind of thing that does occur.' I find that this latter impression

gogic state is substantially identical with the hypnotic state, and she regards it as probably due to cerebral anaemia. She finds it especially marked in children under fifteen, the more so if they belong to the working-class, and rather common among adolescent girls and young women, especially if anaemic, but among adults rarer in women than in men, becoming more frequent in both sexes with old age; the phlegmatic are more liable to it than the sanguine or the nervous.

appears, like the former, after vivid dreams which contain no physical impossibility, but which the full waking consciousness refuses to recognise as among the things that are probable. As an example quite unlike that just recorded, I may mention a dream in which I imagined that I was proving the frequency of local intermarriage by noting in directories the frequency of the presence of people of the same name in neighbouring towns and villages. On half-awaking I still believed that I had actually been engaged in such a task—that is, either that the dream was real or that it referred to a real event—and it was not until I was sufficiently awake to recognise the fallacy of such a method of investigation that I realised that it was purely a dream.

This phenomenon has long been known, although its significance has not been perceived. Brierre de Boismont pointed out that certain vivid dreams are not recognised as dreams, but are mistaken for reality after waking, though he scarcely recognised the normal limitation of this mistake to the hypnagogic state. Moll compared such dreams, thus continued into waking life, to continuative post-hypnotic suggestions. Sully mentioned awaking from dreams which 'still wear the aspect of old acquaintances, so that for the moment I think they are waking realities.'[1] Colegrove, in his study of memory, recorded many cases

---

[1] Sully, *The Human Mind*, vol. ii. p. 317. Foucault (*Le Rêve*, p. 300), briefly notes that he has often had the illusion of seeming to remember a fact which does not exist, and of recollecting a person he has never seen.

MEMORY IN DREAMS

in which young people mistook their dreams for actual events.[1]

This persistence of the memory illusion of sleep into the subsequent hypnagogic state is obviously related to the allied persistence, more occasionally found, of the visual, auditory, and other sensory hallucinations of sleep into the hypnagogic state.[2] Visions thus seen persisting from dreams for a few moments into waking life are often very baffling and disturbing, as has already been pointed out, to ignorant and untrained people. Such visions may occur in the hypnagogic state, even when there has been no conscious precedent dream, and it is indeed probable, as Parish has argued, that it is precisely in the hypnagogic state, the narthex of the church of dreams, as I may term it, that hallucinations are most liable to occur. That illusions may momentarily occur in this state is obvious; thus falling asleep for a few minutes when seated before a black hollow smouldering fire, with red ashes at the bottom, I awake with the illusion that I see a curtain on fire, and have already leaned forward to snatch it away before I realise my mistake.

Under normal conditions, the liability of a dream memory to be mistaken for an actual event seems to be

[1] F. W. Colegrove, 'Individual Memories,' *American Journal of Psychology*, Jan. 1899.

[2] See *e.g.* for such cases in sane persons, Hack Tuke, 'Hallucinations,' *Brain*, vol. xi., 1889. A man with chronic systematised delusions writes: 'I am obsessed at nights; that is, I am made the recipient of projected thoughts which become translated into dreams, and on several occasions I have found, just after waking, and while still in a very passive state, that some one was speaking to me in the ear.'

greater when an interval has elapsed before the dream is remembered, such an interval making it difficult to distinguish one class of memories from the other, provided the dream has been of a plausible character. Thus Professor Näcke has recorded that his wife dreamed that an acquaintance, an old lady, had called at the house; this dream was apparently forgotten until forty or fifty hours afterwards when, on passing the old lady's house, it was recalled, and the dreamer was only with much difficulty convinced that the dream was not an actual occurrence. When we are concerned with memories of childhood, it not infrequently happens that we cannot distinguish with absolute certainty between real occurrences and what may possibly have been dreams.

In normal physical and mental health, however, it seems rare for the hallucinatory influence of dreams to extend beyond the hypnagogic state, but any impairment of the bodily health generally, and of the brain in particular, may extend this confusion. Thus in a case of heart disease terminating fatally, the patient, though in health he was by no means visionary or impressionable, became liable during sleep in the daytime to dreams of an entirely reasonable character which he had great difficulty in distinguishing from the real facts of life, never feeling sure what had actually happened, and what had been only a dream. In disordered cerebral and nervous conditions the same illusion becomes still more marked. This is notably the case in hysteria. In some forms of insanity, as

MEMORY IN DREAMS

many alienists have shown, this mistake is sometimes permanent and the dream may become an integral and persistent part of waking life. At this point, however, we leave the normal world of dreams and enter the sphere of pathology.

In the normal persistence of the dream illusion into the hypnagogic state with which we are here concerned, the dream usually presents a possible, though, it may be, highly improbable event. The half-waking or hypnagogic intelligence seems to be deceived by this element of life-like possibility. Consequently a fallacy of perception takes place strictly comparable to the fallacious perception which, in the case of an external sensation, we call an illusion. In the ordinary illusion an externally excited sensation of one kind is mistaken for an externally excited sensation of another kind. In this case a centrally excited sensation of one order (dream image) is mistaken for a centrally excited sensation of another order (memory). The phenomenon is, therefore, a mental illusion belonging to the group of false memories, and it may be termed hypnagogic paramnesia.

The process seems to have a certain interest, and it may throw light on some rather obscure phenomena. When we are able to recall a vivid dream, usually a fairly probable dream, with no idea as to when it was dreamed, and thus find ourselves in possession of experiences of which we cannot certainly say that they happened in waking life or in dream life, it seems probable that this hypnagogic paramnesia has come into action ; the half-waking consciousness dismisses the vivid and life-like dream as an old and familiar experience, shunting it off into temporary forgetfulness, unless some accident again brings it into consciousness with, as it were, a fragment of that wrong label still sticking to it. Such a paramnesic process may thus also help to account for the mighty part which, as so many thinkers from Lucretius onwards have seen, dreams have played in moulding human action and human belief. It is a means whereby waking life and dream life are brought to an apparently common level.

By hypnagogic paramnesia I mean a false memory occurring in the ante-chamber of sleep, but not necessarily before sleep. Myers's invention of the word 'hypnopompic' seems scarcely necessary even for pedantic reasons. I take the condition of consciousness to be almost the same whether the sleep is coming on or passing away. In the Chesterfield dream it is indeed impossible to say whether the phenomenon is 'hypnagogic' or 'hypnopompic' ; in such a case the twilight consciousness is as much conditioned by the sleep that is passing away as by the sleep that is coming on.

If this memory illusion of the half-waking state may be regarded as a variety of paramnesia, a new horizon is opened out to us. May not the hypnagogic variety throw light on the general phenomenon of paramnesia which has led to so many strange and complicated theories ? I think it may.

Paramnesia, as we have seen, is the psychologist's

MEMORY IN DREAMS 239

name for a hallucination of memory which is sometimes called 'pseudo-reminiscence,' and by medical writers (who especially associate it with epilepsy) regarded as a symptom of 'dreamy state,'[1] while by French authors it is often termed 'false recognition' or 'sensation du déjà vu.' Dickens, who seems himself to have experienced it, thus describes it in *David Copperfield*: 'We have all some experience of a feeling that comes over us occasionally, of what we are saying and doing having been said or done before, in a remote time, of having been surrounded, dim ages ago, by the same faces, objects, and circumstances, of our knowing perfectly what will be said next, as if we suddenly remembered it.' Sometimes it seems that this previous occurrence can only have taken place in a previous existence,[2] whence we probably have, as St. Augustine

[1] Hughlings Jackson (*Practitioner*, May 1874, also *Brain*, July 1888, and *Brain*, 1899, p. 534) applied this term to the intellectual aura preceding an epileptic attack and considered that 'pseudo-reminiscence' itself might indicate a slight epileptic paroxysm in persons who show other symptoms of epilepsy. Gowers also (*Epilepsy*, 2nd ed., p. 133) considers 'dreamy state' to be closely associated with minor attacks of epilepsy; and Crichton-Browne (*Dreamy Mental States*) holds the same view. It should be added that 'dreamy state' by no means necessarily involves pseudo-reminiscence; see *e.g.* S. Taylor, 'A Case of Dreamy State,' *Lancet*, 9th Aug. 1890, p. 276, and W. A. Turner, 'The Problem of Epilepsy,' *British Medical Journal*, 2nd April 1910, p. 805. Leroy found that pseudo-reminiscence is usually rare in association with epilepsy.

[2] 'The feeling of pre-existence,' writes Dr. J. G. Kiernan in a private letter, 'frequently occurs as a consequence of delusions of memory in epilepsy. The case on which George Sand built her story of *Consuelo* was one reported of an epileptic who during the epileptic states had delusions of living in a distant historic past of which he retained the memory as facts during the normal state. I know of two epileptic theosophists who base their belief in transmigration on the memories of their epileptic period. In my judgment a large part of Swedenborg's visions were instances of delusions of memory.'

seems first to have suggested, the origin of the idea of metempsychosis, of the transmigration of souls; sometimes it seems to have happened before in a dream; sometimes the subject of the experience is totally baffled in the attempt to account for the feeling of familiarity which has overtaken him. In any case he is liable to an emotion of distress which would scarcely be caused by the coincidence of resemblance with a real previous experience.[1]

Paramnesia of this kind is known, according to the observations of Lalande,[2] to thirty people in a hundred, and Heymans found it in a considerable proportion of students of both sexes. Such estimates are probably too high if we take into consideration the general population. This experience seems, as Dugas and others have noted,[3] to affect educated people, and notably people of more than average intellect, who use their brains much, especially in artistic and emotional work, to a very much greater degree than the ignorant and phlegmatic manual worker.[4] Dickens has already been mentioned; many other notable

---

[1] Professor Grasset ('La Sensation du "Déjà Vu,"' *Journal de Psychologie Normale et Pathologique*, Nov.-Feb. 1904) considers that a feeling of anguish is the characteristic accompaniment of a true paramnesic manifestation. This statement is too pronounced. There is usually some emotional disturbance, but its degree depends on the temperament of the person experiencing the phenomenon. Sometimes the sensation of pseudo-reminiscence may be accompanied, as a medical man subject to epilepsy (mentioned by Hughlings Jackson) found in his own case, by 'a slight sense of satisfaction,' as in the finding of something that had been sought for.

[2] *Revue Philosophique*, November 1893.

[3] *Revue Philosophique*, January 1894.

[4] Heymans found that students liable to paramnesia tended to possess an aptitude for languages and an inaptitude for mathematics.

MEMORY IN DREAMS

writers have referred to this or some allied feeling, stating that they had experienced it, and Sir James Crichton-Browne brings forward a number of passages from the poets in evidence of their familiarity with such phenomena.[1] Shelley (who appears on at least two occasions to have experienced hallucinations also) underwent what may be regarded as an experience of paramnesia (described in his *Speculations on Metaphysics*) which is of interest in the present connection because it brings this phenomenon into relation with dreams. He was walking with a friend in the neighbourhood of Oxford, when he suddenly turned the corner of a country lane and saw 'a common scene' of a windmill, etc., which, it immediately seemed to him, he recollected having seen before in a dream of long ago. Five years afterwards he was so agitated in writing this down that he could not finish the account. The real resemblance of 'a common scene' with a similar dream scene, even supposing it could be recollected when the two experiences were separated by a long interval, would scarcely be a coincidence likely to cause agitation. The emotion aroused seems to mark the experience as belonging to the class of paramnesic illusions which so often make a peculiarly vivid impression on those to whom they occur.

[1] Paul Bourget, the novelist, in an interesting letter published by Grasset (*loc. cit.*) states that this experience has been habitual with him from as long back as he can remember, occurring in regard to things heard or felt more than to things seen, and accompanied by an emotional trouble similar to that experienced in dreams of dead friends who appear as living, though even in his dreams the dreamer knows that they are dead. Bourget adds that he is of emotional temperament, and that the phenomenon was more pronounced in childhood than it is now.

A great many theories have been put forward by psychologists and others to account for this paramnesic phenomenon. The most ancient explanation, long anterior to the beginnings of scientific psychology, was the theory that the occurrence which, as it now happens, strikes us as so overwhelmingly familiar had actually occurred to us in a previous existence long ages before ; thus Pythagoras, according to the ancient story, when he visited the temple of Juno at Argos recognised the shield he had worn ages before when he was Euphorbus and fought with Menelaus in the Trojan war. A much more recent theory runs to the opposite extreme and claims that all or nearly all these cases of recognition indicate a real but confused reminiscence of past events in our present life, dim recollections which the subject is unable definitely to locate. This is the explanation largely relied on by Ribot, Jessen, Sander, Sully, Burnham, and many others. It was perhaps largely due to ignorance of the phenomenon ; Ribot, when he wrote his book on the diseases of memory, considered that only three or four cases had been recorded, for an abnormal phenomenon always seems rare until it is recognised and definitely searched for. Undoubtedly, this theory will explain a considerable proportion of cases, but not really typical cases in which the subject has an overwhelming conviction that even the minute details of the present experience have been experienced before. We may read a new poem with a vague sense of familiarity, but such an experience never puts on a really

MEMORY IN DREAMS

paramnesic character, for we quickly realise that it is explainable by the fact that the writer of the poem has fallen under the influence of some greater master. The only experience I can personally speak of as at all approaching true paramnesia occurred on visiting the ruins of Pevensey Castle many years ago. On going up the slope towards the ivy-covered ruins, bathed in bright sunlight, I experienced a strange and abiding sense of familiarity with the scene. Three theories might account for this experience (for I refrain from including the Pythagorean theory that I experienced a reminiscence of the experience of a possible ancestor coming from across the Thames to the assistance of Harold against William the Conqueror at this spot): (1) that it was a case of true paramnesia; (2) that I had been taken to the spot as a child; (3) that the view was included among a series of coloured stereoscopic pictures with which I was familiar as a child, and which certainly contained similar scenes. I incline to this last explanation. Here, as elsewhere, there are no keys which will unlock all doors.

A modification of the theory that the pseudo-reminiscence is an unrecognised real reminiscence is furnished by Grasset, who considers that the phenomenon is due to a subconscious impression previously received, but only reaching consciousness under the influence of the new similar impression. This theory would include the revival of dream images, and is therefore related to the theory of Lapie and Méré, according to which the feeling of many of these subjects that what they now experience had happened before in a dream is the correct explanation of the phenomenon.[1]

We enter on a different class of explanations with the early theory of Wigan that such cases are due to the duality of the brain, the two hemispheres not acting quite simultaneously. This is a somewhat crude conception, though it may seem approximately on the lines of more recent theories. The theory of the duplex brain, each hemisphere being supposed capable of acting independently, was at one time invoked to explain many phenomena, but it is no longer regarded as tenable.[2]

We may dismiss these theories, which have been effectively criticised by others, and revert to our clue in the sleeping and hypnagogic state. The hypnagogic state is a transition between waking and sleeping. It is thus a condition of mental feebleness and suggestibility doubtless correlated with a condition of irregular brain anaemia. A plausible suggestion under such conditions is too readily accepted. Does ordinary paramnesia occur under similar conditions of mental feebleness and suggestibility ? It is rare to find descriptions of paramnesic experiences by scientific observers who are alive to the importance of accurately

[1] Paul Lapie, *Revue Philosophique*, March 1894; Charles Méré, *Mercure de France*, July 1903; Sully, Tannery, and Buccola also considered that this is a factor in the explanation of the phenomenon. Freud (*Zur Psychopathologie des Alltagsleben*, 1907, p. 122) brings forward a modification of this theory, and believes that false recognition is a reminiscence of unconscious day-dreams.

[2] For a minute and searching criticism of the theory of the duplex brain, see especially four articles by Bonne in the *Archives de Neurologie*, March-June 1907.

MEMORY IN DREAMS

recording all the conditions, but there is some reason to think that paramnesia does occur in states produced by excitement, exhaustion, and allied causes. The earliest case of paramnesia recorded in detail by a trained observer is that described by Wigan as occurring to himself at the funeral of the Princess Charlotte. He had passed several disturbed nights previous to the ceremony, with almost complete deprivation of rest on the night immediately preceding ; he was suffering from grief as well as from exhaustion from want of food ; he had been standing for four hours, and would have fainted on taking his place by the coffin if it had not been for the excitement of the occasion. When the music ceased the coffin slowly sank in absolute silence, broken by an outburst of grief from the bereaved husband. 'In an instant,' Wigan proceeds, 'I felt not merely an *impression*, but a *conviction*, that I had seen the whole scene before on some former occasion.' Such a condition may fairly be regarded as an artificial reproduction, by means of emotion, excitement, and exhaustion, of the condition which occurs simply and naturally in sleep or on its hypnagogic borderland.

The frequency—if it may be taken to be a fact—of the occurrence of pseudo-reminiscence in epileptics, noted by various medical observers, whether at the onset of the fit or independently of any obvious muscular convulsion, may be significant in this connection. There is no good reason to suppose that pseudo-reminiscence has a true relation to epilepsy, and still less that it necessarily constitutes a minor epileptic paroxysm. But the special sleep-like condition of contracted cerebral circulation in epilepsy renders it favourable to paramnesia as well as to hallucinatory phenomena.[1]

Independently of epilepsy, any condition of temporary and perhaps chronic nervous exhaustion may produce, or at all events predispose to, the paramnesic delusion of recognising present experiences as familiar. Thus Rosenbach has recorded the case of a sane and healthy man, who, after severe mental labour, followed by sleeplessness, seemed to know all the people he met in the street, though on close examination he found he was mistaken.[2] Such a condition may even be almost congenital. Thus of Anna Kingsford, who was of highly strung and neurotic disposition, we are told that, as a child, ' all that she read struck her as already familiar to her, so that she seemed to herself to be recovering

[1] 'Epilepsy,' wrote Binns long ago (*Anatomy of Sleep*, 1845, p. 431), ' is a disease which in some of its symptoms strongly resembles abnormal sleep.' The conditions under which a paramnesic manifestation may really replace an epileptic fit are well described by a literary man with hereditary epilepsy whose case has been recorded by Haskovec of Prague (*XIIIe. Congrès International de Médecine: Comptes Rendus*, vol. viii., ' Psychiatrie,' p. 125): ' One day at the theatre, under the influence of the heat and perhaps the music, I experienced extreme excitement and fatigue. I thought I was about to have an attack, and resisted with all my strength, and it failed to take place. But I found myself in a strange psychic state. On leaving the theatre I seemed to be dreaming. I saw and heard everything and talked as usual. But everything seemed strange. Nothing seemed to reach directly *me* or to be a real impression, but merely the automatic reproduction of something learnt, only I felt that I had lived it all before and felt it; at that moment I simply seemed to be observing it.'

Centralblatt für Nervenheilkunde, April 1886. In some forms of insanity the false recognition of a person may become a fixed delusion. This question has been studied by Albès in his Paris thesis, *De l'Illusion de Fausse Reconnaissance*, 1906.

old recollections rather than acquiring fresh knowledge.'¹ '

It is noteworthy that artificial anaesthesia by drugs which produce an abnormal sleep also favours paramnesia. Thus Sir William Ramsay ² has stated that when, under an anaesthetic, he heard a slight noise in the street, 'I not merely knew that it had happened before, but I could have predicted that it would happen at that very moment.'

In all these conditions we appear to be in the presence of an enfeebled, excited, and impaired state of consciousness approximating to the true confusion of dream consciousness. It seems as if externally aroused sensations in such cases are received by the exhausted cerebral centres in so blurred a form that an illusion takes place, and they are mistaken for internally excited sensations, for memories.

That paramnesia is a fatigue product—even though often a product of nervous hyperaesthesia—is indicated by the statements of many who have described it. Anjel long ago emphasised this fatigue, and Bonatelli, also at an early period, found that illusions of memory were specially liable to occur in states of unusual nervous irritability. During recent years this characteristic of paramnesia has been more and more frequently recognised. Bernard Leroy, who devoted a lengthy and important Paris thesis to pseudo-reminis-

---

[1] E. Maitland, *Anna Kingsford*, vol. i. p. 3. Lalande (*Revue Philosophique*, November 1893, p. 487) gives a precisely similar case in a child.

[2] As quoted by Jastrow, *The Subconscious*, p. 248.

cence,[1] showed that a certain proportion of cases indicated the presence of fatigue or distraction. Heymans found that it was in the evening, when his subjects were in a passive condition, tired, exhausted, or engaged in uncongenial work, that they were most liable to the experience.[2] Féré brought forward a case in which, as he pointed out, pseudo-reminiscence in a healthy man, convalescent from influenza, was associated with fatigue and disappeared with it.[3] Dromard and Albès declare that pseudo-reminiscence is ' a phenomenon of exhaustion,' and one of them makes the significant statement : ' I become more easily the prey of this illusion when, by chance and without thinking of it, I simultaneously apply my attention to an external object and an internal thought.'[4] Dugas, again, considers that all the various forms of paramnesia have ' one common character, which is that they occur as the result of prolonged or intense fatigue ';[5] he adds that most of the cases of paramnesia he has noted in young people during fifteen years coincided with periods of anaemia and nervous weakness.

[1] Leroy, *Etude sur l'Illusion de Fausse Reconnaissance*, 1898, with forty-nine new observations. Leroy states, however (in declared opposition to my view), that only a minority of his cases actually mention fatigue.

[2] Heymans, 'Eine Enquête über Depersonnalisation und Fausse Reconnaissance,' *Zeitschrift für Psychologie und Physiologie der Sinnesorgane*, November, 1903 ; also a further paper in the same journal confirming his conclusions, January 1906.

[3] Féré, 'Deuxième Note sur la Fausse Reconnaissance,' *Journal de Neurologie*, 1905.

[4] Dromard et Albès, ' L'Illusion dit de Fausse Reconnaissance,' *Journal de Psychologie Normale et Pathologique*, May-June 1905

[5] Dugas, ' Observations sur des Erreurs " Formelles " de la Mémoire,' *Revue Philosophique*, July 1908.

MEMORY IN DREAMS

It is not, however, necessary to believe that fatigue, in the ordinary sense of the word, whether physical or mental, is the invariable accompaniment of paramnesia. If it is the presence of a condition resembling that of sleep or the hypnagogic state which predisposes to the experience, that condition may be produced by other circumstances. Distraction, excited hyperaesthesia simulating increased power, and various chronic psychic states hue to a highly-strung or over-strained nervous system may all tend in the same direction, even though no sense of exhaustion is felt.[1] This is doubtless why it is that so many poets, novelists, and other men of strenuous intellectual aptitude are liable to this experience.

It has been argued by some who admit that there is often an element of fatigue in paramnesia,[2] that the real cause of the false memory is an abnormal celerity of perception, perhaps due to hyperaesthesia. The scene would thus be perceived so quickly that the subject

[1] A friend, liable to this form of paramnesia, wrote to me after the publication of my first paper on the subject: 'I find, as you foretold, that it is difficult to recall an experience of this kind in all its details. I feel sure, however, that it is not necessarily allied with an enfeebled or overwrought nervous system. It was commonest with me in my youth, at a time when my life was a pleasant one, and my brain not fagged as now. I still [aged 43] have it occasionally, but not so frequently as twenty years ago.' It may be added that my friend, of Highland family, was a man of keen and emotional nervous temperament, a strenuous mental worker—whence at one time a serious breakdown in health—and had published two volumes of poems in early life. The greater liability to paramnesia in early life, which is generally recognised, is comparable to the special liability of children to hypnagogic visions, both phenomena being probably due to the greater excitability and easier exhaustibility of the youthful brain.

[2] For instance, by Allin, 'Recognition,' *American Journal of Psychology*, January 1896.

concludes that he must have had this experience before. That the subject often has a feeling of unusual rapidity of perception may very well be admitted. But there is no reason whatever to suppose that the perception actually is received with any such unusual rapidity. The probabilities are in the other direction. We know that many influences (such as drugs like alcohol) which produce a feeling of heightened and quickened perceptions really have a slowing and dulling effect, in the same way as the wise and beautiful things we utter in dreams are usually found on awaking to be commonplace, if not meaningless. There is no evidence to show that paramnesia is accompanied by a real heightening of perception, while, as we have seen, a broad survey of the facts makes it more reasonable to suppose that we have, on the contrary, a sudden fall towards the dream state, a state in which, as Tissie and others have pointed out, there are many stages.

It must be remembered in this connection that in the hypnagogic and other states related to sleep we are not able to estimate time conditions consciously, though, as the frequent ability to wake at fixed moments indicates, we may do so subconsciously. Time is long, short, or non-existent in dream-like states. This is always true of the onset of the hypnagogic state. When I am suddenly awakened at night by a voice or a bell or other stimulus, I often find it very difficult to say whether I was or was not already awake, and have frequently replied, when so awakened, that I was already awake. That is an illusion, as is shown by the frequency

MEMORY IN DREAMS

with which elderly people who fall asleep in the day time, will declare, though they may have been snoring a moment before, that they have never been asleep. By a somewhat similar paramnesic illusion we can never fix the exact moment when we awake. When we become conscious that we are awake it always seems to us that we are already awake, awake for an indefinite time, and not that we have just awakened. If I had to register the exact moment I awake in the morning I should usually feel that I was considerably late in making the observation. It seems that the imperfect hypnagogic consciousness projects itself behind. At the first onset, consciousness is not sufficiently developed to be able to realise that it is beginning, and when it becomes sufficiently developed to make such a statement the moment when it can be correctly made is already past. Consciousness is only able to assert that it has been continuing for an indefinite time. And that assertion involves a paramnesic illusion of putting back a present experience into the past, analogous to the illusion of pseudo-reminiscence.[1]

[1] The explanation of paramnesia here set forth received on its first publication the approval of Léon Marillier, who considered it 'ingenious and seductive,' and as adequately accounting for the phenomena, provided we bear in mind that the loss of a clear feeling of time is characteristic of hypnagogic and allied states, the perception of each moment being immediately transferred into an ancient memory, and consequently recognised (*L'Année Biologique*, third year, 1897, p. 772). This necessity for taking into account the co-existence of perception and illusory remembrance has largely moulded several of the theories of paramnesia. Thus Jean de Pury (*Archives de Psychologie*, December 1902), while affirming that pseudo-reminiscence is due to an *anteriorisation* of actual perceptions, regards it as of the nature of a double refraction such as that simultaneously produced on two faces of a prism by the same image; under the influence

If we realise these characteristics of paramnesia we can scarcely fail to conclude that we are concerned here with illusions which, while they fall within the sphere of memory, are largely conditioned by the whole psychic condition. As in dreams, it is inattention, failure of apperception, defective association of the mental contents, which make the paramnesia possible. Paramnesia is, as Fouillée has said, a kind of diplopia or seeing double in the mental field. 'I have the impression,' says one of the writers on this subject who himself experiences the sensation, 'that the present reality has a *double*.' Actual double vision is due to the failure of that muscular co-ordination which, as Ribot and others have insisted, is of the very essence of attention. This wider psychic basis on which paramnesia rests has of late been recognised by several psychologists. Thus Léon-Kindberg states that in paramnesia there is an absence of mental attention, of the effort of synthesis necessary to grasp an actual occurrence, which is, therefore, perceived with the same

---

of conditions he is unable to define, an image appears for the moment on the plane both of the past and of the present, and psychically we see double just as physically we see double when the parallelism of our visual rays is disturbed. Piéron, again, taking up a theory at one time favoured by Dugas, and previously suggested in one form or another by Ribot and Fouillée, assumes the formation of two images: one which, owing to distraction or fatigue, reaches consciousness after having traversed subconsciousness, and so takes on a dream-like and effaced character, and almost simultaneously with this a direct perception which has not thus changed its character; the shock of the conflict between these two produces the pseudo-reminiscence ('Sur l'Interpretation des Faits de Paramnésie,' *Revue Philosophique*, August 1902) Albès, in his Paris thesis, criticises this explanation, pointing out that a sequence of this kind very frequently occurs, but produces no pseudo-reminiscence.

MEMORY IN DREAMS

facility as a memory not requiring synthesis, with the resulting illusion that it is a memory.[1] Ballet, again, regards paramnesia as a transitory or permanent psychasthenic state, due to dissociation.[2] Dugas, also, who has repeatedly returned to this subject during many years, in his latest contributions attaches primary importance to this broader factor of paramnesia. In analysing memory, he says, there is an element which, though often overlooked, is capital: the recognition of a state of consciousness not merely as passed, but as bound up with our own personal past; when that synthetic function ceases to be accomplished, or is only accomplished defectively, then memory is lacking or perverted. Nervous weakness, he proceeds, produces failure of attention, the inhibitory power of attention being no longer exerted, and the psychic elements fall back to anarchy. Now many psychic states, such as sensations, recollections, and images, differ from each other less by their substance than by the way in which the mind takes hold of and apprehends them. The mind seizes a sensation with a stronger grasp than a recollection, and a recollection with a stronger grasp than an image. When attention is relaxed the line of demarcation between these psychic states tends to be effaced; the sensation becomes vague and floating like the recollection and the image, while the recollection and the image, on the contrary,

[1] Michel Léon-Kindberg, 'Le Sentiment du Déjà Vu,' *Revue de Psychiatrie*, April 1903, No. 4.
[2] G. Ballet, 'Un Cas de Fausse Reconnaissance,' *Revue Neurologique*, 1904, p. 1221.

become objective and acquire something of the brilliance and relief of the sensation. The very same cause —enfeeblement of attention—thus produces opposite effects, on the one side raising the tone, on the other lowering it, so that states of mind which are ordinarily distinct tend to be approximated and confused, as we may observe in the hypnagogic condition.[1]

Although Dugas makes no reference to Janet, it is not difficult to see that he has assimilated some of the views of that distinguished investigator of psychic mysteries. Janet, as we know, in various morbid psychic conditions, attaches great explanatory force to the individual's loss of hold, through psychic weakness, of his own personality, and to the diminished sense of reality and even depersonalisation thence ensuing. It so happens that Janet himself has set forth a theory of pseudo-reminiscence which is characteristic of his own attitude, and also harmonises with the wider outlook which now marks the attempts to explain these perversions of memory. Janet declares that pseudo-reminiscence is a negative phenomenon and belongs to a group in which various other feelings of diminished sense of reality belong. These people all say in effect : ' It seems to me that these things are not real ; it seems to me that these events are not actual or present.' The essence of this form of paramnesia

---

[1] Dugas, ' Observations sur des Erreurs "Formelles" de la Mémoire, *Revue Philosophique*, July 1908; *ib.* June 1910. Dugas makes no reference to Janet, nor to my paper on Hypnagogic Paramnesia, but his statement of the matter to some extent combines and harmonises those of the two earlier writers.

is thus more a negation of the present than an affirmation of the past. 'The function of adaptation to the present moment,' Janet remarks, 'is the most complicated and the most recent of all. The function of the real is the most elevated and the most difficult of all cerebral functions.' Under various influences there is a diminution of nervous and psychic tension, and such suppression of the high tension of the mind leaves only the lower functions subsisting. When that fall of tension is rapid, there may be a crisis of which pseudo-reminiscence is one of the symptoms.[1] Janet would thus place pseudo-reminiscence among the manifestations of psychasthenia, though he leaves untouched the difficult question of its precise mechanism.

The most comprehensive attempt to explain the mystery of paramnesia in recent years is certainly that made in an elaborately eclectic study by one of the most distinguished of living French thinkers, Professor Bergson.[2] He first casts a glance over what he considers the two main groups of explanations of this puzzling phenomenon : (1) those, advocated by Ribot, Fouillée, Lalande, Arnaud, Piéron, Myers, etc., which involve the more or less simultaneous existence in consciousness of two images, of which one is the reproduction of the other ; (2) those advocated by Janet, Heymans, Léon-Kindberg, Dromard and

[1] P. Janet, 'A Propos du Déjà Vu,' *Journal de Psychologie Normale et Pathologique*, July-August 1905.

[2] H. Bergson, 'Le Souvenir du Présent et la Fausse Reconnaissance,' *Revue Philosophique*, December 1908. It should be remarked that, except in the attempt to explain why paramnesia is not normally habitual, Bergson's paper is based on the ideas or suggestions of previous writers.

Albès, etc., which insist on the lower mental tone, the diminished attention, the lack of synthetising power, which mark the condition in which paramnesia occurs. Bergson is quite ready to accept the principles of both these groups of explanations, and to combine them. But, he argues, to understand the phenomenon adequately, we must go deeper ; we must analyse the normal mechanism of memory. And he finds, if we do this, that not merely the moment of a paramnesic illusion, but every moment of our life, offers two aspects, actual and virtual, perception on one side, and memory on the other. The moment itself, indeed, consists of such a scission, for it is always moving, always a fleeting boundary between the immediate past and the immediate future, and would be a mere abstraction if it were not ' precisely the mobile mirror which ceaselessly reflects perception in recollection.' When the matter is thus regarded a recollection is seen to be, in reality, not something which has been, but something which is, proceeding *pari passu* with the perception it reproduces. It is a recollection of the moment taking place at that moment. Belonging to the past as regards its form, it belongs to the present as regards its matter. It is recollection of the present. Now this is exactly the state in which the paramnesic person consciously finds himself, and the only problem before us, therefore, is to ascertain why every one at every moment is not conscious of the same experience. Bergson replies that nothing is more useless for present action than the recollection of the present. It has

MEMORY IN DREAMS

nothing to tell us ; we hold the real object, and to give up that for its recollection would be to sacrifice the substance to the shadow. Therefore we obstinately and persistently turn away from the recollection of the present. It emerges consciously only under the influence of some abnormal or pathological disturbance of attention. Paramnesia is an anomaly of this kind, and it is due to a temporary enfeeblement of the general attention to life, a momentary arrest of the forward movement of consciousness. ' False recognition,' Bergson concludes, 'may thus be regarded as the most inoffensive form of inattention to life. It seems to result from the combined play of perception and memory given up to their own energy. It would take place at every moment if it were not that will, ceaselessly directed towards action, prevents the present from folding in on itself by pushing it indefinitely into the future.'

So far as my own explanation is concerned, it will be seen that I still place weight on the general condition of temporary or chronic nervous fatigue as the soil on which paramnesia arises—a belief now accepted by most psychologists [1]—and that I think we must search for the clue to the mechanism of the illusion in

---

[1] Before the appearance of my paper, as already mentioned, Anjel had emphasised the significance of fatigue in the production of paramnesia (*Archiv für Psychiatrie*, Bd. viii. pp. 57 *et seq.*). His theory, indeed (only known to me through brief summaries)—according to which the pseudo-reminiscence is due to the tardy apprehension by the fatigued mind of a sensation which is thus degraded to the level of a reproduced impression —seems practically identical with that which I independently reached in the light of hypnagogic phenomena.

those dreaming and hypnagogic states in which it most often occurs. As regards a definite explanation of the mechanism we must, in the face of so many ingenious and complicated theories, perhaps still await more general agreement.[1] What I have suggested, and am still inclined to maintain, is that the psychic enfeeblement, temporary or chronic, which is the general preliminary condition of paramnesia, whether or not there is any subjective sensation of increased power, may account for the paramnesia by bringing an externally aroused perception down to a lower and fainter stage on which it is on a level with an internally aroused perception—a memory. Just as in hypnagogic paramnesia the vivid and life-like dream, or internal impression, is raised to the class of memories, and becomes the shadow of a real experience, so in waking paramnesia the external impression is lowered to the same class. Perception is alike dulled in each case, and the immediate experience follows the line of least resistance—this time too carelessly or too prematurely—to join the great bulk of our experiences.

[1] I disregard those theories which invoke histological explanations, as by some peculiar disposition of the neurons. Such explanations are as much outside the psychologist's sphere as the old-fashioned explanations by reference to God and the Devil. A known physiological or pathological process may, indeed, quite properly be recognised by the psychologist; such, for instance, as the disturbance of the heart associated with some dreams. Even minute changes in the brain, when they have been properly determined by the histologist, may be effectively invoked by the psychologist if they seem to supply an exact physical correlative to his own findings. But for the psychologist to go outside his own field, and invent a purely fanciful and arbitrary neuronic scheme to suit a psychic process, explains nothing. It is merely child's play. The stuff that the psychologist works with must be psychical, just as the stuff of the physicist's work must be physical.

MEMORY IN DREAMS

We thus realise how it is that that doubling of experience occurs. The mind has for the moment become flaccid and enfeebled ; its loosened texture has, as it were, abnormally enlarged the meshes in which sensations are caught and sifted, so that they run through too easily. In other words, they are not properly *apperceived*. To use a crude simile, it is as though we poured water into a sieve. The impressions of the world which are actual sensations as they strike the relaxed psychic meshwork are instantaneously passed through to become memories, and we see them in both forms at the same moment, and are unable to distinguish one from the other.

In sleep, and in the hypnagogic state, as in hypnosis, we accept a suggestion, with or without a struggle. In the waking paramnesic state we seem to find, in a slighter stage of a like condition, *the same process in a reversed form.* Instead of accepting a representation as an actual present fact, we accept the actual present fact as merely a representation. The centres of perception are in such a state of exhaustion and disorder that they receive an actual external sensation in the feebler shape of a representation. The actual fact becomes merely a suggestion of far distant things. It reaches consciousness in the enfeebled shape of an old memory—

'. . . like to something I remember
A great while since, a long, long time ago.'

Paramnesia is thus an internal hallucination, a reversed hallucination, it is true, but while so reversed, the stream of consciousness is still following the line of least resistance.

It is along some such lines as these, it seems to me, that we may best attempt to explain the phenomena of paramnesia, phenomena which are of no little interest since, in earlier stages of culture, they may well have had a real influence on belief, suggesting to primitive man that he had somehow had wider experiences than he knew of, and that, as Wordsworth put it, he trailed clouds of glory behind him.

CHAPTER X

CONCLUSION

The Fundamental Nature of Dreaming—Insanity and Dreaming—The Child's Psychic State and the Dream State—Primitive Thought and Dreams—Dreaming and Myth-Making—Genius and Dreams—Dreaming as a Road into the Infinite.

IN the preceding chapters we have traced some of the elementary tendencies which prevail in the formation of dreams. These tendencies are in some respects so unlike those that rule in waking life—slight and subtle as their unlikeness often seems—that we are justified in regarding the psychic phenomena of sleeping life as constituting a world of their own.

Yet when we look at the phenomena a little more deeply we realise that, however differentiated they have become, dream life is yet strictly co-ordinated with other forms of psychic life. If we pierce below the surface we seem to reach a primitive fundamental psychic stage in which the dreamer, the madman, the child, and the savage alike have their starting point, and possess a degree of community from which the waking, civilised, sane adult of to-day is shut out, so that he can only comprehend it by an intellectual effort.[1] It thus happens that the ways of thinking and

---
[1] Certain phases of waking psychic life are, however, closely related to dreaming. This is obviously the case as regards day-dreaming or reverie. (See *e.g.* Janet, *Névroses et Idées Fixes*, vol. i. pp. 390-6.) It would also

feeling of the child and the savage and the lunatic each furnish a road by which we may reach a psychic world which is essentially that of the dreamer.

The resemblance of insanity to dream life has, above all, impressed observers from the time when the nature of insanity was first definitely recognised. It would be outside the limits of the present book to discuss the points at which dreams resemble or differ from insanity, but it is worth while to touch on the question of their affinity. The recognition of this affinity, or at all events analogy, though it was stated by Cabanis to be due to Cullen, is as old as Aristotle, and has constantly been put forward afresh. Thus in the sixteenth century Du Laurens (A. Laurentius), in his treatise on the disease of melancholy, as insanity was then termed, compared it to dreaming.[1] The same point is still constantly brought forward by the more philosophic physician. 'Find out all about dreams,' Hughlings Jackson has said, 'and you will have found out all about insanity.' From the wider standpoint of the psychologist, Jastrow points out that not only insanity, but all the forms of delirium, including the drug-intoxications, are 'variants of dream consciousness.'

The reality of the affinity of dreaming and insanity

appear that wit is the result of a process analogous to that fusion of incompatible elements which we have found to prevail in dreams. Our dreams are sometimes full of usually ineffective wit; I could easily quote dreams in illustration. (Freud has, from his point of view, studied the analogy between wit and dreaming in *Der Witz und seine Beziehung zum Unbewussten*.)

[1] In more recent times Moreau of Tours, especially, argued (*Du Haschich et de l'Aliénation Mentale*, 1845) that *haschisch*-intoxication is insanity, and that insanity is a waking dream.

CONCLUSION 263

is well illustrated by a case, coming under the observation of Marro, in which a dream, formed according to the ordinary rules of dreaming, produced a temporary fit of insanity in an otherwise perfectly sane subject.[1] In this case a highly intelligent but somewhat neurotic young man was returning to Italy after pursuing his studies abroad, and reached Turin, on the homeward journey, in a somewhat tired state. In the train he believed that he had detected some cardsharpers, and that they suspected him of finding them out, and bore him ill-will in consequence. This produced a state of general nervous apprehension. At the hotel his room was over the kitchen ; it was in consequence very hot, and to a late hour he could still hear voices and catch snatches of conversation, which seemed to him to be directed against himself. His suspicions deepened, he heard noises, in reality due to the kitchen utensils, which seemed preparations for his murder, and he ultimately became convinced that there was a plot to set fire to his room in order to force him to leave it, when he would be seized and murdered. He resolved to escape, got out of the window with his revolver in his hand, found his way to another part of the house, encountered a man who had been awakened by his movements, and shot at him, believing him to be a party to the imaginary conspiracy. He was seized and taken to the asylum, where he speedily regained calm, and realised the delusion into which he had fallen.

[1] In insane subjects a dream not uncommonly forms the starting point of a delusion, and many illustrative examples could be brought forward.

When questioned by Marro, on reaching the asylum, he was unaware that he had ever fallen asleep during the night ; he could not, however, account for all the time that had elapsed before he left the room, and it was probable, Marro concludes, that he was in a state between waking and sleeping, and that his delusion was constituted in a dream. Fatigue, nervous apprehension, an unduly hot bedroom, the close proximity of servants' voices, and the sound of kitchen utensils, had thus combined, in a state of partial sleep, to produce in an otherwise sane person, a morbid condition in every respect identical with that found in insane persons who are suffering from systematised delusions of persecution.[1]

The resemblance of the child's psychic state to the dream state is an observation of less ancient date than that of the analogy between dreaming and insanity, but it has frequently been made by modern psychologists. ' In dreams,' says Freud, ' the child with his impulses lives again,'[2] and Giessler has devoted a chapter to the points of resemblance between dream life and the mental activity of children.[3]

I should be more especially inclined to find the dream-like character of the child's mind at three points : (1) the abnormally logical tendency of the child's mind

[1] Marro, La Pubertà, pp. 286-92.
[2] Freud, Die Traumdeutung, p. 13. Elsewhere (p. 135) Freud remarks: ' The deeper we go in the analysis of dreams the more frequently we come across traces of childish experience which form a latent source of dreams.' The same point had been previously emphasised by Sully, ' The Dream as a Revelation,' Fortnightly Review, March 1893.
[3] C. M. Giessler, Die Physiologischen Beziehungen der Traumvorgänge, ch. iv.

CONCLUSION 265

and the daring mental fusions which he effects in forming theories; (2) the greater preponderance of hypnagogic phenomena and hallucinations in childhood, as well as the large element of reverie or day-dreaming in the child's life, and the facility with which he confuses this waking imagination with reality ; and (3) the child's tendency to mistake, also, the dreams of the night for real events.[1] This last tendency is of serious practical import when it leads a child, in all innocence, to make criminal charges against other persons.[2] This tendency clearly indicates the close resemblance which there is for children between dream life and waking life ; it also shows the great vividness which children's dreams possess. In imaginative children, it may be added, a rich and vivid dream life is not infrequently the direct source of literary activities which lead to distinction in later life.[3]

[1] Jewell, who gives illustrations in evidence, concludes (*American Journal of Psychology*, January 1905, pp. 25-8) that 'the confusion of dreams with real life is almost universal with children, and quite common among adolescents and adults.'
[2] Hans Gross, the distinguished criminologist, refers (*Kriminalpsychologie*, p. 672) to two cases of children who brought criminal charges which were apparently based on dreams. Gross mentions that this may often be suspected when the child says nothing at the time, and shows no excitement or depression until a day or two after the date of the alleged event. For confusion of dream with reality, see also Gross, *Gesammelte Kriminalistische Aufsätze*, vol. ii. p. 174.
[3] Thus Rachilde (Mme. Vallette) writes that as a young girl her dreams were so vivid that ' I would often ask myself if I had not an existence in two forms : my waking personality and my dreaming personality. Sometimes I was deceived and imagined that my real life was dreams.' She instinctively began to write at the age of twelve, and it was by completing her dreams that she became a novelist (Chabaneix, *Le Subconscient*, p. 49). George Sand's early day-dreams, of which she gives so interesting an account (*Histoire de ma Vie*, part III. ch. viii), developed

The child, we are often told, is the representative of the modern savage and the primitive man. That is not, in any strict sense, true, nor can we assume without question that early man and modern savages are identical. But we can have very little doubt that in our dreams we are brought near to ways of thought and feeling that are sometimes closer to those of early man, as well as of latter-day savages, than are our psychic modes in civilisation.[1] So remote are we to-day from the world of our dreams that we very rarely draw from them the inspiration of our waking lives. For the primitive man the laws of the waking world are not yet widely differentiated from the laws of the sleeping world, and he finds it not unreasonable to seek illumination for the problems of one world in the phenomena of the other. The doctrine of animism, as first formulated by Tylor (more especially in his *Primitive Culture*) finds in dreams the chief source of primitive religion and philosophy. Of recent years there has been a tendency to reject the theory of animism.[2] Certainly it is possible to rely too exclusively on dreams as the inspiration of early man ; if the evidence of dreams had

around the central figure of Corambé, first seen in a real dream. Corambé was, at the same time, a divine being, to whom she erected an altar. So that of the child it may be said, as Lucretius said of primitive man, that the gods first appear in dreams.

[1] ' In sleep,' says Sully (*Fortnightly Review*, March 1893), ' we have a reversion to a more primitive type of experience.' ' Dreaming,' says Jastrow (*The Subconscious*, p. 219), ' may be viewed as a reversion to a more primitive type of thought.'

[2] This tendency is notably represented by Durkheim ('Origines de la Pensée Religieuse,' *Revue Philosophique*, January 1909) and Crawley (*The Idea of the Soul*, 1909).

not been in a line with the evidence that he derived from other sources, there is no reason why the man of primitive times should have attached any peculiar value to dreams. But if the animistic conception presents too extreme a view of the primitive importance of dreaming, we must beware lest the reaction against it should lead us to fall into the opposite extreme. Durkheim argues that it is unlikely that early man attached much significance to dreams, for the modern peasant, who is the representative of primitive man, appears to dream very little, and not to attach much importance to his dreams. But it is by no means true that the peasant of civilisation, with his fixed agricultural life, corresponds to early man who was mainly a hunter and often a nomad. Under the conditions of civilisation the peasant is fed regularly and leads a peaceful, stolid, laborious, and equable life, which is altogether unfavourable to psychic activity of any kind, awake or asleep. The savage man, now and ever, as a hunter and fighter, leads a life of comparative idleness, broken by spurts of violent activity ; sometimes he can gorge himself with food, sometimes he is on the verge of starvation. He lives under conditions that are more favourable to the psychic side of life, awake or asleep, than is the case with the peasant of civilisation.

Moreover, it must be remembered that all the peoples whom we may fairly regard as in some degree resembling early man possess a specialised caste of exceptional men who artificially cultivate their psychic activities, and thereby exert great influence on their fellows. These are termed, after their very typical representatives in some Siberian tribes, *shamans*, and combine the functions of priests and sorcerers and medicine men. It is nearly everywhere found that the shaman—who is often, it would appear, at the outset a somewhat abnormal person—cultivates solitude, fasting, and all manner of ascetic practices, thereby acquiring an unusual aptitude to dream, to see visions, to experience hallucinations, and, it may well be, to acquire abnormally clairvoyant powers. The shamans of the Andamanese are called by a word signifying dreamer, and in various parts of the world the shaman finds the first sign of his vocation in a dream. The evocation of dreams is often the chief end of the shaman's abnormal method of life. Thus, among the Salish Indians of British Columbia, dreams are the proper mode of communication with guardian spirits, and 'prolonged fasts, bathings, forced vomitings, and other exhausting bodily exercises are the means adopted for inducing the mystic dreams and visions.' [1]

When we witness the phenomena of Shamanism in all parts of the world it is difficult to dispute the statement of Lucretius that the gods first appeared to men in dreams. This may be said to be literally true; even to-day it often happens that the savage's totem, who is

[1] Hill Tout, *Journal*, Anthropological Institute, January-June 1905, p. 143; Sidney Hartland, in his presidential address to the Anthropological Section of the British Association, in 1906, emphasised the significance of dreams in Shamanism, and Sir Everard im Thurn, in his *Among the Indians of Guiana*, shows how practically real are dreams to the savage mind.

CONCLUSION 269

practically his tutelary deity, first appears to him in a dream.[1] An influence which seems likely to have been so persistent may well have had a large plastic power in moulding the myths and legends which everywhere embody the religious impulses of men. This idea was long ago suggested by Hobbes. 'From this ignorance of how to distinguish dreams and other strong Fancies,' he wrote, 'from Vision and Sense, did arise the greatest part of the Religion of the Gentiles in time past, that worshipped Satyrs, Fauns, Nymphs, and the like.'[2]

Ludwig Laistner, however, appears to have been the first to argue in detail that dreams, and especially nightmares, have played an important part in the evolution of mythological ideas. 'If we bear in mind,' he said in the Preface to his great work, 'how intimately poetry and religion are connected with myth, we encounter the surprising fact that the first germ of these highly important vital manifestations is not to be found in any action of the waking mind, but in sleep, and that the chief and oldest teacher of productive imagination is not to be found in the experiences of life, but in the phantasies of dream.'[3] The pictures men formed of

[1] See, e.g., as regards the American Indians, Thornton Parker in the *Open Court*, May 1901.
[2] *Leviathan*, part I. ch. ii.
[3] Laistner, *Das Rätsel der Sphinx*, 1889, vol. I. p. xiii. While Laistner was chiefly concerned with the exploration of the religious myths, he pointed out that epics and fairy-tales (Amor and Psyche, the stories of the Nibelung and Baldur, etc.) may be similarly explained. It seems probable that his investigations received a stimulus in the earlier experiments of J. Boerner (*Das Alpdrücken*, 1855) on the production of nightmare. Laistner has had many followers, notable C. Ruths (*Experimental-Untersuchungen über Musikphantome*, 1898), who argues (pp. 415-46) that the old Greek myths had their chief root in dream phenomena, in delirium,

the over-world and the under-world have the character of dreams and hypnagogic visions, and this is true even within the sphere of Christianity.[1] The invention of Hell, Maudsley has declared, would find an adequate explanation, if such is needed, in the sufferings of some delirious patients, while the apocalyptic vision of Heaven with which our Christian Bible concludes, is, Beaunis remarks, nothing but a long dream.[2] And if it is true, as Baudelaire has said, that 'every well conformed brain carries within it two infinites : Heaven and Hell,' we may well believe that both Heaven and Hell find their most vivid symbolism in the spontaneous action of dreams.

In migraine and the epileptic aura visions of diminutive creatures sometimes occur, and occasionally micropsic vision in which real objects appear diminished. It has been suggested by Sir Lauder Brunton that we may here have the origin of fairies, at all events for

and in the visions aroused in some persons by hearing music, while he considers that many fabulous monsters and dragons have arisen from the combinations seen in dreams. We know that the Greeks, who were such great myth-makers, much occupied themselves in lying in wait for dreams, and in oneiromancy and necromancy (*e.g.*, Bouché-Leclercq, *Histoire de la Divination dans l'Antiquité*, vol. I. Bk. ii. ch. i. pp. 277-329). In this way alone it is doubtless true that, as Jewell says, ' dreams have had a great effect upon the history of the world.'

[1] For evidence regarding the high esteem in which many of the greatest Greek and Latin Fathers held dreams as divine revelations, see *e.g.*, Sully, Art. ' Dreams,' *Encyclopædia Britannica*.

[2] There is still a natural tendency in the uninstructed mind to identify spontaneous visual phenomena with Heaven. ' When I gets to bed,' said an aged and superannuated dustman to Vanderkiste (*The Dens of London*, p. 14), ' I says my prayers, and I puts my hands afore my eyes—so [covering his face with his hands] ; well, I sees such beautiful things, sparkles like, all afloating about, and I wished to ax yer, sir, if that ain't a something of Heaven, sir.'

CONCLUSION 271

some races of fairies ; for fairies, though diminutive in some countries, as in England, are not diminutive in others, as in Ireland. A more normal and frequent channel of intercourse with such creatures is, however, to be found in dreams. This is illustrated by the following dream experienced by a lady : ' I saw a man wheeling along a cripple. Eventually the cripple became reduced to about the size of a walnut, and the man told me that he had the power of becoming any size and of going anywhere. To my horror he then threw him into the water. In answer to my remonstrances that he would surely be drowned, the man said that it was all right, the little fellow would be home in a few hours. He then shouted out, " What time do you expect to get back ? " The tiny creature, who was paddling along in the water, then took out a miniature watch, and replied : " About seven ! " '[1] In a dream of my own I saw little creatures, a few inches high, moving about and acting on a diminutive stage. Though I regarded them as really living creatures, and not marionettes, the spectacle caused me no surprise.

The dream-like character of myths, legends, and fairy tales is probably, however, not entirely due to direct borrowing from the actual dreams of sleep, or even from the hallucinations connected with insanity, music, or drugs, though all these may have played their part. The greater nearness of the primitive

---

[1] This was the only traceable element in the dream. The dreamer was accustomed to look at her watch on awaking in the morning, and, if it was seven or later, not to go to sleep again.

mind to the dream-state involves more than a tendency to embody in waking life conceptions obtained from dreams. It means that the waking psychic life itself is capable of acting in a way resembling that of the sleeping psychic life, and of evolving conceptions similar to dreams.

This point of view has in recent years been especially set forth by Freud and his school, who argue that the laws of the formation of myths and fairy tales are identical with the laws in accordance with which dreams are formed.[1] It certainly seems to be true that the resemblances between dreams and legends are not adequately explained by supposing that the latter are moulded out of the former. We have to believe that on the myth-making plane of thought we are really on a plane that is more nearly parallel with that of dreaming than is our ordinary civilised thought. We are in a world of things that are supernormally enormous or delicate, and the emotional vibrations vastly enlarged, a world in which miracles happen on every hand and cause us no surprise. Slaughter and destruction take place on the heroic scale with a minimum expenditure of effort; men are transformed into beasts and beasts into men, so that men and beasts converse with each other.[2]

[1] Freud, 'Der Dichter und das Phantasieren' (1908), in second series of his *Sammlung Kleiner Schriften zur Neurosenlehre*; K. Abraham, *Traum und Mythus* (1909); and O. Rank, *Der Mythus von der Geburt des Helden* (1909), both published in the *Schriften zur angewandten Seelenkunde*, edited by Freud.

[2] Synesius refers to conversations with sheep in dreams, and he was probably the first to suggest that such dream phenomena may be the

CONCLUSION 273

Finally, it may be observed that the atmosphere into which genius leads us, and indeed all art, is the atmosphere of the world of dreams. The man of genius, it is often said, has the child within him ; he is, according to the ancient dictum, which is still accepted, not without an admixture of insanity, and he is unquestionably related to the primitive myth-maker. All these characteristics, as we see, bring him near to the sphere of dreaming, and we may say that the man of genius is in closer touch with the laws of the dream world than is the ordinary civilised man. ' It would be no great paradox,' remarks Maudsley, ' to say that the creative work of genius was excellent dreaming, and dramatic dreaming distracted genius.'[1] This has often been recognised by some of the most typical men of genius. Charles Lamb, in speaking of Spenser, referred to the analogy between dreaming and imagination. Coleridge, one of the most essential of imaginative

<small>origin of fables in which animals speak. The dog and the cat, as we should expect, seem most frequently to speak in the dreams of civilised people. Thus I dreamed that I had a conversation with a cat who spoke with fair clearness and sense, though the whole of her sentences were not intelligible. I was not surprised at this relative lack of intelligibility, but neither was I surprised at her speaking at all. I have also encountered a talking parrot whose speech was more relevant than that of most talking parrots ; this somewhat surprised me. In legends a wider range of animals are able to speak, no doubt because the primitive legend-makers were familiar with a wider range of animal life. How natural it is to the uninstructed mind to treat animals like human beings is well shown by the experiences of Helen Keller, the blind deaf-mute, who writes (*The World I Live in*, p. 147) : ' After my education began, the world which came within my reach was all alive. . . . It was two years before I could be made to believe that my dogs did not understand what I said, and I always apologised to them when I ran into or stepped on them.'
[1] *Journal of Mental Science*, January 1909, p. 16.</small>

S

men, argued that the laws of drama and of dreaming are the same.[1] Nietzsche, more recently, has developed the affinity of dreaming to art, and in his *Birth of Tragedy* argued that the Appollonian or dream-like element is one of the two constituents of tragedy. Mallarmé further believed that symbolism, which we have seen to be fundamental in dreaming, is of the essence of art. 'To name an object,' he said, 'is to suppress three-quarters of the enjoyment in a poem which is made up of the happiness of gradually divining; to suggest—that is our dream. The perfect usage of this mystery constitutes symbolism: to evoke an object, little by little, in order to exhibit a state of the soul, or, inversely, to choose an object, and to disengage from it a state of the soul by a series of decipherments.'[2] It may be added that imaginative and artistic men have always been prone to day-dreaming and reverie, allowing their fancies to wander uncontrolled, and in so doing they have found profit to their work.[3] From Socrates onwards, too, men of genius have some-

[1] 'Images and thoughts,' he said, 'possess a power in and of themselves independent of that act of the judgment or understanding by which we affirm or deny the existence of a reality correspondent to them. Such is the ordinary state of the mind in dreams. . . . Add to this a voluntary lending of the will to this suspension of one of its own operations, and you have the true theory of stage illusion.'

[2] Quoted by Paul Delior, *Remy de Gourmont et son Œuvre*, p. 14.

[3] Thus even Leonardo da Vinci (Solmi, *Frammenti*, p. 285) acknowledged the benefit which he had gained by gazing at clouds or at mud-bespattered walls; and recommended the practice to other artists, for thereby, he says, they will receive suggestions for landscapes, battle-pieces, 'and infinite things,' which they may bring to perfection. He compared this to the possibility of hearing words in the sounds of bells. Some other distinguished artists have adopted somewhat similar practices which are fundamentally the child's habit of seeing pictures in the fire.

CONCLUSION

times been liable to fall into states of trance, or waking dream, in which their mission or their vision has become more clearly manifested;[1] the hallucinatory voices which have determined the vocation of many great teachers belong to psychic states allied to these trances.

It is scarcely necessary to refer to the occasional creative activity of men of genius during actual sleep or to the debts which they have acknowledged to suggestions received in dreams.[2] This has perhaps, indeed, been more often exaggerated than overlooked. There can be no doubt that a great many writers and thinkers, including some of the highest eminence, have sometimes been indebted to their dreams. We might expect as much, for most people occasionally have more or less vivid or suggestive new ideas in dreams,[3] and it is natural that this should occur more often, and to a higher degree, in persons of unusual intellectual force and activity. But it is more doubtful whether the creative activity of normal dreams ever reaches a sufficient perfection to take, as it stands, a very high place in a master's work. Coleridge's 'Kubla Khan' has the most notable claim to be an exception to this

[1] Thus Tennyson (*Memoir*, by his son, vol. i. p. 320) was subject from boyhood to a kind of waking trance. 'This has generally come upon me,' he wrote, 'through repeating my own name two or three times to myself silently.' (It thus seems to have been a sort of auto-hypnotisation.) In this state, individuality seemed to dissolve, he said, and he found in it a proof that the extinction of personality by death would not involve loss of life, but rather a fuller life. We are so easily convinced in these matters!

[2] See *e.g.*, De Manacéïne, *Sleep*, p. 314; Arturo Morselli, 'Dei Sogni nei Genii,' *La Cultura*, 1899.

[3] Thus I once planned in a dream a paper on the Progress of Psychology, which seemed to me on awakening to present a quite workable though not notably brilliant scheme.

rule. This poem was written by Coleridge in 1788, soon after 'Christabel,' and at a time when the poet was suffering much from depression, and taking a great deal of laudanum. We are entitled to assume, therefore, that the poem was composed under the influence of opium, and not in normal sleep. It may be added that it is difficult to believe that Coleridge could have recalled the whole poem from either a normal or abnormal dream ; as a rule, when we compose verses in sleep we can usually recall only the last two, or at most four, lines.[1] Moreover, there is reason to believe that the first draft of 'Kubla Khan' was not the poem as we now know it.[2]

After Coleridge's 'Kubla Khan' the most important artistic composition usually assigned to a dream is the *Trillo del Diavolo* sonata of Tartini, the eighteenth-century composer and violinist, who has been called the prototype of Paganini. Tartini, who was a man of nervous and emotional temperament, seems to have possessed real genius, and this sonata is his principal work. But there is not the slightest ground for stating that it was composed in a dream, and Tartini himself made no such claim.[3]

---

[1] Sante de Sanctis, however (*I Sogni*, p. 369), reproduces a dream poem of twelve lines.

[2] See note in J. D. Campbell's edition of Coleridge's *Poetical Works*, p. 592.

[3] Tartini composed the sonata—a noble and beautiful work which still survives—at the age of twenty-one. In old age he told Lalande the astronomer (as the latter relates in his *Voyage d'un Français en Italie*, 1765, vol. ix. p. 55) that he had had a dream in which he sold his soul to the Devil, and it occurred to him in his dream to hand his fiddle to the Devil to see what he could do with it. 'But how great was my astonishment when I heard him play with consummate skill a

CONCLUSION

The imaginative reality of dreams is perhaps appreciated by none so much as by those who are deprived of some of their external senses. Thus a deaf and dumb writer of ability who has precise and highly emotional dreams—which sometimes remind him of the atmosphere of Poe's tales, and are occasionally in organised sequence from night to night—writes : ' The enormous reality and vividness of these dreams is their remarkable point. They leave a mark behind. When I come to consider I believe that much that I have written, and many things that I have said and thought and believed, are directly due to these dream-experiences and my ponderings over how they came. Beneath the superficiality of our conscious mind—prim, smug, self-satisfied, owlishly wise—there lies the vast gulf of a subconscious personality that is dark and obscure, seldom seen or even suspected. It is this, I think, that wells up into my dreams. It is always there—always affecting us and modifying us, and bringing about strange and unforeseen new things in us—but in these dreams I peer over the edge of the conscious world into the giant-house and Utgard of the subconscious, lit by one ray of sunset that shows the weltering deeps

sonata of such exquisite beauty as surpassed the boldest flights of my imagination. I felt enraptured, transported, enchanted ; my breath was taken away, and I awoke. Seizing my violin I tried to retain the sounds I had heard. But it was in vain. The piece I then composed, the " Devil's Sonata," was the best I ever wrote, but how far below the one I had heard in my dream ! ' The dream, it will be seen, was of a fairly common type, and to Tartini's excitable temperament it served as a stimulus to his finest energies. But the real ' Devil's Sonata ' was hopelessly lost. (See the articles on Tartini in Fetis, *Biographie Universelle des Musiciens*, and Grove's *Dictionary of Music and Musicians*.)

of it. And the vivid sense of this is responsible for many things in my life.'[1]

Dreaming is thus one of our roads into the infinite. And it is interesting to observe how we attain it—by limitation. The circle of our conscious life is narrowed during sleep; it is even by a process of psychic dissociation broken up into fragments. From that narrowed and broken-up consciousness the outlook becomes vaster and more mysterious, full of strange and unsuspected fascination, and the possibilities of new experiences, just as a philosophic mite inhabiting a universe consisting of a Stilton cheese would probably be compelled to regard everything outside the cheese as belonging to the realm of the Infinite. In reality, if we think of it, all our visions of the infinite are similarly conditioned. It is only by emphasising our finiteness that we ever become conscious of the infinite. The infinite can only be that which stretches far beyond the boundaries of our own personality. It is the charm of dreams that they introduce us into a new infinity. Time and space are annihilated, gravity is suspended, and we are joyfully borne up in the air, as it were in the arms of angels; we are brought into a deeper communion with Nature, and in dreams a man listens to the arguments of his dog with as little surprise as Balaam heard the reproaches of his ass. The un-

[1] Helen Keller, the blind deaf-mute, has written some interesting chapters on her dreams in *The World I Live in*. For the most part it would seem that the dream life of the blind (which has been studied by, among others, Jastrow, *Fact and Fable in Psychology*, pp. 337 *et seq.*) is not usually rich or vivid.

CONCLUSION

expected limitations of our dream world, the exclusion of so many elements which are present even unconsciously in waking life, impart a splendid freedom and ease to the intellectual operations of the sleeping mind, and an extravagant romance, a poignant tragedy, to our emotions. 'He has never known happiness,' said Lamb, speaking out of his own experience, 'who has never been mad.' And there are many who taste in dreams a happiness they never know when awake.[1] In the waking moments of our complex civilised life we are ever in a state of suspense which makes all great conclusions impossible; the multiplicity of the facts of life, always present to consciousness, restrains the free play of logic (except for that happy dreamer, the mathematician), and surrounds most of our pains and nearly all our pleasures with infinite qualifications; we are tied down to a sober tameness. In our dreams the fetters of civilisation are loosened, and we know the fearful joy of freedom.

In this way the Paradise of dreams has been a reservoir from which men have always drawn consolation and sweet memory and hope, even belief, the imagination and gratification of desires that the world restrained, the promise and proof of the dearest and deepest aspirations.

Yet, while there is thus a real sense in which dreams produce their effect by the retraction of the field of consciousness and the limitation of the psychic activities which mark ordinary life, it remains true that if

[1] See *e.g.*, Marie de Manacéine, *Sleep*, p. 313.

we take into account the complete psychic life of dreaming, subconscious as well as conscious, it is waking, not sleeping, life which may be said to be limited.[1] Thus it is, as we have seen, that the most fundamental and the most primitive forms of psychic life, as well as the rarest and the most abnormal, all seem to have their prototype in the vast world of dreams. Sleep, Vaschide has said, is not, as Homer thought, the brother of Death, but of Life, and, it may be added, the elder brother.

'We dream, see visions, converse with chimæras,' said Joseph Glanvill, the seventeenth-century philosopher; 'the one half of our life is a romance, a fiction.' And what of the other half? Pepys tells us how another distinguished man of the same century, Sir William Petty, ' proposed it as a thing that is truly questionable whether there really be any difference between waking and dreaming.'[2] Our dreams are said to be delusions, constituted in much the same way as the delusion of the insane. But, says Godfernaux, 'all life is a series of systematised delusions, more or

[1] This aspect of dreaming has been set forth by Bergson (*Revue Philosophique*, December 1908, p. 574). 'The dream state,' he remarks, 'is the substratum of our normal state. Nothing is added in waking life; on the contrary, waking life is obtained by the limitation, concentration, and tension of that diffuse psychological life which is the life of dreaming. The perception and the memory which we find in dreaming are, in a sense, more natural than those of waking life: consciousness is then amused in perceiving for the sake of perceiving, and in remembering for the sake of remembering, without care for life, that is to say for the accomplishment of actions. To be awake is to eliminate, to choose, to concentrate the totality of the diffused life of dreaming to a point, to a practical problem. To be awake is to will; cease to will, detach yourself from life, become disinterested : in so doing you pass from the waking ego to the dreaming ego, which is less *tense*, but more *extended* than the other.'

[2] Pepys, *Diary*, 2nd April 1664.

less durable.' Men weary of too much living have sometimes found consolation in this likeness of the world of dreams to the world of life. 'When thou hast roused thyself from sleep thou hast perceived that they were only dreams which troubled thee,' wrote the Imperial Stoic to himself in his *Meditations*; 'now in thy waking hours look at these things about thee as thou didst look at those dreams.' Dreams are true while they last. Can we, at the best, say more of life?

We set out to study as carefully as possible the small field of dream consciousness belonging to a few persons, not, it may be, abnormal, of whom it was possible to speak with some assurance. The great naturalist, Linnæus, once said that he could spend a lifetime in studying as much of the earth as he could cover with his hand. However small the patch we investigate, it will lead us back to the sun at last. There is nothing too minute or too trivial. I have often remembered with a pang, how, long years ago, I once gave pain by saying, with the arrogance of boyhood, that it was foolish to tell one's dreams. I have done penance for that remark since. 'Il faut cultiver notre jardin,' said the wise philosopher of the eighteenth century. I have cultivated, so far as I care to, my garden of dreams, and it scarcely seems to me that it is a large garden. Yet every path of it, I sometimes think, might lead at last to the heart of the universe.

INDEX

ABRAHAM, K., 65, 272.
After-images, 26.
Albès, 246, 248, 252, 256.
Alcohol, 250.
Aliotta, 102.
Allin, 249.
Analogy in dreams, 41.
Andamanese shamans, 268.
Anaesthesia from drugs, 101.
Andrews, Grace, 84, 108.
Animism and dreaming, 210, 266.
Anjel, 247, 257.
Antoninus, 281.
Apperception in dreams, 68, 259.
Apraxia, 97.
Aristotle, 17, 31, 65, 92.
Arnaud, 255.
Artemidorus of Daldi, 157.
Atavistic dreams, alleged, 133.
Attention in dreams, 24 et seq.; 67, 219, 229, 252.
Auditory element in dreams, 77 et seq.
Augustine, St., 239.
Aural origin of some dreams, alleged, 139.
Autoscopy, 163.

BACH, 153.
Baldwin, 2, 4, 68.
Ballet, G., 253.
Bancroft, H. H., 37.
Baudelaire, 152.
Beaunis, 14, 33, 72, 132, 145, 203, 211, 224, 270.
Beddoes, T., 199.
Benson, Archbishop, 224.
Bergson, 137, 255 et seq., 280.
Binet, 56, 57, 58, 201.
Binns, 246.
Binswanger, L., 144.
Birds in dreams, 37.

Bladder as a stimulant to dreams, 88, 96, 163, 164.
Bleuler, 150, 154.
Blind, dreams of the, 278.
Blood, dreams of, 183.
Bode, 2.
Boerner, J., 269.
Bolton, F. E., 133.
Bolton, J., 69.
Bonatelli, 247.
Bonne, 244.
Bouché-Leclercq, 270.
Bourget, 241.
Bradley, F. H., 97.
Bramwell, J. M., 188.
Brill, 165.
Brodie, Sir B., 13.
Brown, Horatio, 30, 108.
Browning, 146.
Brunton, Sir Lauder, 270.
Buccola, 244.
Buchan, 90.
Burnham, 230, 242.

CABANIS, 13.
Calkins, 17.
Capuana, 92.
Cardiac stimuli of dreams, 88, 90, 136, 140.
Carpenter, W., 14.
Cerebral light, 27.
Cervantes, 129.
Chabaneix, 130, 143, 206, 265.
Child, psychic state of, 189, 264.
Childhood, hypnogogic hallucinations of, 28 et seq., 232.
Chloroform anaesthesia compared to dreaming, 16, 32, 34, 135, 137.
Christina the Wonderful, 144.
Cicero, 129.
Claparède, 171, 174.
Clarke, E. H., 30, 119.

Classification of dreams, 17, 71.
Clavière, 150, 215, 216.
Cleland, 155.
Colegrove, 234.
Coleridge, 273, 275.
Colour in dreams, 33.
Colour associations, 149.
Coloured hearing, 150.
Comar, 163.
Confusion in dreams, 36 *et seq*.
Consciousness, definition of, 2.
Contrast dreams, 175, 208.
Cooley, 189.
Corning, L., 79.
Crawley, 266.
Crichton-Browne, 108.
Criminals, dreams of, 120.
Curnock, N., 228.

DAURIAC, 79, 152.
Day-dreams, 167, 244, 261, 274.
Dead, dreams of the, 194 *et seq*.
Delacroix, 60.
Delage, 31.
Delbœuf, 5, 23.
Delior, 274.
Descartes, 13.
Dickens, 239.
Dircks, H., 2.
Dissociation in dreams, 66, 148, 185, 195, 221.
Dissolving view, dreams compared to, 36, 47.
Dogs, sleep of, 15, 101.
Dramatic element in dreams, 180 *et seq*.
Dreaming, alleged dreams of, 65.
Dreamless sleep, 14.
Dreamy state, 239.
Dromard, 248, 255.
Drowning, hallucinations of the, 145, 214.
Dugas, 240, 248, 252, 253.
Duplex brain, theory of, 244.
Durkheim, 266.
Dying, hallucinations of the, 145, 161.

ECSTASY, HYSTERICAL, 144.
Egger, 213, 216.
Ellis, Havelock, 28, 37, 165, 168, 179, 191, 197.

Emotion in dreams, 94 *et seq*.
Epilepsy and pseudo-reminiscence, 239, 245.
Epileptic dreams, 139.
Erotic dreams, 88, 126, 177.
Erotic symbolism, 65, 179.
Extrospection, 172.

FAIRIES AND DREAMS, 270.
Falling, dreams of, 129 *et seq*.
False recognition in dreams, 230 *et seq*.
Fear in dreams, 121, 174.
Féré, 92, 139, 156, 163, 248.
Ferenczi, 168.
Ferrero, 151.
Fish, dreams of, 163.
Floating, dreams of, 143.
Flournoy, 174, 187.
Flying, dreams of, 129 *et seq*.
Forman, Simon, 30.
Foucault, 5, 6, 7, 8, 13, 17, 22, 24, 174, 187, 195, 202, 215, 216, 224, 234.
Fouillée, 252, 255.
Freud, 52, 56, 65, 89, 99, 119, 120, 127, 133, 164 *et seq*., 210, 216, 217, 244, 262, 264, 272.
Fusion of dream imagery, 36 *et seq*.

GALTON, SIR F., 149.
Gassendi, 65, 202.
Genius and dreaming, 273.
Giessler, 22, 72, 174, 187, 189, 264.
Gissing, 170.
Glanvill, J., 280.
Glossolalia, 225.
Goblot, 6, 32, 154.
Godfernaux, 280.
Gods first appeared in dreams, 268.
Goethe, 70, 208.
Goncourt, E. de, 203.
Goncourt, J. de, 142.
Goron, 140.
Gowers, Sir W. R., 139, 239.
Grasset, 240, 243.
Greenwood, F., 66, 113, 163, 228.
Griesinger, 208.
Gross, Hans, 265.
Gruithuisen, 32.
Gustatory dreams, 85.

INDEX

Guthrie, 76, 108, 138.
Guyon, E., 29, 31.

HALL, STANLEY, 29, 65, 133, 174, 189.
Hallam, Florence, 74.
Hallucinations, 26, 159, 182, 188, 235, 271.
Hammond, 14, 65, 92, 104.
Hartland, E. S., 268.
Haschisch, 98, 215, 262.
Haskovec, 246.
Hawthorne, 228.
Head, H., 34, 121.
Headache and dreams, 34, 91, 116, 177.
Hearn, Lafcadio, 108, 133, 138, 209.
Heaven and dreams, 270.
Heine, 152.
Hell and dreams, 270.
Hermes, 129.
Herodotus, 89.
Herrick, C. L., 107.
Hervey de Saint-Denis, 159.
Heymans, 240, 248, 255.
Hilprecht, 220.
Hinton, James, 63.
Hippocrates, 13.
Hobbes, 31, 109, 269.
Holland, Sir H., 13.
Howells, W. D., 121.
Hutchinson, H., 132, 138.
Hypermnesia, 218 et seq.
Hypnagogic hallucinations, 15, 28 et seq., 67, 141, 160, 181, 215, 232, 265.
Hypnagogic paramnesia, 232 et seq.
Hypnopompic state, 238.
Hypnotism, 79, 231, 232, 234.
Hyslop, J. H., 27.
Hysteria, 67, 143, 162, 168, 187, 217, 219.

ICARUS, 130, 138.
Ida of Louvain, St., 144.
Imagery in dreams, 21 et seq., 64, 104, 120.
Insane, hallucinations of, 34, 271.
Insanity compared to dreaming, 48, 69, 105, 170, 188, 231, 262 et seq.
Isserlin, 165.

JACKSON, HUGHLINGS, 239, 240, 262.
James-Lange theory of emotion, 109.
Janet, 67, 144, 187, 229, 254, 255, 261.
Jastrow, J., 14, 64, 96, 220, 247, 262, 266, 278.
Jerome, St., 129.
Jessin, 242.
Jesus, 147, 210.
Jewell, 92, 99, 138, 140, 199, 211, 228, 265, 270.
Johnson, Dr., 185.
Joseph of Cupertino, St., 144.
Jones, Elmer, 32, 34, 135, 137.
Jones, Ernest, 165.
Jung, C. J., 89.

KALEIDOSCOPE, DREAM PROCESS COMPARED TO, 21, 28.
Keller, Helen, 273, 278.
Kiernan, 92, 239.
Kingsford, Anna, 119, 247.
Kraepelin, 48, 230.
Krauss, F. S., 157.

LAISTNER, 269.
Lalande, 240, 247, 255.
Lalanne, 105.
Lamb, C., 273.
Languages remembered in sleep, 225.
Lapie, 243.
Laud, 176.
Laurentius, 17, 262.
Legends, symbolism in, 156, 209.
Leibnitz, 13.
Léon-Kindberg, 252, 255.
Leroy, 26, 60, 161, 239, 247.
Lessing, 14.
Levitation, 144.
Liepmann, 97, 170.
Lilliputian hallucinations, 161, 270.
Little, Graham, 108.
Linnæus, 281.
Locke, 14.
Logic of dreams, 5 et seq., 56 et seq.
Logorrhœa, 170.
Lombard, E., 225.
Lombroso, 208.
Lorrain, Jacques le, 105.
Löwenfeld, 165.
Lubbock, 210.

Lucretius, 15, 129, 238, 268.

MACARIO, 92.
Macaulay, Lord, 221.
MacDougall, R., 79, 107, 138, 208, 229.
Macnish, 14.
Maeder, 156, 160, 164, 166.
Magnification of dream imagery, 104 et seq., 135, 160.
Maine de Biran, 26, 94.
Maitland, E., 119, 247.
Mallarmé, 274.
Manacéïne, Marie de, 119, 163, 187, 199, 229, 232, 275, 279.
Marillier, 251.
Marro, 263.
Marshall, H. R., 57.
Masselon, 92.
Maudsley, 119, 270, 273.
Maurier, G. du, 206.
Maury, 31, 32, 47, 186, 203, 213.
Memory and dreams, 8 et seq., 212 et seq.
Mercier, C., 2, 110.
Méré, 243.
Mescal, 27, 28.
Metamorphosis of dream imagery, 22.
Metaphysics and dreams, 63.
Metchnikoff, 174.
Meunier, R., 84, 92, 108.
Migraine, 34, 270.
Millet, J., 150.
Miner, J. B., 138, 152.
Mitchell, Sir A., 13.
Mitchell, Weir, 32.
Moll, 234.
Monboddo, Lord, 158, 226.
Monroe, W. S., 74, 83.
Moral attitude in dreaming, 118 et seq.
Moreau of Tours, 262.
Morphia dreams, 140.
Morselli, A., 275.
Mosso, 136.
Mourre, Baron, 24.
Movement in dreams, 20, 45, 96, 97 et seq.
Movement in sleep, 15.
Müller, J., 32.
Murder, dreams of, 111 et seq., 142.

Murray, Elsie, 110.
Music, symbolism of, 151.
Music in dreams, 77 et seq.
Myers, 255.
Myth-making and dreaming, 210, 269 et seq.

NÄCKE, 13, 119, 175, 202, 208, 236.
Nayrac, 68.
Neologisms in dreams, 48.
Neurasthenia, 27.
Newbold, 220.
Newman, E., 153.
Nietzsche, 274.
Nightmare, 99, 181.
Night-terrors, 30, 96, 108.
Nitrous oxide anaesthesia, 101, 135.
Nocturnal enuresis, 90.
Number-forms, 149.

OLFACTORY DREAMS, 83.
Oneiromancy, 156, 270.
Opium visions, 28, 140.
Orpheus, 210.

PARAMNESIA, 230 et seq.
Paraphasia, 48.
Parish, E., 67, 184, 235.
Parker, Thornton, 269.
Partridge, G. E., 29.
Paul, St., 191.
Pepys, 202, 280.
Periodicity in memory, 224.
Personality in dreams, division of, 187.
Peter, St., 146.
Petty, Sir W., 280.
Philostratus, 157.
Pick, 97.
Piderit, 155.
Piéron, 92, 145, 159, 162, 215, 216, 252, 255.
Pirro, 153.
Pliny the Elder, 157.
Prel, Carl du, 221.
Premonitory dreams, 91, 163.
Presentative dreams, 17, 71, 166.
Primitive psychic state, 266.
Prince, Morton, 174, 187.
Prodromic dreams, 91, 157, 163.

INDEX

Prophetic dreams, 93, 157.
Pseudo-reminiscence in dreams, 230 et seq.
Psychasthenia, 255.
Punning in dreams, 51.
Purcell, 153.
Pury, Jean de, 251.
Pythagoras, 242.

QUINCEY, DE, 28, 30.

RACHILDE, 143, 265.
Raffaelli, 130.
Railway travelling, dreams of, 81, 119.
Rank, O., 272.
Rapidity of dreams, alleged, 213 et seq.
Raymond, 229.
Reasoning in dreams, 56 et seq.
Renan, 203.
Representative dreams, 17, 71, 167.
Respiratory stimuli to dreams, 134 et seq.
Retinal element in dreams, 23, 26, 31, 183.
Rhythm, 138.
Ribot, 25, 26, 79, 85, 242, 252, 255.
Rochas, Colonel de, 79, 131, 144.
Rosenbach, 246.
Ruths, C., 79, 129, 211, 269.

SAGERET, 41.
Saints, alleged levitation of, 144.
Salish Indians, 210, 268.
Sand, George, 239, 265.
Sante de Sanctis, 92, 120, 168, 199, 208, 276.
Savage, psychic state of, 190, 266.
Savage, G. H., 33.
Schaaffhausen, 13.
Scherner, 88, 135, 159, 163, 164.
School, dreams of return to, 83, 195.
Schopenhauer, 175.
Schroeder, T., 191.
Schweitzer, 153.
Scripture, E. W., 27.
Secondary self in dreams, 187.
Segre, 96.
Sensory impressions in sleep, 71 et seq.
Shamans, 268.

Shelley, 241.
Silberer, 141.
Simon, Max, 91.
Skin sensations in dreams, 74 et seq., 117, 135, 137.
Sleep, dreamless, 14.
Smith, Hélène, 187.
Snakes, dreams of, 65.
Sollier, 144, 163, 188.
Solmi, 274.
Somnambulism, 95.
Spencer, Herbert, 130, 210.
Spontaneous character of dream imagery, 24.
Ssikorski, 145.
Stekel, 168.
Stewart, Dugald, 104.
Stoddart, 34, 221.
Stomach on dreams, influence of, 108 et seq.
Storms as cause of dreams, 81.
Stout, 2, 4, 68, 98, 195.
Stevenson, R. L., 217.
Stretton, 2.
Strümpell, 14, 135.
Suarez de Mendoza, 150.
Subconscious, definition of, 4.
Subconsciousness in dreams, 23, 63.
Suggestibility in dreams, 230.
Sully, 17, 234, 242, 244, 264, 266, 270.
Sunshine in dreams, 2.
Sutton, Bland, 133.
Swedenborg, 239.
Swoboda, 224.
Syllogistic arrangement of dreams, 58.
Symbolism in dreams, 81, 91, 109, 141, 148 et seq.
Symonds, J. A., 30, 108.
Synaesthesias, 149.
Synesius, 65, 129, 157, 227, 272.

TACTILE SENSATIONS IN DREAMS, 74 et seq., 85, 137.
Tannery, 5, 6, 66, 244.
Tartini, 276.
Taste dreams, 85.
Taylor, S., 239.
Therapeutic use of music during sleep, 79, 84.

Theresa, St., 144.
Thurn, Sir E. im, 268.
Tennyson, 275.
Time in dreams, estimate of, 250.
Tissié, 17, 72, 250.
Titchener, 85.
Tobolowska, 60, 216.
Toothache as a cause of dreams, 116.
Tout, Hill, 268.
Tuke, Hack, 235.
Turner, J., 231.
Turner, W. A., 239.
Tylor, 210, 266.

URBANTSCHITSCH, 155.

VANDERKISTE, 270.
Vaschide, 13, 92, 159, 162, 172, 199, 280.
Verbal transformations in dreams, 47.
Vesical dreams, 88, 96, 163, 164.
Vesme, C. de, 131.
Vigilambulism, 144.
Vinci, L. da, 274.

Visceral stimuli of dreams, 87 et seq., 121, 164.
Vision in dreams, 20.
Visual stimuli of dreams, 86, 108 et seq.
Vold, Mourly, 32.
Volkelt, 89.
Vurpas, 172.

WAGNER, 153, 183.
Weed, Sarah, 74.
Weygandt, 14, 72, 199.
Wigan, 244, 245.
Wiggam, 176, 208.
Wilks, Sir S., 214.
Wilson, A., 187.
Winslow, Forbes, 92.
Wish-dreams, 89, 165 et seq.
Wordsworth, 215.
Wright, H., 96.
Wundt, 14, 23, 57, 72, 135, 136, 195, 210.

ZENOGLOSSIA, 225.

Printed in Great Britain by T. and A. CONSTABLE LTD.
at the Edinburgh University Press